Managing Global Finance
in the Digital Economy

Managing Global Finance in the Digital Economy

Francisco Carrada-Bravo

PRAEGER

Westport, Connecticut
London

Library of Congress Cataloging-in-Publication Data

Carrada-Bravo, Francisco.
  Managing global finance in the digital economy / Francisco Carrada-Bravo.
    p. cm.
  Includes bibliographical references and index.
  ISBN 1–56720–527–5 (alk. paper)
    1. International finance. 2. International business enterprises—Finance. I. Title.
HG3881.C3158 2003
658.15'99—dc21   2001058936

British Library Cataloguing in Publication Data is available.

Library of Congress Catalog Card Number: 2001058936
ISBN: 1–56720–527–5

First published in 2003

Praeger Publishers, 88 Post Road West, Westport, CT 06881
An imprint of Greenwood Publishing Group, Inc.
www.praeger.com

Printed in the United States of America

The paper used in this book complies with the
Permanent Paper Standard issued by the National
Information Standards Organization (Z39.48–1984).

10 9 8 7 6 5 4 3 2 1

I wish to dedicate this book to the memory of my parents and my brother Jose Luis. Also, I want to dedicate it to my brothers Teodoro and Gustavo, my wife Lilia, and my lovely daughters Lilia del Carmen, Maria Elena, and Patricia. And last but not least, to the future carrier of the family torch, Alejandro Navarro Carrada.

Contents

Illustrations

A. FIGURES

B. TABLES

Preface

This book is the fruit of countless hours of work dedicated to the review of academic materials related to global finance, and to travel and meet with corporate executives from various continents to get from them ideas and experiences that helped to shape the content of this book.

One topic that surfaced continuously during the research period was the disappointment held by many executives and students with the lack of progress in the curriculum of finance to incorporate the various aspects of globalization into the subject matter. To shorten this gap, this book was written with the intent of providing the reader interested in learning global finance in the context of the digital business environment of the new century, with the finance tools required to solve the problems faced by multinational corporations in world markets.

To fulfill the objectives set for the manual, the book was divided into fourteen chapters covering the following topics:

- Fundamentals of value creation in the digital economy
- Interpreting and forecasting financial statements
- The foreign exchange market
- The fundamentals of investing globally
- Inflation, interest rates, and the exchange rate
- Global arbitrage
- Globalization and the balance of payments
- Financing global trade and foreign direct investment
- Exchange rate risk management
- Transaction risk management with futures and options
- Managing economic risk
- Interest and currency international swaps

- Valuing a foreign business
- Value creation in the digital economy

Each chapter is organized logically around subject matters related to optimizing corporate funds in the global market place. To maintain continuity in the learning process, all of the chapters share the same structure. They begin with an introduction followed by a brief explanation describing the purpose of the chapter. Subsequently, there is a description of the finance tools needed to fulfill the purpose of each chapter, and various applications of these tools to corporate experiences in a variety of settings around the globe. To close the chapter, there is a summary of the topics included in each section.

To help the reader to master the content of the book, at the end of each chapter are exercise sets designed to let the reader apply the financial tools learned and to extend the practicality of this book. Also, in selected chapters, there are cases strategically placed throughout the text to provide the reader with a rich variety of circumstances to frame a fluid, challenging, and exciting learning environment.

Faculty, business executives, and students from Argentina, Bahrain, Brazil, Canada, Chile, China, Colombia, Cuba, Guatemala, Honduras, Indonesia, Japan, Mexico, South Africa, Saudi Arabia, Singapore, Spain, Taiwan, the United States, and Uruguay reviewed and applied the material included in this volume. They contributed with comments and suggestions that helped to sharpen the financial tools included in various chapters of the book, to fine-tune the pedagogical value of the book, and to improve the focus of chapters and cases.

Finally, this book was made possible thanks to the assistance provided by Hilary Claggett, Meg Fergusson, and Patricia Carrada who reviewed the original version of the manuscript and provided extensive advice and suggestions on how to improve the style and content of the document.

Georgia Lessard, of the Instructional Design & Support department at Thunderbird, The American Graduate School of International Management, also provided a very valuable assistance. She turned raw drafts into chapters meeting the standards set by the publisher. However, as is customary, any remaining shortcomings and oversights in the text are mine alone.

Introduction

THE DOMAIN OF GLOBAL FINANCE

While tradition dictates that we differentiate between corporate and global finance, practice indicates that all finance has become global and interrelated, as is suggested throughout this volume. Therefore, this book focuses in the delivery of business experiences associated with the financial interaction between entities of two or more regions of the world, via the Internet or other form of electronic communication.

For international managers and government officials engaged in global affairs, the knowledge of global finance in the context presented in this book is very important in several ways. First, it helps them to judge how external shocks may affect the economy of a country or the finance of a firm. Second, global finance will provide them with guidance regarding what steps should be taken to profit from the disturbances associated to currency variations or technological changes in global communication. Otherwise, it suggests ways to isolate institutions from the harmful aspects of external shocks originating in either the digital economy or the change in communications technology.

This book is also helpful to assist the business executive, regardless of their function, in building the necessary judgment required to make wise financial decisions in the current business environment.

WHO SHOULD READ THIS BOOK

This manuscript was designed for business executives and government officials interested in meeting the challenges posed by corporate finance in the context of globalization.

The personal application of global finance to understanding corporate performance is not limited only to managers of very large and sophisticated multinational corporations or government officials of wealthier nations. Rather, regardless of location and professional training, it extends to managers of any size businesses and the government officials of ministries engaged in world affairs. This extensive coverage is possible due to the fact that the book presents experiences in various fields of corporate finance from companies of the Americas, Europe, Asia, and Africa engaged in e-commerce or software businesses, as well as the challenges faced by a variety of countries worldwide.

1

The Fundamentals of Value Creation in the Digital Economy

The fundamental principle guiding this book is that every business executive, regardless of his or her principal activity, has to manage the resources of the firm with the objective of increasing the market value of the corporation.

The explanation of how to manage in order to create value will be provided in the context of recent technological changes that continues to reshape existing commercial relationships in the global economy. This explanation will encompass the methods and tools that will help the executive to determine whether the firm's current investments are creating value. If it is not creating value, this book also suggests measures that can remedy existing shortcomings in global investment strategies. The topics of this book will enable the executive to determine whether a new business proposal has the potential to increase the value of the firm. Examples of decisions to be considered are replacing or upgrading existing capital equipment, launching a new product, acquiring another firm, or restructuring existing operations.

The content of this and other chapters will present several important advantages involved in managing, with the goal of increasing the value of a firm. First, it provides an integrated financial management system. Second, it helps the reader to appraise actual business performance. Third, it will contribute to making sound business decisions and to designing effective financial programs that match the interests of management with that of the stockholders.

To attain the goals designed for this book, this chapter reviews the most challenging issues confronted by global finance and provides a general but comprehensive overview of global finance. Although the topics of this chapter are examined in greater detail in other chapters, many of the key terms and concepts are introduced and defined here. These include:

- The importance of managing a multinational corporation for value creation
- How to measure the value created by a business proposal such as an investment project, a change in the financial structure of a corporation, a business acquisition, or the decision to invest in the global market
- The significance of the firm's cost of capital and how to measure it
- What are financial markets and the importance of these markets as a source of corporate funding and value creation
- The business cycle of a firm and the importance of growth
- The structure and logic of financial statements and how they can be used to assess the profitability of the company and its ability to generate cash
- The importance of risk, how to measure risk, and how the different forms of risk affect sales, profits, and the cost of capital
- The meaning of market value added, and economic value added and how both concepts relate to the goal of managing for value creation

THE DECISION-MAKING PROCESS AND VALUE CREATION

Normally, the process of creating value starts with the identification of a market need. An example would be the introduction of a new product. If a firm has the assets and the technology to manufacture the product at a lower cost than its competitors, then this company can manufacture the product and sell it at a profit. The content of this proposal raises several questions that need to be resolved before the company engages in the new venture. For example, should the firm go ahead with this project? If so, how will the project be financed? What will be the sources of funding? Will the project produce enough revenue to cover the cost of the funds required to launch the project? Moreover, will the firm be more valuable because of this project?

Debt holders are those lending money to the firm whereas shareholders normally finance a new venture, such as launching a new product. The cash contributed by the shareholders is called equity capital. Contributions by debt holders are considered debt capital.

Similar to other resources, capital provided by the stockholders or debt holders is not free. Debt holders are willing to fund a project if it can be shown that the profitability of the project is great enough to meet the cost of debt capital. However, this information is not sufficient to convince the stockholders to approve the project. The individuals owning a firm will be inclined to accept a venture only if it increases the value of the firm. This objective is met only when the expected return on a new project exceeds its financing cost.

In short, the approval of a new business proposal on the part of the stockholders will depend on whether the proposed business project can increase the market value of the firm. If the initial evaluation of the project leads to the conclusion that the launching of a new product will increase the value of the firm, then the corporation should go ahead with the new business proposal. Otherwise, the firm should abandon it.

The premise of market value creation also applies to current business operations. If some existing line of business is destroying rather than creating value, the firm should take immediate corrective action. If these actions do not improve the value of the firm, then the company should consider alternative courses of action such as selling that line or shutting it down.

THE FUNDAMENTAL PRINCIPLE OF CORPORATE FINANCE

A business proposal increases the value of a firm when the present value of the future stream of net cash flow exceeds the initial cash outlays required to implement it.[1] This principle suggests the existence of several important finance tools and concepts. The first concept is the *present value* of the future stream of expected net cash benefits. It is the dollar amount that makes the owners of the firm indifferent to choosing between owning that sum today or receiving the expected future cash flow stream as it matures. An example of this choice is the alternative faced by the stockholders of receiving a cash dividend of $100,000 today or expecting a cash dividend of $112,000 next year. In this case, $100,000 is the present value of $112,000 expected a year later.

The comparison of present value with the initial cash outlay required to launch a new business proposal leads to another very important finance concept known as *net present value* (NPV). This is defined as the difference between the present value of a proposal and the initial cash outlay required to implementing it: NPV = – Initial cash outlay + Present value of future net cash benefits.

This new concept can be used to restate the fundamental principle of finance in simple terms: *A business proposal increases the value of a firm if the NPV of the proposal is positive.* By contrast, it destroys value if the NPV is negative.

To estimate the NPV of a business project, consider the previous example and assume that the request requires an initial investment of $90,000 today to generate the $112,000 in dividends next year. In this case, the NPV of the proposal is the difference between $100,000 (the present value of the $112,000) and the $90,000 initial cash outlay (Figure 1.1).

NPV of proposal = – $90,000 + $100,000 (present value of $112,000)
= – $90,000 + $100,000
= $10,000

Given that the NPV of the proposed business plan is positive, then the project should be implemented because it creates $10,000 value for the firm implementing it. This value will accrue to the stockholders, who could sell their equity stake in the company, including the project, for $10,000 more than they could get if the project did not exist. This is true even if the business proposal is in the planning stage and the project has not been undertaken yet. The ability of the firm to identify the project and the markets' expectation that the firm will execute the project successfully, create an immediate increase both in the firm's value and the wealth of its stockholders.

Figure 1.1
Discounting Expected Cash Flows

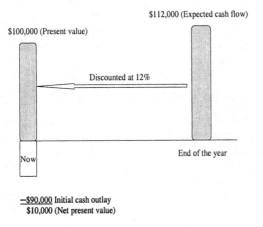

$112,000 (Expected cash flow)

$100,000 (Present value)

Discounted at 12%

End of the year

Now

$-$90,000 Initial cash outlay
$10,000 (Net present value)

If the firm implementing the project has 100,000 shares of common stock traded on a stock exchange, then the price of the stock will increase. The stock price increase can be estimated by dividing the increase in the value of the firm ($10,000) by the number of shares on the day the project is announced.[2]

THE RELEVANCE OF CASH

The fundamental principle of finance requires that both the initial investment needed to undertake the project and the stream of net future benefits that the project is expected to generate be measured in cash.[3] From the perspective of investors (stockholders and debt holders), only cash matters. They have invested cash in the firm and are only interested in cash returns. Therefore, managers must also be concerned about the cash flow associated with operations.

DISCOUNT RATES

The proposal previously discussed is expected to generate $112,000 in one year. The present value of that future cash flow is $100,000. This dollar value ($100,000) is the amount of cash that makes the owners of the company indifferent to receiving this cash today or receiving $112,000 in one year. This is equivalent to stating that the stockholders expect to receive a return of 12% from the project because $100,000 invested at 12% will yield $112,000 in one year. This percentage is known as the *discount rate*. It is the rate at which the future cash flow must be discounted to find its present value.

To estimate the NPV of a business proposal, it is necessary to discount the future cash flow stream to find its present value and to deduct from that present value the initial cash outlay required to implement the project.

In the previous example, the discount rate was known because the expected future cash flow and the present value were already known. In practice, this is not usually the case. To determine the value of the discount rate associated with a business proposal, it is necessary to find the cost of financing the proposal and use this information as the discount rate.

THE COST OF CAPITAL

Normally, corporations finance their investment needs with a combination of *equity capital* and *debt capital*. To fund a project, both shareholders and debt holders require a return from their contribution to the financing of the firm. When a project is funded with both equity and debt, the cost of capital is the weighted average of the cost of equity and the after-tax cost of debt. The weights are the proportion in which equity and debt capital enter into the total financing of a new project.

To illustrate the estimation of the cost of capital when the source of funding is a combination of equity and debt, consider a project financed with 30% equity costing 12% and 70% debt capital with an after-tax cost of debt of 8%. Given this information, the weighted average cost of capital, or WACC, is 9.2%.

Project cost of capital WACC = (30% × 12%) + (70% × 8%)
= 3.6% + 5.6%
= 9.2%

This example suggests that the contribution of equity financing to the cost of the project is 3.6% (30% of 12%), and debt financing 5.6% (70% of 8%).[4]

VALUE CREATION AND CORPORATE DECISION-MAKING

Every day, executives working for a corporation are confronted with myriad problems that require a solution. For instance, the finance executive makes decisions related to:

- *Capital budgeting*—whether the firm should accept or reject a project

- *Capital structure*—how much of the firm's assets should be financed with debt and how much with capital

- *Business acquisition*—how much a firm should pay to acquire another business

- *Foreign direct investment*—how to invest in a foreign country, how to consider multiple currency cash flows and how to measure the risk of operating in a foreign country

This book provides in other chapters the financial tools that will assist the executive in the decision-making process. In the remainder of this chapter, the reader is supplied with an overview of how the corporate decisions previously described relate to value creation.

THE CAPITAL BUDGETING DECISION

The capital budgeting decision is a major resolution affecting the long-term performance of a corporation. This is also known as the capital expenditure decision. The key parameters used to frame a capital expenditure decision are the NPV and the internal rate of return, both of which are direct applications of the fundamental principle of finance.

THE NET PRESENT VALUE RULE

The NPV rule is a direct application of the fundamental principle of finance, because it states that a project should be accepted only if it produces value. This happens only when the NPV of the project is positive. In this case, there is value creation because the present value of expected future cash flows is greater than the initial cash outlay required to initiate the business proposal.

THE INTERNAL RATE OF RETURN RULE

The internal rate of return is the discount rate for which the NPV of a business proposal is zero. To determine whether a project creates value, business executives normally compare the internal rate of return of a proposal with the WACC. If the internal rate of return exceeds the cost of capital, then the project is predicted to add value to the firm.

To illustrate how the internal rate of return relates to value creation, consider the case of a project requiring an initial investment of $100,000, which is expected to generate a cash flow of $105,000 in one year. At a 5% discount rate, the NPV of the project is zero. If the WACC is only 3%, then the project should be accepted since it will add 2% of $100,000 ($2,000) of value to the firm.

THE CAPITAL STRUCTURE DECISION

This decision is related to the relocation of assets and the net effect of this change on the cash position of a corporation. If the management of a business entity decides to replace equity with debt or to switch from debt to equity, then management is making a capital structure decision. This decision creates value for the firm when the NPV of the future cash flows, traced to the change in the cash position, increases as a result of a capital structure decision.

To illustrate a capital structure decision and its effect on value creation, consider the following case. On March 28, 2001, Agere, the semiconductor and optical component arm of Lucent Technologies placed a large initial public offering (IPO). However, due to poor IPO market conditions, Lucent raised $2.5 billion less than the company had hoped for. To cover the unexpected cash shortfall, Lucent began to draw funds from a $6.3 billion credit facility arranged in February 2001. The use of the credit facility by Lucent caused some uneasiness in the financial market given that bankers get concerned when investment grade companies draw on credit lines, which act as insurance, in case they are not able to sell short-term commercial paper, an infrequent act. The cash withdraw forced the banks to price the line of credit like a non investment grade deal and to request from both Agere and Lucent collateral to secure the loans.

The poor timing of the offering forced Lucent to create a new and unwanted capital structure. This had major implications for value creation within Lucent since it damaged the credit ratings of the company and led to an increase in the cost of borrowing.[5] Both aspects were at the cause of a sharp deterioration in the stock price of Agere, which dropped from $6.23 on March 30, 2001, to $5.05 on April 9, 2001.[6]

THE BUSINESS ACQUISITION DECISION

The purchase of one company by another corporation is another form of investing. An acquisition creates value for the shareholders of the acquiring firm if the NPV of the future cash flows to be generated by the target firm after the acquisition exceeds the price paid by the acquirer. The NPV of an acquisition is as follows:

NPV (acquisition) = − Price paid to acquire the target company + present value of the cash flows generated by the target company during the post acquisition period.

The decision to acquire a target company creates value for the shareholders of the acquiring firm when the NPV of the cash flows to be generated by the acquisition is positive. The value created in an acquisition is closely related to the type of the acquisition. If the acquisition takes the form of a pure conglomerate merger (the business to be purchased is unrelated to the professional activity of the acquiring firm), then the benefits of the acquisition are simply related to the cash flows generated by the assets of the target company standing alone. If the business activity of the two companies is similar or complementary, then the acquisition can produce additional benefits associated with their synergies.

To assess the contribution of these synergies on value creation, it is necessary to consider the increase of the cash flows of the acquiring and target companies. The synergies can take the form of an increase in the volume of sales for the two companies or a reduction in the operating cost of the two entities. An example of an acquisition based on synergy considerations is provided by the acquisition of Top Tier by SAP on April 7, 2001. SAP, Europe's largest business software maker, bought Top Tier, a U.S. portal business software maker for $400 million, in cash. This acquisition was valued at 20 times the sales value of the target company in the year 2000, which amounted to only $20 million. SAP justified the acquisition and the price paid on the ground that the purchase of the U.S. corporation could help SAP increase sales in the enterprise portal, customer relationship management, supply chain management, and marketplace software sectors. In addition, it could provide SAP with experienced engineering staff from the United States and a base of important clients (Daimler-Chrysler, Hewlett Packard, GMAC, Universal Studios, and Wells Fargo).[7]

THE FOREIGN DIRECT INVESTMENT DECISION

An overseas capital expenditure, similarly to other forms of investment, requires spending cash now with the expectation that the NPV of future net cash flows generated by the foreign investment will be higher than the initial cash outlay. In this instance, the fundamental principle also applies—except that the assessment of value creation in foreign direct investment is more complicated than the one required to estimating the benefits of a local investment. The difficulties associated with assessing foreign direct investment are related to currency risk and political or country risk.

Currency risk refers to the peril associated with unanticipated changes in the value of a currency in which the cash flows are denominated. Country risk is related to the unforeseen variations in the government policies of the host country that may affect the value of the cash flows measured in the currency of the host country. For example, the unexpected increase in foreign level of taxation or the sudden application of exchange controls to the repatriation of profits.

THE ROLE OF THE FINANCIAL MARKETS AND GLOBAL FINANCE

The financial market includes several important sectors, such as the equity, money, capital, and foreign exchange markets. The *equity market* is the realm in which the participants buy and sell stock. In the *money market*, traders exchange short-term debt (public and corporate). The *capital market* is a notional location where the participants trade long-term debt (corporate and government bonds). The *foreign exchange market* is the place where banks, corporations, and individuals buy and sell currencies.

The stock market plays a very important role in the process of business growth and value creation by performing primary and secondary market functions. In the primary stock market, cash-rich individuals or corporations provide funding to cash-strapped new business ventures in exchange for certificates that recognize the right of the holder to receive a share of the cash flows to be generated by the new venture. The secondary stock market provides an efficient mechanism to trade securities already issued. The primary and secondary stock markets are closely interrelated given that the price of securities in the secondary markets often determines the price of the stock in the primary market. For instance, investment or merchant banks use the price of stock observed in the secondary market as a benchmark to set the price of a new public offering in the primary market. The price of a new offering is not static. At the end of a trading day, the last price may move away from the opening or initial price. The last or closing pricing of a new offering may affect the value of stock already issued.

One of the best known equity markets is the New York Stock Exchange (NYSE), which houses over 80% of the American securities traded. To be listed in the NYSE, the company needs to have earnings equivalent to $2.5 million before taxes, tangible net assets of $40 million, and 1.1 million publicly held common shares. However, these conditions are not cast in iron. The NYSE ultimately judges the viability of each company based on its own merits, some of which may be greater or less than the conditions previously listed.[8]

EXTERNAL AND INTERNAL FUNDING

The stock, money, and capital markets when functioning as primary markets are very important sources of external funding. Corporations can raise equity capital by issuing shares of common stock. Similarly, companies can raise funds in the money and capital markets by issuing short or long-term debt. To raise funds in any one of these three markets, corporations usually resort to the services provided by investment bankers. These bankers do not arrange for corporate loans. Rather, they help the corporations place new stock as an IPO, issue commercial paper in the money market, or sell corporate bonds in the capital market.

By nature, debt financing is always an external source of corporate funds since it can take the form of a loan from a commercial bank. It exists as a new issue of commercial paper in the money market or a new issue of corporate bonds in the capital or bond market. In contrast, equity financing can be either internal or external. Internal equity financing takes place when a corporation retains a portion of the profits for investment purposes. The proportion of profits retained within the firm is called the *profit retention rate*. The percentage paid out in the form of cash dividend is known as the *dividend payout ratio*.

The retention of profits can be total or partial. The degree of profit retention will depend on the corporation's availability to obtain external financing and the cost of it. When external funds are scarce and the cost of equity capital is high, firms tend to increase their profit retention rate. Profit retention is also associated with the cost of collecting external funds, such as the fees that the companies have to pay to investment banks and the costs incurred by a firm to comply with the rules that govern external equity funding. Normally, the expenses associated with a new public offering are complex and costly. As a result, companies are normally more inclined to raise equity through earnings retention.

THE GROWTH OF A FIRM: THE CASE OF CNH IN CHINA

To describe the factors influencing the growth of a firm, this section uses the case of a Chinese subsidiary of CNH.

CNH is a U.S. company with manufacturing operations in 16 countries. It was created in November 1999 through the business merger of Case Corporation and New Holland N.V. It distributes products in 160 countries through a network of 10,000 dealers and distributors and is considered the largest manufacturer of tractors in the world and the third largest producer of construction equipment. In addition, it has one of the world's largest equipment financing companies.

The pattern of growth of a corporation like CNH is determined by the firm's ability to raise external funds and retain earnings. To explain the role of these two items on corporate growth, this section uses the creation of the new CNH subsidiary in China as an example. This proposal requires an initial investment of $2 million funded with 50% equity capital and 50% debt capital. The relationship between debt and capital implicitly leads to a capital structure of 1 (the capital structure is measured by the ratio of debt to equity). All the funds are allocated to purchase assets ($2 million), which allow the company to sell $4 million and produce a net profit of $600,000.

The proportion of sales to assets and net profits to sales is reflected in two very important ratios. The first is known as the efficiency of assets, which uses the ratio of sales to assets as equal to 2. The second is the net profit margin, which is the ratio of net profits to sales. This is equivalent to 15%.

Once profits are generated, the owners of the firm are confronted with the decision of how to distribute them. In the example under consideration, it is assumed that CNH decides to disburse $200,000 in dividends and retain the rest ($400,000). This yields a retention rate of 67% (the ratio of retained earnings to net profits). To maintain the same capital structure of 1 in the next business cycle, the firm needs to borrow $400,000. The process of corporate growth is described in Figure 1.2.

At the beginning of 2001, equity capital has increased $400,000, which is 20% of the initial capital. At the end of the second cycle, the equity has increased $562,800. This is also 20% of equity capital at the beginning of the second business cycle. The rate of equity growth (20%) permits a net profit margin of 15%, which is known as *the rate of self-sustainable growth*. The fastest growth rate in sales that the firm can maintain if it keeps its operating and financing policies unchanged is a debt to equity ratio of 1, a sales to assets ratio of 2, a net profit margin of 15%, and a retention rate of 67%.

Figure 1.2
The Growth of a Firm

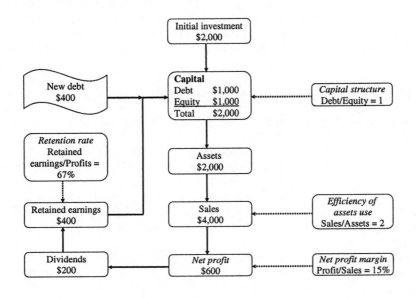

Table 1.1
Business Cycle and Corporate Growth

	Cycle 1, year 2000 ($ Thousands)	Ratio	Cycle 2, year 2001 ($ Thousands)	Ratio
Initial investment	2,000			
Additional investment			800	
Debt capital	1,000		400	
Equity capital	1,000		400	
Capital structure, Debt/Equity		1		1
Assets	2,000		2,800	
Sales	4,000		5,600	
Efficiency of assets use, Sales/Assets		2		2
Net profits	600		840	
Net profit margin Net profits/Sales		15%		15%
Distributed earnings	200		277.20	
Retained earnings	400		562.80	
Retention rate Retained earnings/Net profits		67%		67%
Additional debt	400		562.80	
Available capital for next cycle	800		1,125.60	
Self-sustainable rate growth = Retained earnings plus new debt/initial equity		20%		20%

The self-sustainable growth rate it is a very important indicator of business performance and should be a key component in the financial strategy of a firm in the digital economy. For a more detailed description of the different aspects of corporate growth, see Table 1.1.

THE FINANCIAL STATEMENTS OF CNH

To keep track of its performance throughout the world, CNH integrates, like any other multinational corporation, two financial statements: the balance sheet and the income statement.

The balance sheet is a statement that describes the value of the assets owned by CNH Global, such as cash, inventory, plant, and equipment. It also shows how much the company owes, which is called liabilities. Both the assets and liabilities describe the financial situation of the company at a specific date, usually the end of the year. The difference between assets and liabilities is an accounting estimate of how much equity capital the shareholders have invested in CNH. This difference is called the book value of equity, which depends on the accounting method used to value assets and liabilities.

The income statement, also known as the profit-and-loss statement, is used to provide an estimate of the change in the book value of equity over a period of time. This change can be measured from quarter to quarter or from year to year.

The change in the value of equity is equal to the difference between revenues and expenses, which results in a *net profit* if the results are positive or a net loss if negative. *Revenue* is any transaction occurring during the accounting period that increases the book value of equity. An *expense*, by contrast, is any transaction that reduces the book value of equity.

The Balance Sheet of CNH

The balance sheets for 2000 and 2001 (Table 1.2) reflect on the left side, the value of the assets held by CNH during each one of the periods. The right side lists the value of the liabilities of the corporation and the equity of the shareholders.

The assets listed on December 31, 2000, include $200,000 cash, $300,000 of account receivable, $500,000 of inventories, and $1,200,000 of fixed assets. *Accounts receivable* reflects the amount of cash owed to CNH by its customers for sales made on credit. *Inventory* reflects the value of raw materials, work in process, and finished goods held by the company. *Net fixed assets* represent the value of long-term assets held by the CNH such as equipment, machinery, and buildings. To estimate the net value of fixed assets, the firms deducts from the purchase price of the assets, accumulated depreciation expenses to account for the loss in value of these assets due to wear and tear.

The right side of the balance sheet for the year 2000 provides an indication of how CNH financed the acquisition of the assets during this year. The first source of funding listed is $400,000 of short-term debt borrowed from banks. The next source of funding is $200,000 of accounts payable, which is debt owed by CNH to suppliers of raw materials for purchases made on credit and have not been settled yet. The remainder of funding is $600,000 of long-term debt and $1,000,000 in equity.

The Managerial Balance Sheet of CNH

This is a simplified and more meaningful balance sheet focusing on the concept of working capital. To explain the idea of working capital, consider the business activity of CNH, which is producing and distributing machinery and equipment. To perform these functions CNH must hold both account receivables and inventories because sales are not paid in cash right away and goods need to be manufactured and stored before they can be sold. Luckily, CNH does not have to provide all the capital needed to finance accounts receivables and inventories, since the suppliers of the company provide partial funding is in the form of interest free accounts payable.

The net investment in working capital for December 2000 is equal to $600,000, resulting from a $300,000 accounts receivable plus $500,000 of inventories minus $200,000 of accounts payable. The transfer of accounts payable to working capital on the right-hand side of the balance sheet and the meshing of this account with both accounts receivable and inventories of CNH in the year 2000 turns the accounting balance sheet into a managerial one. This late version of the balance sheet presents a more realistic picture of the financial position of CNH and is described in Table 1.3.

Table 1.2
CNH Balance Sheet, 2000 and 2001

Assets ($ 000)	2000 31 Dec.	2001 31 Dec.	Liabilities ($ 000)	2000 31 Dec.	2001 31 Dec.
Cash	200	320	Short-term debt	400	560
Accounts receivable	300	420	Accounts payable	200	280
Inventories	500	700	Long-term debt	600	840
Net fixed assets	1,200	1,640	Owners' equity	1,000	1,400
			Total liabilities		
Total assets	2,200	3,080	and equity	2,200	3,080

Table 1.3
The Managerial Balance Sheet of CNH

Assets $ 000	31 Dec. 2000	31 Dec. 2001	Liabilities $ 000	31 Dec. 2000	31 Dec. 2001
Cash	200	320	Short-term debt	400	560
Working capital	600	840	Long-term debt	600	840
Net fixed assets	1,200	1,640	Owners' equity	1,000	1,400
			Total liabilities		
Total assets	2,000	2,800	and equity	2,000	2,800

The Income Statement of CNH

The first item of the income statement (Table 1.4) is total revenues (sales), which amounted to $4,000,000 in the year 2000. To produce this revenue, CNH had to spend $3,400,000. This expenditure includes operating expenses of $2,920,000 (including $200,000 of depreciation), interest payments for $80,000 estimated at 8% of debt ($1,000,000), and a tax liability of $400,000. The taxes are estimated at 40% corporate tax rate on a pretax profit of $1,000,000.

The income statement contains several key concepts. The difference between sales and operating expenses, known as earnings before interest and taxes (EBIT) is estimated at $1,080,000 for the year 2000 ($4,000,000 of sales minus $2,920,000 of operating expenses). The second concept is earnings before taxes (EBT) assessed at $1,000,000 ($1,080,000 of EBIT minus interest expenses of $80,000). Finally, there are earnings after taxes (EAT) or profits of $600,000 ($1,000,000 of EBT minus $400,000 tax liabilities). The company retains $400,000 and distributes the remaining $200,000 to the stockholders as dividend payments.

EBIT can also be viewed as the total profit generated by the activity of the firm that has to be distributed to three parties: the debt holders, the tax authority, and the stockholders of the firm. Debt holders are entitled to receive $80,000 interest payment. The Internal Revenue Service is entitled to $400,000 and shareholders have the right to claim the remaining $600,000. This ordering suggests that the debt holders have the first claim on profits followed by the tax authority and the stockholders. It also indicates that the stockholders have only a residual ownership on the pretax operating profits of the company.

Table 1.4
CNH in China, Income Statement, 2000 and 2001

Income Statement, 2000 ($ Thousands)		Income Statement, 2001 ($ Thousands)	
Sales	4,000	Sales	5,600
Less operating expenses Including $200 of depreciation expenses	2,920	Less operating expenses Including 200 of depreciation expenses	4,088
EBIT	1,080	EBIT	1,512
Less interest expenses (8% x $1,000)	80	Less interest expenses (8% x 1,400)	112
Earnings before taxes	1,000	Earnings before taxes	1,400
Less tax expense (40% x EBT)	400	Less tax expense (40% x EBT)	560
EAT	600	EAT	840
Retained earnings	400	Retained earnings	560
Dividend payments	200	Dividend payments	280

The Profitability of CNH in China

The information presented in the balance sheet and the income statement can be used to estimate several ratios that can help to rate the corporate performance of CNH in China. Perhaps the most important ratio is the *return on equity,* also known as ROE. This index, which is measured as the ratio of earnings after taxes to equity, provides an indication of the profitability of CNH in China from the perspective of the owners of the corporation. The stockholders of CNH invested $1,000,000 that brought in $600,000 profits. This resulted in a return on equity of 60%.

ROE = Earnings after taxes/Equity = $600,000/$1,000,000 = 60%

The Profitability of Total Investment

Another important measure of corporate performance is the ratio of after-tax operating profit to invested capital, known as the *return on total investment* (ROIC). In the year 2001, after-tax operating profit is $952,000 (profits after taxes of $840,000 plus interest payments $112,000). The dollar value of invested capital in the year 2000 was $2,000,000 and the return on total investment is 48%.

ROIC = After-tax operating profit/Invested capital
= $952,000/ $2,000,000
= 48%

Return on invested capital is also known as *return on net assets* (RONA) or *return on capital employed* (ROCE). These relationships are justified by the fact that invested capital is equal to net assets, and both are equal to capital employed. According to the information presented in the managerial sheet described in Table 1.3, the capital employed by CNH in December 2000 is equal to $2,000,000 consisting of $200,000 cash, $600,000 working capital, and $1,200,000 in net fixed assets.

The Cash Flow of the Operation

The analysis of the cash flow associated with a business proposal is crucial to judge the ability of the proposal to generate or destroy value for a firm. The continuous observation of the cash flows associated with a new project constitutes a key managerial activity, which verifies that the project is creating value.

The level of cash flow generated by CNH in China can be found by comparing the amount of cash held by the firm in 2000 and 2001. A quick view of the information presented in the balance sheets indicates that at the end of the 2000 and 2001, CNH had $200,000 and $320,000 in cash, respectively. The difference implies a net cash increase of $120,000 generated by CNH in 2001. It is the net outcome of all cash transactions (all cash receipts minus all cash payments) made by CNH in China in 2001.

Sources of Cash

Corporations obtain cash from three sources: They can borrow or issue new equity (a financing decision), they can sell some of the assets (a divesting or asset disposal decision), or they can generate the cash from operations (operating decision). All the three sources of cash creation are important, but from the perspective of the stockholder the most relevant aspect of a cash flow analysis is the determination of operating cash flow. It is easy to understand the importance attached by the stockholders to this item. A firm that does not generate cash flows from its operation over a period of time will face financial distress. The financial difficulties associated with poor operating cash flows can be corrected temporarily by borrowing or by selling assets. Eventually, the sources of cash will dry up if the firm is not able to reverse a poor operating cash flow performance.

The Cash Flow from the Operation

To estimate the cash flow generated by a business activity, it is necessary to deduct from sales ($5,600,000), operating expenses ($4,088,000) and taxes ($560,000). The second item (operating expenses) includes depreciation ($200,000), which is a cash-generating expense. To account for the cash contribution of this item to the firm, depreciation has to be added back.

The implementation of all the previous transactions leads to a net dollar amount of $1,152,000. To arrive at the final value of the cash flow, it is necessary to take away from $1,152,000 the portion of cash used to fund the growth of working capital ($240,000). Once this adjustment is made, the net cash flow generated by the operation in the year 2001 is $912,000. A detailed analysis of how to estimate operating cash flow is presented in Table 1.5.

Cash Flow from Investing and Financing

To meet the increase in sales, CNH invested $800,000 in new capital expenditures. This expense is reflected in Table 1.5 as a net outflow.

Table 1.5
CNH, Sources of Cash Flow, 2001

Cash Flow from Operating Activities	($ Thousands)	
Sales	5,600	
Less operating expenses		
Including $200 of depreciation expenses	4,088	
Less tax expense (0.4*EBT)	560	
Plus depreciation expense	200	
Less cash used to finance the growth of working capital	240	
A. *Net operating cash flow*	*912*	*912*
Cash Flow from Investing Activities		
Capital expenditures	800	
B. Net cash flow from investing activities		−800
Cash Flow from Financing Activities		
New borrowing	400	
Less interest payments (8%*1,400)	112	
Less dividend payments	280	
C. Net cash flow from financing activities	8	8
Total net cash flow (A + B + C)		120
Cash Flow Analysis Using Balance Sheet Information		
Cash held at the beginning of the year 2001		200
Cash held at the end of the year 2001		320
Cash difference		120

With respect to the cash movements related to financing activities, the income statement, presented in Table 1.4, shows CNH compensating its debt holders (commercial banks) with $112,000.[9] In addition, the company distributed $280,000 in dividend payments. Both the interest and dividend cash outflows are partially offset by a $400,000 borrowing. Overall, the financing activities net $8,000.[10]

Overall Cash Position of CNH

The cash flow analysis presented in the two previous sections is summarized in Table1.5. It shows how the operating, investing and financing activities contributed to the overall cash position of the corporation. It also describes operations contributing to a $912,000 cash inflow, investing consuming $800,000, and financing adding $8,000. The net result of these transactions is a net cash inflow of $120,000, which is equal to the difference in cash held between periods. CNH has $200,000 and $320,000 at the end of the years 2000 and 2001. The difference is the net cash contribution of all the cash transactions in 2001.

The cash flow analysis conducted so far was based on the presumption that the operation results were certain. In practice, this is not the case. Firms are always exposed to several risks, which often prevent the firms from achieving their proposed goals. Therefore, to complement the content of this section it is advisable to conduct a risk analysis of CNH.

Uncertainty and Risk

The major decisions taken by the stockholders are usually based on their anticipation of the conditions of the economy and the market structure of the industry related to the main activity of the firm. These predictions often fail to materialize and so the financial results of the corporation become different from those anticipated by the shareholders. The potential discrepancy between the predicted and actual results is known as risk. This variable can take several forms. The first one, known as *economic risk,* is related to the effect of monetary and fiscal polices and the market structure of the firm on sales. The second risk, identified as *operational risk*, is related to the ability of the firm to adjust its operating expenses to a variation in sales. The flexibility of a firm to adjust to changing demand conditions depends on the proportion of fixed and variable expenditures to total operating expenses. Firms having a large proportion of fixed expenses to total operating expenses have a lesser ability to adjust their cost structure to changes in the environment surrounding the firm. [11] In contrast, corporations having a large proportion of variable cost to total cost can adjust quickly. [12]

Both economic and operational risks determine the degree of *business risk*. To illustrate the concept of business risk, consider an unexpected slowdown in economic activity. If this change increases the volume of inventories, the firm may be forced into cutting operating expenses. If the proportion of fixed to total operating expenses is very high, the firm may not be able to reduce expenses by as much as needed. The cumulative effect of a decrease in sales and a decrease in operating expenditures could lead to a lower than expected dollar value of EBIT.

Business risk is related to *unanticipated changes* in the economic environment surrounding the firm. If the changes in the environment are anticipated, they do not constitute risk since these expectations are incorporated into the decision making of the firm.

If the economic slowdown is related to an unforeseen increase in the interest rate, then the change in the interest rate will be reflected in unexpected increase in the cost of borrowing (financial risk). The *financial risk*, reflected in a higher than anticipated increase in the interest rate, contributes to a deterioration of EAT. The combined effect of business and financial risk constitutes *total risk*.

To minimize economic risk, the stockholders estimate a sales outcome based on the weighted average of a family of possible sales scenarios, each having a certain degree of probability. For example, consider the case of a firm anticipating equally likely sales scenarios of $80, and $110, each yielding profits of $8 and $11.

Most likely dollar value of sales and profits:
Sales = 0.5 × $80 + 0.5 × $110 = $95
Profits = 0.5 × $8 + 0.5 × $11 = $9.5

Figure 1.3
Uncertainty and Risk

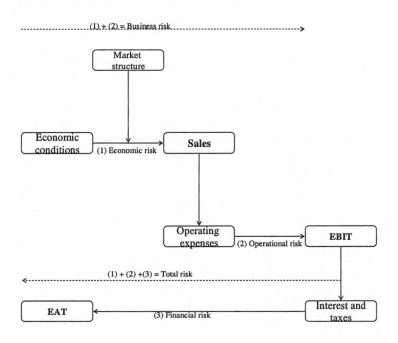

The risk transmission mechanism from disturbances related to the economic environment and the market structure of the industry within which the firm operates is described in Figure 1.3.

Value Creation and the Activities of CNH in China

A reader will find throughout the pages of this book and other books on finance several measures of corporate performance. However, the ultimate test of success is the ability of the firm to create value. In previous sections, it was explained how a single project or business proposal contributes to creating value. In this section we do not consider a proposal in isolation but rather one in relation to the firm as a whole. To measure the ability of the firm to create value, consider the corporation as an entity integrated by a family of projects or business activities. These projects and activities are coordinated by a centralized management system, where each activity has been financed and is producing a flow of benefits. In this context, the firm creates value for its owners only when the NPV of the stream of benefits generated by all the activities of the firm is positive. This occurs only when the market value of the capital of the firm exceeds the total capital employed. This difference is known as *market value added* (MVA) and is expressed as follows:

NPV (MVA of the entire corporation) = Market value of capital − Total capital employed by the firm.

The market value of the capital of the firm is simply the market value of debt and equity. The value of the total capital employed is the book value of the total liabilities of the firm found in the balance sheet.

To provide an example of how to estimate MVA assume CNH has on December 31, 2001, 1 million shares outstanding selling at $2 each and a market value of debt equal to its book value. Consider the information presented in the balance sheet (Table 1.3).

NPV = MVA of the entire corporation = Market value of the capital $_{(Dec. 31, 2001)}$ − Total capital employed $_{(Dec. 31, 2001)}$.

The market value of capital includes $2 million equity plus $1.4 million book value of debt ($560 + $840). Both items add to $3.4 million. The dollar value of capital employed is $2.8 million (see Table 1.3). Given this information and their relationship, the NPV of the entire Chinese operation is $600,000:

MVA = ($2,000,000 market value of equity + $1,400,000 market value of debt) − $2,800,000 value of capital employed = $3,400,000 − $2,800,000 = $600,000.

To better grasp the process of value creation, it is necessary to explore the reasons that create MVA. This is positive when the accumulated flow of benefits generated by all the assets used by the firm exceeds the value of the cost of the capital required to purchase the assets. This relationship is known as *economic value added* (EVA). It is equal to the difference between the dollar value of after-tax profits (the flow of benefits) and the cost of capital employed to generate the profits.

EVA = Profits − cost of the capital employed to generate the profits.

The profit (EAT) in 2001 is valued at $912,000. The initial capital used to generate the profit is $2,000,000 (dollar value at the end of 2000), which was funded with equal proportions of debt and equity capital. The cost of after-tax debt is 4.8% (8% cost of debt × (1 − 40% tax rate)[13] (see Table 1.4). The cost of equity is assumed to be 12%. Therefore, the overall cost of capital is the WACC:

WACC = (50% debt × the after-tax cost of debt) + (50% × the cost of equity)

After-tax cost of debt equity = 8% cost of debt × (1 − 40% tax rate)

= 8% × 60%

= 4.8%

WACC = (4.8% cost of after − tax cost of debt × 50%) + (12% cost of equity × 50%)

= 2.4% + 6% = 8.4%

Cost of capital employed = 8.4% × $2,000,000

= $168,000

Given that profits are $912,000 and the cost of capital employed is $168,000, the dollar value of EVA added for the year 2001 is $744,000.

EVA = after tax operating profit − dollar cost of the capital employed

= $912,000 − (8.4% × $2,000,000)

= $912,000 − $168,000

= $744,000

This result suggests that CNH consumed $168,000 to generate an after-tax profit of $912,000. Consequently, the company generated a net EVA of

$744,000. This number implies that in the year 2001 the corporation generated $744,000 in value for the owners. EVA can be restated as follows:

EVA = After-tax operating profits – (Capital employed × WACC)
= (After-tax operating profit/Capital employed – WACC) × Capital employed

Furthermore, since capital employed is equivalent to invested capital, the profit to capital employed is equivalent to ROIC. As such, EVA can be reinterpreted as follows:

EVA= ROIC – WACC × Invested capital
= ($912,000/$2,000,000 – 8.4%) × $2,000,000
= (45.6% – 8.4%) × $2,000,000
= 37.2% × $2,000,000
= $744,000

EVA shows that the firm will create value for the stockholders as long as the return on invested capital (45.6%) is higher than the cost of capital (8.4%). In the case of CNH, the Chinese operation is clearly a positive addition to the activities of CNH, since the subsidiary is creating a substantial amount of value to the parent company.

SUMMARY

This chapter discusses, at length, the important concept of value creation and provides examples of how firms create wealth. To explain value creation the chapter uses financial information related to the operation of the Chinese subsidiary of a U.S. multinational corporation. This information is organized for purposes of analysis in terms of accounting and managerial balance sheets, and the income statement.

The accounting information is also used to show the reader how to identify the engines of corporate growth and to provide examples of how to estimate cash flow and net operating cash flow from operating, investing, and financing activities.

To understand the risks associated with operating a firm and the risk transmission mechanisms, the chapter includes a review of economic, operational, and financial risks, and how their combination leads to an assessment of total risk.

The chapter also introduces the concept of the WACC and provides some practical applications of this concept.

PROBLEMS

1. Value Creation

    Home Depot is the leading retailer in the home improvement industry and ranks among the 10 largest retailers in the United States. The stores owned by Home Depot sell a wide assortment of building materials, home improvement products, and lawn and garden items. Recently, Home Depot opened up a new subsidiary in Mexico, which is considering three new lines of business to satisfy the taste of local consumers. The characteristics of the three business proposals, presented in dollar terms, are described in the table that follows.

Business Proposals	Initial Investment	Net Revenue
Project 1	$ 88,000	$105,000
Project 2	$169,000	$180,000
Project 3	$230,000	$250,000

The Mexican subsidiary can borrow in dollars at 8% and is subject to a Mexican corporate tax rate of 25%. The estimated cost of equity capital is 12%. The optimal capital structure is reached when the ratio of debt to total capital is 75%. Considering the previous information, indicate:

a. What are the cost of debt and the cost of equity?

b. What is the WACC?

c. Using the NPV rule, identify and rank the projects. Also indicate what are projects creating value for the firms and its stockholders

d. Prior to the analysis of the three projects, the price per share is $1.25 and there are 100,000 shares outstanding. If the company takes on the three projects, and the company's analysis of the projects is credible, what are the new stock price and the new value of the company?

e. If the company decides to borrow $6,250 by repurchasing 5,000 shares at $1.25 each before the implementation of the projects, will this action create value? Explain.

f. If the company decides to issue 5,000 new shares prior to the implementation of the new projects and uses the proceeds to repay debt, will this action create value? If so, how much? What is the price per share and the dollar value of the equity generated by the sale of shares? Also, indicate the dollar value of the company after this action.

2. Growth Potential and Cash Flow Analysis

    Gorky Automobile Plant is a company created by the Russian government in 1932, as a state-owned corporation. It kept this status for many years but was privatized on December 21, 1992, after the demise of the Soviet Union. Gorky Automobile Plant is a vertically integrated company with 80% of the components supplied internally, which makes it quite flexible in the unstable Russian market. The balance sheet for the years 2000 and 2001 and the income statement for the year 2001 are provided. Gorky Automobile Plant can borrow at 12% and its estimated cost of capital is 6.6%. The price per share, at par value, is Ruble 1,000, and there are 6 million shares outstanding.

Gorky Automobile Plant, Balance Sheet (ruble, thousand)					
Assets	12/31/2000	12/31/2001	Liabilities	12/31/2000	12/31/2001
Cash	60,814	499,271			
Marketable securities	353,161	344,196	Short-term debt	637,550	1,115,253
Accounts receivable	2,426,093	3,195,502	Accounts payable	2,939,397	4,130,211
Inventory	1,964,032	2,128,973	Long-term debt	789,046	2,074,945
Net fixed assets	16,100,558	17,319,503	Shareholders equity	16,538,665	16,167,036
			Total liability and		
Total assets	20,904,658	23,487,445	equity	20,904,658	23,487,445

a. Restate the balance sheet and present it in its managerial format. In addition, indicate what is the meaning of working capital.

b. How much cash is generated by the operating activities in the year 2001?

c. What is the cash flow created by operating, financing, and investing activities in the year 2001?

d. Estimate the cash flow for the year 2001.

e. What is Gorky Automobile Plant after-tax operating profitability measured by its return on invested capital?

f. What are the four key ratios shaping the business cycle of Gorky Automobile Plant?

g. Given the information provided, what is the maximum growth rate that Gorky Automobile Plant can sustain?

Gorky Automobile Plant, Income Statement, Year 2001	
Sales (ruble, thousand)	36,229,681
Less operating expenses	34,395,258
Less depreciation (2.5% of net fixed assets)	411,343
Earnings before interest and taxes	1,423,080
Less interest expenses	100,551
Earnings before taxes	1,322,529
Less taxes	241,412
Earnings after tax or net profit	1,081,117

Source: Interfax M&CN, Company Analysis, Russia.

NOTES

1. For example, a new investment, the acquisition of another company, or the restructuring of a corporation.

2. This is true if the announcement is anticipated and the market agrees with the firm on the analysis of a project's profitability.

3. The executive analyzing a NPV should avoid using the accounting numbers associated with the proposal such as the project expected revenues, expenses, and profits that will be recorded in the firm's financial statements because these accounting numbers are usually different from their cash equivalence.

4. The cost of debt is taken after tax because firms can deduct from their pretax profits the interest they pay on the money they borrow. Interest expenses are tax-deductible expense.

5. The cash withdraw fueled the speculation that Lucent was filing for bankruptcy.

6. Lucent Technologies, "Investor Relations," April 9, 2001.

7. Bettina Wessener, "SAP agrees to buy TopTier for $400m," *The Financial Times*, April 2, 2001.

8. For further details of the NYSE, the reader is encouraged to visit www.nyse.com

9. This figure was estimated as follows: short-term ($560,000) and long-term ($840,000) loans, priced at 8%. These two items come from the balance sheet presented in Table 1.3.

10. $120,000 interest payment outflow, $280,000 dividend outflow, and $400,000 loan inflow.

11. High operating leverage.

12. Low operating leverage.

SUGGESTED ADDITIONAL READINGS

Bodie, Z., and Merton, R. *Finance*. Englewood Cliffs, NJ: Prentice-Hall, 2000. See Chapters 7, 8, and 9.

Beal, R., and Stewart, M. *Principles of Corporate Finance*. 6th ed. New York, NY: McGraw-Hill, 2000. See Chapters 1 and 2.

Rappaport, A. *Creating Shareholders Value*. New York, NY: Free Press, 2000. See Chapter 1.

Ross S., Randolph, W., and Jaffe, J. *Corporate Finance*. 5th ed. Homewood, ILL: Irwin, 1999. See Chapter 3.

Young, S., and O'Byrne, E. *EVA and Value Added Based Management: A Practical Guide to Implementation*. New York, NY: McGraw-Hill, 2001. See Chapters 1 and 2.

2

Interpreting and Forecasting Financial Statements

Corporations in the United States are required to make full and fair disclosure of their operations. To meet this goal, businesses publish various financial statements and other reports required by the Securities and Exchange Commission (SEC), the Financial Accounting Standard Board, and the American Institute of Certified Public Accountants.

Some of the reports, like Form 10-K (Annual Report) and Form 10-Q (Quarterly Report), are required by the SEC to make full and fair disclosure of the financial situation of a business. These reports must include the balance sheet, income statement, statement of cash flow, and comments by management on the situation of the company.

The purpose of this chapter is to explain the content and logic of the balance sheet and the income statement, and how these statements relate to each other. To meet this goal, the following sections contain a description of:

- The items included in each of the financial statements and the terminology used to describe them
- The existing relationship between the balance sheet and the income statement
- How business decisions affect the income statement and the balance sheet
- How to combine the financial statements of a U.S. multinational with the business activities of a foreign subsidiary

THE BALANCE SHEET

This statement is a financial picture of a firm at a given point in time. Balance sheet presentations normally describe the financial situation of a firm over two or more periods to provide an indication of the performance of the company at different points in time.

The balance sheet is divided into two parts. One part shows assets and the other describes the liabilities and stockholders' equity. Both parts must always be in balance. The asset column lists all the goods and property owned by the company, as well as the claims against others yet to be collected. The liability side presents all the debts the company owes and stockholders' equity. This last item shows how much the company income revenue would accrue to the stockholders if the company were going to be liquidated at its balance sheet value. To provide a guided tour of the balance sheet, this chapter uses the financial information of Adobe Systems Incorporated hereinafter referred simply as Adobe.

Adobe was founded in 1982, incorporated on October 26, 1983, and made its initial public offering on August 20, 1986.[1] It built software solutions for network publishing including web, print, video, and wireless applications. Web designers, graphic designers, publishers, document-intensive organizations, and consumers use Adobe products. It is the second largest personal computer software company in the United States, with annual revenues exceeding $1.2 billion. It has 2,800 employees and operates in North America, Europe, Asia, and Latin America. Its headquarters is located in San Jose, California, the heart of Silicon Valley.

CURRENT ASSETS

In general, current assets include cash, assets and receivables due in a year or less, and items that can be easily turned into cash during the normal course of business.

Cash and Short-Term Investments

Cash is a form of currency including bills, coins, and money on deposit with a bank. On March 1, 2001, Adobe had $176.262 million in cash (Table 2.1).

Short-term investments, also identified frequently as marketable securities, represent the temporary investment of excess or idle cash for which the company does not have an immediate use. These funds are usually invested for very short periods in securities[2] that can be traded easily and are subject to a minimum price fluctuation. These securities are entered into the balance sheet at cost or market price, whichever is lower. According to the information presented in Table 2.1, Adobe has short-term investments equivalent to $443.957 million.

Table 2.1
Balance Sheet, Adobe Systems Incorporated

Assets	($ Thousands)	1 Mar. 01	1 Mar. 00
Current Assets		**845,375**	**877,912**
Cash		176,262	236,866
Short term investment		443,957	442,987
Accounts (or trade) receivable*		174,902	160,113
Inventories		0	0
Other current assets		50,254	37,946
Noncurrent Assets		*189,260*	*191,504*
Financial assets and intangibles		122,113	127,236
Property, plant and equipment (net)		67,147	64,268
Total Assets		**1,034,635**	**1,069,416**
Liabilities and Equity			
Current Liabilities		*291,898*	*316,872*
Short-term debt		0	0
Accounts payable		38,694	40,280
Accrued expenses		253,204	276,592
Noncurrent Liabilities		*742,737*	*752,544*
Long-term debt		0	0
Stockholders' equity		742,737	752,544
Total Liabilities and Equity		**1,034,635**	**1,069,416**

*This account is net of allowance for doubtful accounts of $9.653 and $8.788 million, respectively.

Accounts Receivable, Inventories, and Total Current Assets

Accounts receivable lists the value of shipments made to customers, which are still in the process of collection. Customers are normally given 30, 60, or 90 days to settle their invoices associated with shipments. The amount that the customers of Adobe owe is valued at $174.902 million. It is important to note that the dollar value of accounts receivable is net of provisions for bad debt. In the case of Adobe, provisions for bad debt amounted to $18.441 million created to cover doubtful accounts for $9.653 and $8.788 million, respectively. The creation of a reserve to cover for nonperforming trade receivables is not unusual because corporations have learned that customers sometimes fail to pay their bills.

Inventories are classified by manufacturing firms as raw materials, partially finished goods, and finished goods inventories. The raw materials and partially finished goods are used to process final products, whereas finished goods are ready for shipment to customers. However, high-tech companies like Adobe do not hold inventories because their business is related to the production and distribution of knowledge stored in electronic devices manufactured by company suppliers.

TOTAL CURRENT AND NONCURRENT OR FIXED ASSETS

Total current assets are listed in a decreasing order of liquidity. *Liquidity* is a measure of the capability of the asset to be used as a medium of exchange. Cash is the most liquid of the current assets because it can be used to pay for any type of business transaction at any time. Another distinguishing feature of current assets is the fact that they are always in constant motion of being converted into cash. For example, inventories of finished goods, when shipped, become accounts receivable. Upon collection, the trade receivables are turned into cash that can be used to pay debts and running expenses.

Noncurrent or fixed assets are also referred to as capital assets, or property, plant, and equipment. These are items expected to produce economic benefits to the firm for a period exceeding one year. This classification includes tangible and intangible fixed assets.

Tangible assets are physical assets, which can be easily identified or bought and sold. These include land, buildings, machinery, equipment, furniture, and transportation equipment held to manufacture, display, store, and transport products. They also include long-term assets such as stock of other companies and loans extended by the firm to other corporations. Fixed assets normally are entered into the balance sheet at cost minus depreciation.

Intangible assets are assets that are not physically present but affect the value of the corporation. These include items such as patents, trademarks, copyrights, and goodwill. To explain this last concept, consider the case of a firm wanting to purchase the assets of another corporation. If the acquiring firm purchases the assets of the target firm at a price exceeding the net book value of the assets in the balance sheet of the target firm, then this difference is entered as goodwill into the balance sheet of the acquiring firm.

For example, consider the case of an acquiring company paying $30 million for assets listed in the balance sheet of the target firm at $25 million. In this case, to account for the difference between book value and the price paid to purchase the assets of the target company, the acquiring firm has to record on its balance sheet a $5 million goodwill entry.

Adobe's fixed assets are worth $67.147 million. This number reflects the net book value of Adobe's fixed assets, which is equal to historical value.[3]

DEPRECIATION

For accounting purpose, depreciation is defined as the decline in the dollar value of an asset due to wear, aging, and obsolescence. There are several methods available to estimate the dollar value of depreciation. In the most commonly used procedure, known as *straight-line depreciation*, the depreciated amount is the same each period. In the less frequently used procedure, known as *accelerated depreciation,* the yearly depreciation amount begins high and declines continuously afterward. To illustrate how to estimate depreciation, consider the case of computer equipment with an acquisition price of $500,000 and a life expectancy of five years. If straight-line method is used to depreciate the asset, yearly depreciation amounts to $100,000, estimated as the ratio of the acquisition price ($500,000) to life expectancy (five years). An accelerated depreciation schedule could be, $200,000 the first year, and subsequent charges of $125,000, $100,000, $50,000, and $25,000 each. Obviously, the asset value reported in the balance sheet will depend on the method used to depreciate the asset, as shown in Table 2.2.

CURRENT LIABILITIES

Current liabilities include all the obligations due within the existing fiscal year such as short-term debt, account payables, and accrued or prepaid expenses.

Short-Term Debt, Accounts Payable, and Accrued Expenses

Short-term debt includes notes payable, bank overdrafts, and drawings on lines of credit. Adobe does not have any short-term debt outstanding, which in the year 2001 was a common characteristic of high-tech companies in the United States.

Accounts payable represent the debt owed by Adobe to the suppliers, which provide the company with goods and services. This debt arises because Adobe, like any other corporation, does not pay its suppliers right away for the goods and services it receives from them. Since Adobe is not a manufacturing company, accounts payable is not very substantial. In March of 2001, this amounted to only $38.694 million.

In addition to short-term debt and accounts payable, Adobe also owes wages to the employees, interest on funds borrowed from banks, fees to attorneys, insurance premiums, and government taxes. All these liabilities are grouped and reported as accrued expenses in the balance sheet as long as they are unpaid. On March 1, 2001, Adobe's accrued expenses amount to $253.204 million.

NONCURRENT LIABILITIES AND EQUITY

Noncurrent liabilities include the obligations of Adobe due to mature in more than a year. Such as long-term debt owed to lenders, pension liabilities owed to employees, and deferred taxes owed to the tax collection agencies of the government. For a manufacturing corporation, noncurrent liabilities are a substantial portion of the total liabilities of the company. However, this is not the case for Adobe. First, Adobe does not have any long-term debt. Second, many of the corporation's employees are temporary, which enables Adobe to not pay retirement funds.

Equity is simply the difference between the book value of Adobe's assets and liabilities at some point in time. For legal and accounting reasons, equity is broken into three categories: capital stock, capital surplus, and accumulated retained earnings. These all amount to $742.737 million in 2001.

Stockholders' equity = Total assets − Total liabilities
= $1,034,635 − $291,898
= $742,737

Table 2.2
Estimation of Net Book Value

Line	($ Thousands)	Year 0	Year 1	Year 2	Year 3	Year 4	Year 5
1	Acquisition price	500					
2	**Straight-line depreciation**		100	100	100	100	100
3	Accumulated depreciation		100	200	300	400	500
4	Net book value = line 1 (year 0) – line 3		400	300	200	100	0
1	Acquisition price	500					
2	**Accelerated depreciation**		200	125	100	50	25
3	Accumulated depreciation		200	325	425	475	500
4	Net book value = line 1 (year 0) – line 3		300	175	75	25	0

Capital Stock: Preferred and Common Stock

The corporation raises capital stock by issuing stock certificates to its stockholders. The certificates or shares may be either preferred or common.

Preferred stock certificates have the highest priority both on dividends and in the distribution of assets in case of bankruptcy, after paying the company's debt with vendors and banks. Corporate charters provide specific provisions related to the conditions under which preferred stock is issued. If preferred stock is stated at $5 cumulative $100 par value, this means that holders of preferred stock are entitled to $5 in dividends prior to the payment of dividends to common stockholders. Cumulative implies that unpaid dividends accumulate and must be paid if profits are available before any dividends are distributed to common stockholders. The only drawback is that preferred stockholders do not have a voice in company affairs.[4]

Regarding common stock, in March 2000, there were 240,609,000 shares of Adobe common stock outstanding in the New York Stock Exchange priced at $42.51 each. Their total market value was $10,228,288,590. The holders of these shares have the right to claim the amount of profits left over after payment to preferred stockholders. As such, there is not a limit on how much a common stockholder can earn. When dividends are high, earnings are high. When profits drop, so do common stock dividends.[5]

Accumulated Retained Earnings

This item is also known as earned surplus. When a company starts up, retained earnings are zero. However, as time passes, the accumulation of retained earnings increases if the firm is profitable and the retention rate is high.[6] If this is the case, a high profit retention rate provides firms with a cash surplus that can contribute to an increase in sales, profits, and the market price of the company's shares. This is the case of Adobe, which has a retention rate of 99% and has allowed the company to accumulate $1,239,240,000 in retained earnings.[7]

THE INCOME STATEMENT

The income statement provides a summary of the operating and financial transactions contributing to change in *shareholders equity* during the accounting period. Some companies in the United States label this statement as the *earnings report* or the *statement of profits and losses*. This report provides valuable information to stockholders and investors interested in acquiring the stock of a company. This is because it shows the operating activities of a firm during a given period and provides a valuable guide to help anticipate future corporate performance.

An income statement contrasts sales and other items of income against all the costs and expenses incurred by the corporation. The costs incurred include cost of goods sold (COGS), research, development, sales, marketing, administrative expenses, amortization of goodwill, depreciation, extraordinary expenses, net interest expenses on investments, and taxes.

The overall result of the comparison is net profits or net losses, also known as earnings after tax.[8] This relationship is the foundation used to construct Adobe's income statement. Revenues are recorded first. Their source is sales of goods and services, the collection of fees, and rental income. Expenses are listed afterwards. Both revenues and expenses are recognized in the income statement when the transaction generating the sales and outlays take place, not when they are settled. Therefore, revenues and expenses increase when sales and expenses are invoiced. When either sales or expenses are paid, net revenues and total assets and liabilities are not affected. When a payment is received, cash increases and accounts receivable decrease by the same amount, therefore, the assets and liabilities entries of the balance sheet remain unchanged.

Revenue or Net Sales, Cost of Goods Sold, and Gross Profits

The revenues of an accounting period, after discounts and allowances for returned merchandise, determine net sales. These represent the primary source of cash received by a company in exchange for goods sold and services rendered. In the case of Adobe, the company had revenues of $ 328.969 million and $ 282.232 million during the years 2001 and 2000 respectively (Table 2.3). This change represents an increase in sales of 17%.

For a manufacturing firm, COGS represents the bulk of the cost incurred by a manufacturing firm in its factories as a factor of production. However, for nonmanufacturing companies like Adobe, this item only represents a relatively minor proportion of sales.[9]

Operating Expenses, Operating Profit, and Extraordinary Items

For modern, high-tech companies serving the digital economy, expenses associated with research and development, sales, marketing, and administrative, determine operating expenses. For Adobe, research and development amounted to $55.687 million, sales and marketing amounted to $103.860 million, and general and administrative expenses amounted to $30.37 million. This totaled to 58% of revenue for Adobe. Sales and administrative expenses are often recognized as overhead expenses because they are unrelated to output and somewhat independent from revenues.

Operating profit is estimated as the difference between gross profits and operating expenses and is a measure of the earnings generated by the normal business activity of a firm.[10] During 2001, Adobe's operating income amounted to $115.454 million. This value is equivalent to 35% of revenues and is 31% higher than the operating income posted by the company the previous year.

The account for extraordinary items represents the gains and losses experienced by a firm during the accounting period, which are related to infrequent transactions not directly related to the main business activity of a firm.

Gross profit is the broadest measure of a firm's income. It is the difference between revenue and the cost of goods sold. In the case of Adobe, gross profits are 94% of total revenue with a 17% rate of growth.

Earnings before Interest and Taxes, and Net Interest Expenses

Earnings before interest and taxes (EBIT) are equal to operating profits less extraordinary items. It is a measure of the profitability of a company, which is not affected either by the borrowing policies of the corporation or the range of its tax liabilities.

This feature of EBIT allows it to play an important role in the rating of corporate performance within or across industries. This is because it enables investors to compare the profitability of firms having different debt policies and varying degrees of corporate taxation.

According to a legally established order, EBIT must be shared among lenders, tax collecting authorities, and the owners of the firm. The lenders have the highest priority for collection and are entitled to receive from the firms interest income for loans granted to them. Companies investing in other firms are also entitled to receive interest income.

Therefore, net interest expenses or nonoperating income is equal to the difference between interest income and interest expenses. Adobe in 2001 had net interest expense of $11.341 million. This result is in sharp contrast with the financial performance of the corporation in the previous year when it reported a net income of $10.327 million.

Earnings before Taxes, Income Tax, and Earnings after Tax

The earnings before taxes (EBT) account is equal to EBIT less net interest expense. In the year 2001, Adobe's EBT is $104.113 million, which is equivalent to 32% of revenue and is 5% higher than the earnings posted by the company the previous year. The amount of taxes paid depends on the level of EBT. These levels of earnings are used by the Internal Revenue Service in the United States to establish the taxable base. Adobe is a distinguished U.S. corporation with a substantial amount of earnings. During 2001, the tax expenses of Adobe amounted to $34.357 million, which is 33% of earnings before taxes.

Table 2.3
Adobe, Consolidated Statements of Income, 2000 and 2001

($ Thousands)	1 Mar. 01	1 Mar. 00
Revenue	328,969	282,232
Less direct cost (including $10,610 of depreciation)	9,406	7,733
Depreciation expenses	10,610	12,989
Gross profit	**308,953**	**261,510**
Less		
Research and development	55,687	57,458
Sales and marketing	103,860	87,760
General and administrative	30,370	26,757
Amortization of good will and intangibles	3,582	1,203
Operating profit	**115,454**	**88,332**
Plus extraordinary items	0	672
EBIT	**115,454**	**89,004**
Investment gains (loss)	-17,038	4,676
Interest and other income	5,697	5,651
EBT	**104,113**	**99,331**
Less tax	34,357	34,766
EAT	**69,756**	**64,565**
Dividends	*3,020*	*2,978*
Retained Earnings	*66,736*	*61,587*

Source: United States Securities and Exchange Commission (SEC), Form 10-Q, March 2, 2001, p 3.

The earnings after taxes (EAT) account is also known as net income, net profits, or the *bottom line*. It takes into consideration all sources of income and all the cost and expenses. It is obtained by deducting tax expenses from EBT. When earnings after taxes are positive, the company is said to be operating in the black. However, if it is negative, the firm is generating a loss and it is said to be operating in the red. Adobe reported in the year 2001 a net income of $69.756 million. This represents 21% of total revenue for the same year and is 8% higher than the earnings reported in the previous period. This amount is also a measure of the net change in equity resulting from the operation of the business in 2001.

CROSS-BORDER TRANSACTIONS

Adobe operates subsidiaries in North America, Europe, Asia, and Latin America. The primary foreign markets are in Japan and Europe. In the Asian country, the company has revenues related to yen denominated licenses. In Europe Adobe licenses in U.S. dollars and has euro-denominated operating expenses. These transactions expose Adobe to foreign exchange rate risk, which is the risk associated with variations in the rate at which yens and euro are exchanged for U.S. dollars. Sensitivity analysis conducted by Adobe indicates that a 10% to 15% appreciation of the yen and euro against the U.S. dollar could increase the dollar value of the foreign currency assets held by the firm from $5.5 to $7.4 million. In contrast, a depreciation of these currencies against the U.S. dollar of the same magnitude would decrease the dollar value of Adobe's foreign currency assets by $3.4 to $4.7 million. These variations are not expected to have a substantial effect on the operations of the company. Nonetheless, these variations pose problems for Adobe. The first challenge is how to translate the value of the yen denominated licenses into dollars, which is considered a foreign exchange translation problem. The second task is how to report in dollar terms, operating expenses stated in euro. This job is considered a foreign exchange transaction problem.

THE TRANSLATION PROBLEM

To solve the foreign exchange translation problems, multinational corporations use any one of the three following translation methods: *current/noncurrent, monetary/nonmonetary*, and *current.*

Current/Noncurrent, Monetary/Nonmonetary, and Current Methods

Under the current/noncurrent method assets and liabilities are grouped according to their maturity. For example, current yen assets and liabilities are translated using the exchange rate prevailing on the date when the balance sheet is issued. In contrast, Nocurrent assets and liabilities are translated at the exchange rate prevailing when the assets were purchased or the liabilities were incurred.

Corporations also use the monetary/nonmonetary method to classify assets and liabilities. Monetary assets and liabilities include accounts that must be stated at current market value and translated at the exchange rate prevailing at the time the balance sheet is issued. Accounts classified as monetary include cash, receivables, payables, and long-term debt. Nonmonetary accounts are items translated at the exchange rate existing when the transaction takes place. For example, the account related to the acquisition of machinery and equipment, is translated using the exchange rate that exists when a plant or building is purchased.

The current method is the simplest and the most widely used translation method. Under this method, all assets and liabilities are translated using the exchange rate existing when the balance sheet is issued. Income statement accounts are translated into dollars using the average exchange rate prevailing over the period of the report, which could be a quarter, six months, or a year. Once the accounts are translated into dollars, dollar gains or losses are computed. The gain or loss can be included in the financial statements of a U.S. corporation in two ways. It can be listed in the income statement as a nonoperating income or charged against the retained earnings account in the balance sheet.

THE TRANSACTION PROBLEM

To separate corporate performance from foreign exchange gains or losses, firms like Adobe use a procedure known as *two-transaction exposure*. This method was designed to determine whether the corporate performance of a subsidiary is related to good or poor management or to foreign exchange gains or losses. The two-transaction exposure separates the dollar value of an event from any ensuing change in the exchange rate by creating three accounts. The first account describes the original transaction. The second account is a balance sheet item designed as loss or gain on foreign exchange. A third account is an item in the income statement labeled as foreign exchange gains or losses.

To illustrate this method, consider Adobe purchasing on January 1, 2001 raw materials in Europe for €1million. At this time, if the exchange rate is $1 = € 0.9, then the dollar value of the inventories held by the European subsidiary on January 1, 2001, is $1.11 million.

Dollar value of European inventories = (€ value) × (exchange rate)
= (€1,000,000) × ($1/€ 0.9)
= (€1,000,000) × ($1.1/€ 1)
= (€1,000,000)/(€1) × ($1.11)
= $1,110,000

In the balance sheet of Adobe, this transaction is entered as $1.11 million of inventories, and $1.11 million of accounts payable. If the dollar depreciates to $1/€ 0.8, on March 1, 2001, then the value of the raw materials in terms of dollars will increase to $1.25 million. As a result of these changes, the dollar balance sheet will include an additional $140,000 in inventories and in accounts payable.

Dollar value of European inventories = (€ value) times (exchange rate)
= (€1,000,000) × ($1/€ 0.8)
= (€1,000,000) × ($1.25/€ 1)
= (€1,000,000)/(€ 1) × ($1.25)
= $1,250,000

If Adobe settles the payable on March 1, 2001, cash and accounts payable will be reduced by $1.25 million.

In the income statement, under a two-transaction method, the use of the inventories is reflected as a charge of $1.1 million to direct cost (cost of goods sold) and $140,000 in exchange rate gains or losses. Table 2.4 presents the effect of the dollar depreciation on the income statement, applying the two-transaction method. It also contrasts its results with those obtained when the exchange rate is ignored (no transaction). This comparison shows that the no transaction method understates the financial performance of the European subsidiary. This also shows how the two-transaction method allows the owners of the company to identify the benefits related to the business operation from foreign exchange rate gains or losses, which in the Adobe case, resulted in a foreign exchange rate gain of $140,000.

Table 2.4
Income Statement, European Subsidiary

($ Thousands)	1 Mar. 01 No transaction	1 Mar. 01 Two-transaction
Revenue	32,897	32,897
Less direct cost (including $1.061 of depreciation)	2,171	2,171
Depreciation expenses	1,061	1,061
Gross profit	**29,665**	**29,665**
Less		
Research and development	5,569	5,569
Exchange rate gains (losses)		140
Sales and marketing	10,386	10,386
General and administrative	3,037	3,037
Amortization of good will and intangibles	358	358
Operating profit	**10,315**	**10,455**
Less extraordinary items	0	0
EBIT	**10,315**	**10,455**
Less		
Investment gains (loss)	−1,704	−1,704
Interest and other income	570	570
EBT	**9,181**	**9,321**
Less tax	3,436	3,436
EAT)	**5,745**	**5,885**

MEASURING CORPORATE PERFORMANCE

There is sufficient information to conduct an analysis of Adobe's corporate performance, but not enough financial tools. These will be provided in following chapters. In spite of this shortcoming, it is possible to issue an initial judgment of how well Adobe has performed by contrasting the financial targets forecasted by Adobe at the beginning of the period with the results posted at the end of the term. For further details see Table 2.5.

Table 2.5
Adobe, Assessment of Corporate Performance

Targets	Actual (1)	Forecast (2)	(1) – (2)	Assessment
Revenue growth	17%	25%	−8%	Less than expected
Gross margin	94%	93%	1%	Better than expected
Research and development margin	17%	18%	−1%	Better than expected
Sales and marketing margin	32%	33%	−1%	Better than expected
General and administrative margin	9%	9%	0%	As expected
Operating profit margin	35%	32%	3%	Better than expected

This comparison indicates that Adobe meets or exceeds most of its internal targets, but it is below expectations in revenue growth, which is a key external target. Adobe attributes its shortcomings to:

- Delays in shipment of new products
- Lack of market acceptance of new products and upgrades
- Adverse changes in economic conditions
- Introduction of new products by major competitors
- Lack of growth in worldwide personal computer
- Renegotiation of royalty agreements

The Equity Account, Composition and Variation

The analysis of the equity account provides additional information that can assist the stockholder to rate the performance of Adobe over the one-year accounting period considered in this chapter.

A detailed analysis of the composition equity and the source of variation of this item are presented in Table 2.6. A visual inspection of how the interaction of the balance sheet and the income statement affect equity is shown in Figure 2.1.

The first source of equity is *common stock*. The dollar value of this item is the number of shares issued by Adobe since its inception times the *par value* or stated value. The par value of common stock is an arbitrary number attached to each share. This number is simply a figure set arbitrarily by the founders of the corporation and is unrelated to the market price of common stock. The accumulated par value of common stock represents the maximum liability of the stockholders if the firm is dissolved.

The second source of equity is *paid-in capital in excess of par*. This value is the difference between the market and par value of common stock or the amount of cash that Adobe received from the sale of the shares less the amount of cash that Adobe would have received if the shares had been sold at par.

Table 2.6
Adobe, Composition and Change of Equity

($ Thousands)	2001	2000	Variation
Common stock, 240,609,000 shares at par value of $0.1	24,061	24,061	0
Paid in capital in excess of par	533,804	506,740	27,064
Accumulated retained earnings	1,239,240	1,172,504	66,736
Other loss	(4,004)	(698)	(3,306)
Treasury stocks at cost	(1,050,364)	(950,063)	(100,301)
Net	**742,737**	**752,544**	**(9,807)**

Source: Adobe Systems Incorporated, SEC, Form 10-Q, March 30, 2001, p. 4.

Figure 2.1
The Link of the Balance Sheet with the Income Statement

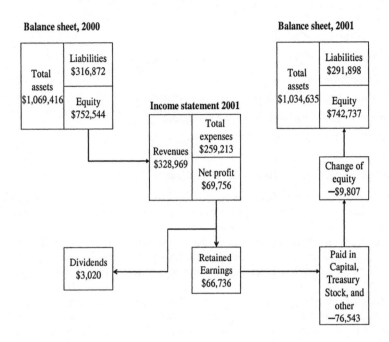

An additional source of equity is *accumulated retained earnings*, or reserves. It shows the accumulation of retained earnings since the inception of Adobe to the date the financial statements were issued. The difference between periods shows the accumulation of retained earnings during the accounting period.

The last major source of equity is *treasury stock*. This item shows the amount of cash spent by the company buying back its own stock since the creation of the company until the date of the balance sheet. The difference between periods indicates how much cash was spent to acquire Adobe stock during the accounting period.

The last line shows the market value at the end of the accounting period. The difference between periods shows the net contribution of the operations of the company during the last period to the net worth of the stockholders.

Unfortunately, during the accounting period, the company reported a decline in equity equivalent to $9.807 million in spite of net accumulation of retained earnings of $66.736 million.

An examination of the information presented in Figure 2.1 leads to the same result. It shows that at the end of the year 2000, Adobe's equity is valued at $752.544 million (see Table 2.1). It also shows the company retaining $66.736 million of earnings. Under normal circumstance, the dollar value of retained earnings would have been reflected as an increase in equity of the same magnitude. However, in the case of Adobe, the effect of earnings accumulation on equity is neutralized by losses experienced in the repurchase of company's shares. This loss is equivalent to $76.543 million. The net result of the two events is a $9.807 million reduction in the value of equity. As a result of this outcome, the value of equity falls to from $752.544 million in the year 2000 to $742.737 million in 2001.

SUMMARY

This chapter defined the meaning of items included in the balance sheet and the income statement, provided guidance on how to prepare a balance sheet and an income statement, and presented some insights on how these two items relate to each other.

To provide the reader with a real-life experience, the explanations provided in the different sections of the chapter were based on the financial information furnished by a digital corporation deeply involved in the global economy.

This information was also used to explain how to prepare the balance sheet and income statement of an e-business, and how the financial statements of this type of corporation relate to each other. In addition, this information was organized to explore the relationship between foreign subsidiaries and their parent companies, how changes in the exchange rate affect this relationship, and how to allocate foreign exchange gains or losses.

NOTES

1. Adobe, "Investor Relations," www.adobe.com. (accessed March 1, 2002).

2. Securities include short-term corporate or government debt such as commercial paper and treasury bills.

3. Historical value is the acquisition price minus accumulated depreciation.

4. This is not the case when companies fail to pay the preferred dividends at the promised date.

5. Profits are not the only source of gain for the holder of a common stock or the only reason to hold the share. Other benefits may arise from high stock prices.

6. A high profit retention rate provides firms with a cash surplus that can contribute to raise sales, profits, and the market price of the stock.

7. United States Securities and Exchange Commission (SEC) Form 10-Q, Adobe Systems Incorporated, March 30, 2001, p. 4.

8. EAT are equal to revenues minus expenses.

9. COGS for Adobe are $20.016 million, including depreciation expenses, or 6% of total revenue.

10. These instruments refer to forward options contracts and bank accounts held by Adobe.

SUGGESTED ADDITIONAL READINGS

Bodie, Z., and Merton, R. *Finance*. Englewood Cliffs, NJ: Prentice Hall, 2000. See Chapter 3.

Hawawini, G., and Viallet, C. *Finance for Executives, Managing for Value Creation*. 2nd ed. Cincinnati, OH: South-Western, 2001. See Chapters 2 and 3.

IBM. "Guide to Financials, A Basic Introduction to Reading Financial Statements." http://www.ibm.com/investor/financialguide/. (Accessed March 21, 2002).

Lycos Small Business. "Preparing Financial Statements." http://business.lycos.com/cch/guidebook.html?lpv=1&docNumber=P06_1570. (Accessed October 23, 2001).

Small Business Administration. "Understanding Basic Financial Statements." http://www.onlinewbc.org/docs/finance/fs_intro.html. (Accessed October 25, 2001).

U.S. Securities and Exchange Commission (SEC). "SEC Fillings and Forms." http://www.sec.gov/edgar.html. (Accessed October 24, 2001).

3

The Foreign Exchange Market

A national currency functions as *medium of exchange,* which is used to make or receive payments. A *unit of account* is used to compare the price of different goods or services in order to determine which one of the items is the most expensive or the cheapest. The *store of value* is a way of gathering money in a savings or checking accounts in a commercial bank. *The standard to defer payments* is to lend money today in exchange for a stream of payments in the future. Residents of a country often conduct business abroad or engage in financial transactions with persons in other countries. As such, there is the need for an international payments or exchange system to settle cross-border transactions from one currency to another.

The mechanism used to facilitate the purchase and sale of foreign currencies is the *foreign exchange market.*[1] This is a financial market where the participants exchange a national monetary unit for another currency and where the price of one currency is always stated in terms of another currency.[2] It is the oldest and largest financial market in the world. In 1977, the purchase and sale of U.S. dollars in the foreign exchange market was estimated at $5 billion a day. In the year 2001, the turnover had increased to $1.5 trillion a day. To put this into perspective, consider that the value of the transactions in the U.S. stock market totaled $21 trillion in the year 2001. The comparison of the two indicates that the dollar value of foreign exchange transactions is 26 times higher than the value of stock trading. Eighty percent of the foreign exchange transactions are related to dollar trading and to the acquisition of the U.S. dollars, euros, and Japanese yen.

The goal of this chapter is to provide the reader with the tools required to understand the operations and mechanics of the foreign exchange market. To meet this goal, the chapter:

- Depicts the nature of the foreign exchange market
- Discusses the benefits of having a market to trade currencies
- Indicates who are the most important players in this market and the reasons why they participate
- Describes the organization and composition of the foreign exchange market and offers an explanation of how to trade in each segment of this market

THE NATURE OF THE FOREIGN EXCHANGE MARKET

The foreign exchange market operates continuously, 24 hours a day, because there is always a financial center open for business in some part of the world and someone buying and selling currencies day or night. This continuous trading is made possible by the interconnection of the markets.

At the beginning of each day, the foreign exchange market starts in Wellington, New Zealand; then Sydney, Australia; followed by Tokyo, Hong Kong, and Singapore. Prior to the closing of Asia, the market opens in Bahrain and the Middle East. When the markets of Asia are still operating, Europe enters the trading. Subsequently, when it is still early afternoon in London, trading begins in New York and other U.S. financial centers. Finally, the cycle is completed when in the late afternoon in the United States, countries in Asia start trading again.

The twenty-four hour trading feature ensures an endless stream of variations in market conditions responding to developments in the world economy. The chain of events taking place in different regions often cause sharp variations in exchange rates during trading and off-trading hours. To avoid being caught unprepared, market players have introduced various strategies allowing them to monitor the market. Some of them keep their offices open 24 hours by organizing into trading teams, which work in shifts.

THE BENEFITS OF TRADING CURRENCIES

The foreign exchange market enables the residents of a country to trade local currency for foreign currencies, which in turn allows them to purchase foreign goods and services. For instance, a resident of the United States can trade dollars for euro in the foreign exchange market and use the euro to import a German-made car. In this instance, the local currency (the dollar) acts as a medium of exchange to allow U.S. residents to import foreign goods or services.

The availability of foreign exchange and exchange rate quotations enables traders to compare the value of a variety of goods and services produced in different locations under a variety of circumstances. To illustrate this point, a U.S. resident is trying to decide whether to import shoes from Japan or purchase them locally in the United States. If a pair of Japanese produced shoes is worth 1,000 yen in Tokyo and the exchange rate quoted in the international currency market is one dollar for 100 Japanese yen ($1/¥100), then the dollar price of the Japanese shoes is $10. If the price in the United States is $12 for shoes of similar quality, then the U.S. resident may want to import the shoes from Japan, because the price there is the lowest. In this example, the U.S. dollar played the role of an international unit of account and let the U.S. resident identify the lowest price for shoes.

Mexican residents wanting to put their savings in dollars can trade local currency, Mexican pesos, for dollars in the foreign exchange market and use the dollar proceeds to open a savings account in a U.S. bank. In this instance, the U.S. dollar acts as a store of value enabling Mexican residents to put their peso savings into the more stable U. S. currency.

Multinational corporations from the United States often need to settle foreign currency denominated accounts payable or accept accounts receivable in terms of foreign exchange. If a U.S. corporation has a 90-day euro payable, when the payable is due, the U.S. firm can trade dollars for euro in the foreign exchange and pay its debt. In this instance, the foreign exchange market uses the euro as a means to settle an international payment.

PARTICIPANTS IN THE FOREIGN EXCHANGE MARKET

The foreign exchange market is made up of individuals, firms, banks, and other private and public institutions from all over the world buying and selling currencies for various reasons. Some are involved in *international trade*, importing and exporting goods or services. Others are engaged in *foreign direct investment,* purchasing overseas plants and equipment, or in *portfolio investment*, acquiring or selling stocks, bonds and other financial assets. Another group uses the *money market* to trade short-term debt instruments internationally.

The foreign exchange participants that are involved in international trade can use the market to *hedge* accounts payable and receivable. Others engage in portfolio investment to *speculate*. Another group looks for opportunities to buy currency where it is cheap and simultaneously sell it in locations where it is expensive. This activity is known as *arbitrage*.

Foreign exchange transactions are often conducted by commercial banks on behalf of corporate customers. These usually take the form of an exchange of bank deposits in currencies from two or more countries. For example, a bank in the U.S. can purchase euro from another bank with dollars for a U.S. customer. This transaction then is settled with an exchange of dollar bank deposits to a euro bank account. This family of foreign exchange transactions, which use commercial banks as intermediaries, has developed into a segment of the financial markets known as the *interbank market*.

Central and commercial banks, multinational corporations, speculators, and arbitrageurs are active players in the foreign exchange market. Central banks are considered the dominant players in this market as a result of their ability to issue or restrict the supply of currencies. They also possess large amounts of foreign exchange reserves that they frequently trade in order to manage the parity of their currencies or those of their trading partners. Central banks of large countries often intervene in the foreign exchange market by selling or buying large sums of dollars and other currencies. The purpose of this trading is to maintain their currencies or the monetary unit of a partner within a desired price range. Central banks also influence the foreign exchange market through their balance of payment policies. For example, a central bank can sell part of their foreign exchange reserve holdings to finance a balance of payments deficit or buy foreign currency to eliminate a balance of payments surplus.

The importance of the commercial banks in the foreign exchange market is that they actively trade on their own behalf or on the interest of their customers. Commercial and investment banks trade foreign currency with each other directly or through brokers. This activity is very profitable for a commercial bank.

Firms participate in the foreign exchange market to settle foreign currency payables, to turn foreign exchange receivables into local currency, to arbitrage, to hedge, to speculate, or to repatriate profits. Usually, their intervention is channeled through commercial banks or brokers who act on behalf of their corporate customers.

Individuals partake in the currency markets either as traders or brokers. A trader purchases or sells currencies for their own benefit. This is usually to facilitate international traveling, to purchase foreign goods, to arbitrage, to speculate, or to convert savings into other currencies. In contrast, the broker is an "order filler" who is paid a fee to execute the instructions of a customer on the trading floors of the exchange. The broker takes a position only in behalf of a client.

THE ORGANIZATION OF THE FOREIGN EXCHANGE MARKET

The international currency markets can be classified according to the pricing procedures ruling the exchange, the time to maturity of the different foreign exchange contracts, the degree of freedom available to market participants, the convertibility of the currencies swapped, and how the currencies are quoted. In general, there are five basic currency markets: the euro, spot, forward, futures, and options markets.

THE EUROCURRENCY AND EURODOLLAR MARKET

The Eurocurrency market originated in London during the 1950s when the Soviet Union acquired a substantial amount of dollar denominated deposit in U.S. banks. These deposits were held to finance Soviet trade with the United States. The Soviet government was fearful of the U.S. government's ability to freeze or seize these deposits if they were held by a U.S. bank. They then asked a group of London banks to transfer the dollar deposits from New York to British banks in London. The European bankers were glad to have these accounts, which were labeled Eurodollars. They were dollar-denominated bank accounts deposits outside the United States. Later, the British banks increased the scope of this market when they opened up a variety of foreign currency denominated bank accounts. Commercial banks from other countries soon copied the British model, which spread the use of foreign currency-denominated bank accounts.

The *Eurocurrency* market is an international money market where commercial banks accept variable interest-bearing deposits in a variety of currencies. In the Eurocurrency market, the commercial banks or *euro banks*, accept foreign currency deposits that are known as *euro deposits*. These accounts are not regulated by the Central bank and therefore, euro banks are not required to hold reserves on Euro accounts or to insure them.

The Eurodollar market is a great success. Today, this market is considered the most competitive and efficient credit market in the world. The transactions in this market are quoted at the bid or offer rate. The *bid rate* is the interest rate at which a euro bank accepts deposits from other euro banks. The *offer rate* is the rate at which a euro bank grants a loan. For example, a euro bank in Panama can accept French franc deposit at a bid rate of 3% and grant French franc loans at the bid rate of 3.2%. The difference between offer and bid rates is called the *interbank spread,* which in the previous example is equal to 0.2%. It is the gross profit resulting from a euro transaction.

THE SPOT MARKET

In the spot market, banks trade currencies for immediate delivery or for release within a period not to exceed 48 hours. They also pre agree on the price, which is known as the *spot rate* and may be stated directly or indirectly. A direct, or *American,* quotation is given when the spot rates are stated in terms of units of local currency per one unit of foreign currency. Direct quotations enable a market participant to understand foreign currency quotations in terms of their own currency. If a quotation is given as $0.90/€1, anyone can understand that it takes 90 cents to purchase one euro. An indirect, or *European,* quotation is stated in terms of the number of units of foreign currency required to purchase one unit of the local currency. For instance, £0.8/US$1 indicates that 80 cents of a British pound are required to purchase one dollar.

Very often, traders cannot find spot quotations on "exotic currencies." For instance, it is not easy to find printed spot quotations for Indian rupees in terms of Mexican pesos (rupee/Mexican peso). To overcome this problem, a trader can use the *chain rule* to estimate the required *cross rate*. To estimate the cross rate between the Indian rupee and the Mexican peso, there has to be a third currency linking them. Typical linking currencies are the U.S. dollar, euro, British pound, or yen.[3] To estimate the Indian rupee (Rs) and the Mexican to Mexican peso (MxP$) cross rate, it is necessary to have both the number rupee per dollar and the dollars per Mexican peso. Given these rates, the cross rate is equal to four Indian rupees per one Mexican peso (Rs4/MxP$1).

	Indian rupee per dollar	Dollars per Mexican peso
Quotations:	Rs40/$1	$0.1/MxP$1

Cross Rate Estimation:

- In the first step, 40 Indian rupees are traded for $1 (Rs40/$1)

- Next, $1 is traded for 10 Mexican pesos, or equivalently, 10 cents of dollar trade for one Mexican peso ($0.1/MxP$1)

- At the conclusion of the cross-transaction 40 Indian rupees are equivalent to 10 Mexican pesos, or similarly, 4 Indian rupees are equal to 1 Mexican peso (Rs4/MxP$1). The cross rate (CR) is estimated as follows:

CR = (Rs40/$1) × ($1/MxP$10) = (Rs40/MxP$10) × ($1/$1)
= (Rs4/MxP$1)

Cross-currency quotations are utilized to identify triangular arbitrage opportunities. This form of arbitrage involves the acquisition of a currency in a location where the monetary unit is cheap and its simultaneous sale in another region where the currency is expensive.

THE FORWARD MARKET

In the forward market, the participants make a commitment to purchase or sell foreign currencies at a quotation known as the *forward rate*. This rate is for delivery at a specified future date, which is beyond the two days required for settlement on a spot transaction. *Forward contracts* are usually stated in 30, 90, and 180 days, but can be arranged for other days. Normally, the size and maturity of the forward contracts is negotiated to satisfy the needs of the customer. *Forward quotations* are restricted to a selected number of currencies, which include the U.S. and Canadian dollars, Euro, British pound, Swiss franc, Italian lira, Japanese yen, and German mark.

Forward rates can also be quoted at a *premium* or *discount* in relation to the spot rate. The dollar is quoted at a premium against a foreign currency when the number of units of this currency are less in the forward than in the spot. In contrast, the dollar is selling at a forward discount when the forward quote is higher in the forward than in the spot.

For example, if a 90-day forward quote for the British pound is $1.56 and the spot is $1.54, then the dollar is selling at a 90-day forward discount of $0.02 against the British pound. In contrast, if the 90-day forward and spot quotations for the same currency are $1.60 and $1.62, then the dollar is said to be selling at a $0.02, 90-day forward premium against the pound.

A forward premium or discount is normally given on yearly basis. Annualized premiums (or discounts) are estimated as follows:

(3.1)   Premium = {[forward rate − spot rate)/spot rate] × 100} × (12/n)
where n is the number of months to maturity of the forward contract.

For instance, if the forward rate is $0.867/€1 and the spot quote is $0.87/€1, then the dollar is selling at a 180-day forward premium, equivalent to −0.344%. The annualized value of the 180-day dollar forward premium is −0.689%. This is estimated by applying the previous forward and spot quotations in Equation 3.1.[4]

Annualized dollar forward premium = [($0.867 − $0.87)/$0.87] × 100 × (12/6)
= (− 0.0034/$0.87) × (100) × (12/6)
= −0.689%

THE FUTURES MARKET

The first futures market in the United States was established in Chicago in 1919 to serve the needs of the American farming community in the Midwest region. In May of 1972, the Chicago Mercantile Exchange (CME) introduced an international money market division, the International Monetary Market (IMM), to trade currencies and securities in the futures market. Trading with futures is subject to strict regulations established by both the Commodities Futures Trading Commission and the exchange.

The futures contract is a commitment made on the trading floor to buy or to sell foreign currencies. Each contract specifies the quantity of the item and the time to delivery or payment. The buyers and the sellers agree on a price today, the futures price, for a currency to be delivered and paid in the future. Delivery dates are the third Wednesday of the month the contract is due. Delivery months are March, June, September and December. The last day of trading is two business days before the third Wednesday of the contract month. The price quotations are always in terms of U.S. dollars per unit of foreign exchange.

Futures Contracts Highlights

For each currency the exchange establishes several important rules. The first is related to the price and size of the contract. Other regulations state a minimum price change, which is given in price points. In addition, there is a limit on how much each futures contract can fluctuate daily.

For example, the CME has established a contract size of 100,000 units for British pounds (See Table 3.1). The minimum price change for this currency is two points, where each point is worth $6.25. Therefore, the minimum price fluctuation for a British pound contract is $12.50. On a daily basis, there are no limits to price changes.[5]

Since exchange rates fluctuate, international investors use futures contracts both to protect an investment and to profit from it. A futures contract is an impersonal agreement between two parties unknown to each other. Yet contracts will not fail because the exchange guarantees the contracts. To fulfill this commitment, the exchange imposes a deposit or *margin* requirement to cover the fluctuations in the value of the contract. The margin has two parts: the *initial margin* and the *maintenance margin*. The exact amount of the initial margin depends on the daily price movement limit set forth in the contract. Any gains or losses are added to or subtracted from the margin. If continuous losses occur and the margin declines below 80% of its required level, then a transfer of margin takes place. This additional margin, which is equivalent to the change in the value of the contract, is called the *variation margin*.

Futures Pricing

The value of a futures contract is equal to the size of the contract times the futures quotation. If the futures quote of a euro is $0.8745 for 125,000 units, then the value of the contract is $109,312.5.

Table 3.1
Chicago Mercantile Exchange Futures, Currency Contract Highlights

Currency	Units per Contract	Minimum Price	Fluctuation Tick, $/point
British pound	62,500	1 pt. = $0. 0001	2.0/pts. = $12.5
Canadian dollar	100,000	1 pt. = $0.0001	1/pt. = $10.0
Euro	125,000	1 pt. = $0.0001	1/pt. = $12.5
Japanese yen	12,500,000	1 pt. = $0.000001	1/pt. = $12.5
Mexican peso	500,000	1 pt. = $0.000025	5/pts. = $12.5
Swiss franc	125,000	1 pt. = $0.0001	1/pt. = $12.5

Source: *Futures and Facts,* Chicago Mercantile Exchange (CME). The contract size specifications are from the CME. Other exchanges may have different contract specifications.

The price of a currency in the futures market is closely related to the spot quotation, but there is a difference related to the date of delivery. This difference is also reflected in the futures price minus spot price and is called the *swap rate.* The swap value approaches zero as the delivery date for future contracts nears. As a result, the futures delivery ultimately becomes a spot delivery. As a result of arbitrage, spot and futures contracts become substitutes for each other as time passes and their value should be equal. This principle is crucial in a futures market because it is the essence of futures pricing.

The swap between the dollar and the euro can be calculated using the following expression:

Swap = (spot rate) × (dollar interest rate – euro interest rate) × (days to delivery/360)

To provide an illustration of how to estimate a swap consider the case of a futures contract due in 90 days when the spot value of the euro is 90 cents of a dollar per one euro ($0.9/€1) and the three-month dollar and euro interest rates are 6% and 4% per year respectively. Given this information, the value of the swap is $0.0045:

Swap = ($0.9) × (0.06 – 0.04) × (90/360)
= ($0.9) × (0.02) × (1/4)
= ($0.9) × (0.02) × (0.25)
= $0.0045

Once the dollar value of the swap is calculated, the next step is to add the swap to the spot rate to determine the futures price. For instance, in the case of the euro, the future price of one euro in dollar terms is $0.9045:

Futures price for the euro = spot rate + swap = ($0.9 + $0.0045) = $0.9045/€1

The swap provides useful information to market participants. To illustrate the important of this concept, consider a situation where the futures price for the euro is 90 cents of a dollar ($0.90/€1). In this instance, the euro in the futures is under priced or "cheap." To benefit from this situation, a trader could sell euros in the spot and simultaneously buy euros back in the futures. If the actual futures price is higher than $0.9045 then the trader should do the reverse and buy euros in the spot and simultaneously sell euros in the futures market. In any one of the previous instances, the trader may end up gaining a profit per unit equivalent to the difference between the current futures price and $0.9045. The gain per contract is equivalent to the difference between the current future price and $0.9045 times the futures contract size for euro.

Futures Pricing and Market Strategies

A trader confronted with the futures market faces a host of futures price quotations, which are always expressed as the dollar price of foreign currency or the number of dollars to one unit of foreign currency. These quotations include the opening price for each of the different maturity periods for each day, the high, low, and settlement prices, the open interest, and the volume traded.

The opening price is the quotation at which the currency is offered at the beginning of the trading day. Traders have the choice to purchase or sell currencies at this price prior to the opening of the exchange. See Table 3.2.

The settlement price denotes the price at which the futures contracts are valued at the end of the day. If the market is very active, the settlement price may be the last price of the day. Otherwise, the exchange's Settlement Committee may estimate it as the weighted average of the last 30 minutes of trading.[6] This determination is important because it will resolve who has profits and losses and the value of the margin since futures contracts settle daily.

The open interest refers to the number of contracts still standing at the end of trading session of the previous day. Each unit represents a buyer and a seller who still have a contract position. The open interest fluctuates during the life of the contract and is used to assess whether the market is "robust" or "weak." Ordinarily, open interest is small in the early stages of a contract. It then increases to a maximum within the four to six weeks before maturity and declines as the contract is close to expiration.

Traders enter into the futures market to hedge or speculate. Hedging is used to protect international business transactions from changes in the exchange rate. Traders may take long or short positions, even though combined positions are also feasible.

A *long position* is taken when an investor buys a futures contract, accepting delivery of a specified amount of currency at the maturity of the contract. It is also when someone has a contract to purchase a currency and still owns it. A *short position* is taken when the trader has sold currency and has an obligation to deliver. The positions taken by the traders usually reveal their market expectations. A trader is "bullish" when he takes a long position. This is because the trader expects the futures price to increase. In contrast, when traders expect a price decline, they adopt a "bear mood" and take a short position.

The Options Market

Trading currencies in the options market is based on the same principles governing the futures markets (Table 3.3).

Trading takes place in a specific site, under fixed rules, with standard size contracts, standard delivery dates, and open trading. Registered brokers, who charge a fee for their service, usually manage options contracts.

Table 3.2
Futures Quotations
Euro CME)—125,000 euros, $ per euro

					Lifetime		Open
	Open	High	Low	Settle	High	Low	Interest
March	.8745	.8752	.8701	.8736	.8720	.8770	56,576
June	.8735	.8772	.8722	.8759	.8738	.8750	1,839
September	.8660	.8694	.8660	.8683	.8625	.8668	270

Estimated volume 24,426; vol. Thursday 35,278; open interest 58,685* – 1,399.
*The sum of the items is listed in the last column and is known as open interest.

Source: *Using Currency Futures,* Chicago Mercantile Exchange.

Nature of the Options Contracts

An options contract gives its owner (or holder) the right to buy or sell foreign currencies prior to the expiration of the contract at a quotation called the strike price. To have this right, the holder of the contract has to pay a fee known as the *premium.*

In the options market, there are two types of options contracts available: put and call. *Put contracts* confer to their "holder" the right to sell foreign currency at the strike price. In turn, the seller of the contract, "the writer," is obligated to buy the foreign currency when the owner wants to exercise the option. *Call contracts* grant to their holder the right to purchase from the "writer" foreign currency at the strike price. In this contractual, the "writer" is obligated to furnish the foreign currency at the holder's request if they want to exercise the option.

When a new euro, Japanese yen, Swiss franc, or British pound, contract is listed, there are 13 put and call strike prices arranged in an ascending order. The price, which is closest to the strike and futures price, is located in the center of this list. For example, if some day in March, the futures price for the Swiss franc closes at $0.60. Then the next day, the strike prices for March puts and calls will be 54 cents, 55 cents, 56 cents, 57 cents, 58 cents, 59 cents ...66 cents; where 60 cents will be the center price and closest to the underlying futures price. For the Canadian and Australian dollars, there are only nine put and call strike prices. The fifth price is the nearest strike to the futures price.

Interpreting Currency Options Information

The first column of Table 3.4 shows the strike price, which is always given in terms of dollars. The next three columns present the expiration months for call contracts (February, March, and April) and the premium attached to the different periods listed. For example, if traders want to buy a call contract (the right to purchase foreign currency) for April at the strike price of 56 cents of a dollar, they have to pay 2.21 dollar cents premium per Swiss franc. If at a certain point in time traders want to exercise the options contract, they will have to pay 56 cents per franc, in addition to the 2.21 cents premium paid up front.

Table 3.3
Chicago Mercantile Exchange Options, Currency Contract Highlights

Currency	Trading Units	Minimum Price Change	Value of 1 point	Strike Price Interval
British pound	62,500	$0.0001	$6.25	$2.5 cents
Canadian dollar	100,000	$0.0001	$10.00	$5 cents
Euro	125,000	$0.0001	$12.50	$1 cents
Japanese yen	12,500,000	$0.000001	$12.50	$0.01 cent
Swiss franc	125,000	$0.0001	$12.50	$1 cent

Source: *Futures and Facts*, Chicago Mercantile Exchange (CME). The contract size specifications are from the CME. Other exchanges may have different contract specifications.

The estimated volume shows the number of options contracts negotiated during the last two days of trading. Each unit represents both a buyer and a seller. The open interest shows the number of option contracts that are still open at the end of a day.

A premium, either on call or put contracts, is the price per unit of the option. For example, if traders want to purchase a put options contract to sell Swiss francs in February at 58 cents of a dollar, they have to pay a premium of 1.14 cents of dollar per unit. Since the contract has 125,000 units, the value of the premium per contract is $1,425:

Premium = $0.0114 × 125,000 = $1,425

The dollar value of the premium varies constantly. These variations are related to possible discrepancies between spot and strike prices, the life span of the contract, and the price variability of the currency.

The higher the spot relative to the strike price, the higher the call premium. This is due to the higher risk incurred by the seller (or writer) of the contract who might be obligated to deliver foreign currency at the maturity of the options contract at a price below the spot price.

Table 3.4
Option Quotations
Swiss franc (IMM)—125,000 francs, $ cents per Swiss franc

Strike Price	Calls—Settle			Puts—Settle		
	February	March	April	February	March	April
56	1.63	1.87	2.21	0.28	0.52	0.65
57	0.96	1.27	1.60	0.60	0.91	....
58	0.50	0.80	....	1.14	1.44	....
59	0.25	0.50	....	....	2.13	....
60	....	0.30	....	....	....	....

Estimated volume 8,145; Thursday volume 9,077 calls, 9,024 puts; open interest Thursday.; 47,855 calls, 47,767 puts.

Source: *Using Currency and Options*, Chicago Mercantile Exchange.

In the options market a distant maturity carries a higher premium to compensate the seller of the option contract for the time-risk normally implicit in long waiting periods.

Another element playing a role in the determination of a premium is price variability of a currency. The greater the price variability associated with a currency, the higher the probability that the spot rate will differ from the strike price, therefore, the higher the price variability of a currency, the higher the premium.

SUMMARY

The foreign exchange market is oldest and largest financial market in the world. It operates 24 hours a day to facilitate the purchase and sale of foreign currencies. This system allows residents to import and export goods and services and to engage in foreign direct investment and portfolio investment. The participants involved in international trade can use the exchange market to hedge and arbitrage. Others enter into portfolio investment or speculation.

The foreign exchange market includes a large variety of segments, classified according to several factors. These factors include the following: pricing rules, the time to maturity of the contracts, formalizing a foreign exchange transaction, the freedom allowed to market participants, the marketability and convertibility of the currencies swapped, and the way the currencies are quoted. Given these elements, it is possible to identify five key segments: the Euro currency, spot, forward, futures, and options markets.

The Euro currency market is a worldwide market having interest-bearing deposits in a variety of currencies. In the spot market, the participants trade currencies from every country of the world for immediate delivery at a pre-agreed price known as the spot rate. In the forward market, the traders commit to purchase or sell foreign exchange at a forward rate, for delivery at a date that suits the need of the trader. In the futures market, the participants commit to buy or sell a reduced number of currencies selected by the exchange, according to the rules set by the exchange. These regulations define the pricing mechanism, the time to maturity of the contracts, and the maximum variations in the price of the contract on each transaction. In the options market trade takes place only in the exchange and under fixed rules related to contract size, delivery dates, and put and call options contracts. The options contract classified as American provides their owner with the right to trade foreign currency prior to the expiration of the contract at an explicit quotation known as strike price. To have this right, the contract holder has to pay a fee, known as a premium.

PROBLEMS

1. If the spot rates are 84 yen per dollar and $0.87 per one euro, what is the yen-euro exchange rate (yen/€1)?

2. If a German corporation desires to avoid exchange rate risk on a 90-day Japanese yen payable, would you recommend the European company to sell yen in the forward market?

3. An exporter in Canada must sell foreign currency received from exports to Switzerland (Swf), the United States ($), and Singapore (S$). She received the quotes listed below. Should the exporter sell her currency to the Canadian or the foreign banks? Explain.

Spot Quotes from Canadian Banks	Spot Quotes from Foreign Banks
$0.59/Swf1	Swf1.7/$1
$0.63/Can$1	Can$1.15/$1
$0.55/S$1	S$2.1/$1

4. If a US firm's cost of goods sold exposure is much greater than its sales exposure in euro, what will be the effect of a depreciation of the euro on the profit position of this firm?

5. If the euro is expected to appreciate against the U.S. dollar, what is the best strategy for a speculator operating in the futures market?

6. The Dai-Kal Corporation is a U.S. exporter invoicing its exports to Italy in euro. If the company expects, with certainty, an appreciation of the euro against the dollar, what is the firm's best strategy to hedge, assuming that it is limited to operate in the options markets?

NOTES

1. Foreign exchange can be cash, funds available on credit and debit cards, traveler's checks, bank deposits, or other short-term claims denominated in a monetary unit different from the local currency. Within the United States, any money denominated in a currency different from the U.S. dollar, is foreign exchange. For example, one British pound bank deposit constitutes a unit of foreign exchange in the United States.

2. If the dollar price of one British pound is 1.60, then a typical quotation in the foreign exchange market is $1.60/£1.

3. The most widely used linking currency is the U.S. dollar.

4. Also, it can be said that the euro is selling in Europe at a 0.689% annual discount against the U.S. dollar.

5. For further details see, The Chicago Mercantile Exchange, Contract Specification for Currency Products, www.cme.com/clearing/spex/XMLReports/currencyGroup. (Accessed March 12, 2002).

6. Ultimately, the Settlement Committee decides the settlement price based on what considers being a reasonable and fair price.

SUGGESTED ADDITIONAL READINGS

Bank of England. "Financial Markets." www.bankofengland.co.uk/markets/forex/. (Accessed March 13, 2002).

Caves, R., Frankel, J., Jones, R. *World Trade and Payments.* 9th ed. Boston, MA: Thompson Steele, Inc., 2002. See Chapter 16.

Federal Reserve Bank of New York. *The Foreign Exchange Market in the United States.* www.ny.frb.org/pihome/addpub/usfxm/. (Accessed March 13, 2002).

Financials.Com. "Currency Library." http://currencies.thefinancials.com/. (Accessed March 12, 2002).

Krugman, P., and Obstfeld, M. *International Economics, Theory and Policy.* 5th ed. Reading, MA: Addison Wesley, 2000. See Chapter 13.

4

The Fundamentals of Investing Globally

Global managers have to consider a host of complex and important decisions related to value creation. The most important decision is perhaps, related to how and where to invest. This decision is associated with spending in assets that should be placed where they can provide a sustained source of cash flow to the firm in the future. If the decision is successful, the manager will be commended for his skills and vision in identifying potentially successful projects and for carrying them to conclusion. However, if the project fails to perform, it can prevent the firm from generating positive cash flows and from attracting new sources of capital. Considering these two alternatives, it is very important for managers and stockholders to identify good and bad investment projects.

From the perspective of the fundamentals of finance, a good proposal increases the market value of the firm's equity. This happens when the NPV (NPV) of the project is positive and when the value of future cash flows directly linked to the operation of capital is higher than the cash initially spent in the acquisition of a productive asset. However, comparing the value of future cash flows with the initial capital expenditures is not possible because the two flows have a different time value. A dollar today is considered more valuable than a dollar to be received later. One reason for this is that firms or individuals holding cash can earn revenue if the cash is placed in an interest-bearing bank account or other profitable activity. Interest revenues are known as the *time value of money*.

Fortunately, the field of finance provides several tools that can help the business executive and the stockholder to overcome the problem of compatibility between the time value of current and future cash flows. One of these provisions is the discount mechanism used to convert future cash flows into current cash flow equivalents. This cash flow transformation is recognized as *present value* or discounted value. For example, a $110 cash flow available a year from now, is worth $100 today if it earns 10% on an interest-bearing bank account free of risk. The $100 is the present value or discounted value of a future cash inflow of $110 discounted at a rate of 10%.

In addition to the time value of money, discounting is also related to risk. For most professional activities, there is the anticipation that a future cash flow may not be realized exactly as expected. Consequently, a proper discounting process has to incorporate both risk and the time value of money. This concept is identified in finance as the *discounted cash flow model.*[1]

For a global corporation, a proper discounted cash flow model specification has to incorporate at least three aspects: the proper estimation of future cash flow, a suitable discount rate, and a reasonable assessment of the future value of the exchange rate. This chapter presents a discounted cash flow model entirely devoid of exchange rate considerations. The exchange rate variable will be introduced in a later chapter. It is assumed that cash flows and discount rates are known. Therefore, this chapter focuses on calculating the NPV, explaining what it is measuring, describing the process to estimate it, and interpreting it. To meet these goals the chapter contains:

- A description of the aspects to consider in a capital budgeting decision
- How to estimate the NPV of a stream of future cash flows
- How to interpret the future value, present value, and NPV estimates
- How to use the NPV rule to choose between projects dissimilar in size and life expectancy
- How to incorporate and interpret risk in NPV models

THE CAPITAL BUDGETING DECISION

The most important aspect of sustained corporate success is finding and assessing new business opportunities. To promote the development of new ideas, management has to create a corporate environment conducive to uncovering new opportunities that can lead to a prosperous long-term investment.

Once new business ventures are identified, the next step is to evaluate them from the perspective of NPV rules. To apply this concept, it is necessary to have information related to the life span of the project, some anticipation regarding the dollar value of future cash flows, and a good grasp of how to discount them. Fortunately, at this stage, the focus will be on the process of estimating NPVs, assuming that all the relevant parameters are known.

IDENTIFYING NEW BUSINESS OPPORTUNITIES

One line of new business investment is related to complying with safety, health, and environmental regulations. The estimation of these expenses is easy because these expenditures are usually provided by the institutions that control these business activities.

Sometimes, new business expenditures are used to replacing old machinery for more efficient and modern equipment. In this case, the focus of an NPV calculation will be on replacing old equipment and the cost savings generated by the new machinery. The estimation of these two items is not difficult because they are normally provided by companies supplying the new equipment.

Expanding a business activity represents another investment opportunity. Obtaining the information required to assess a proposal of this nature is more difficult than previous ones because it requires more information on sales, revenues, and working capital.

Another investment opportunity is the creation of a new line of business. This opportunity is the most difficult to evaluate because estimating expenditures, cash flows, and discount rates is less precise due to management and firm inexperience in the new activity.

Once a new capital investment is accepted, it has to be implemented and monitored. The last aspect is important to determine whether the project is succeeding or falling short of expectations initially set at the time it was approved. Auditing projects is vital in deciding to continue projects meeting the firm's expectations or terminating those activities failing to comply with their proposed goals.

Project Comparability

Before addressing the aspects of how to estimate the return and NPV of a project, it is best to first review various aspects relevant to corporate investment. The first and foremost important consideration is risk. Two or more projects are comparable as long as they belong to the same risk class. Projects belonging to the same risk family offer convenience in that they can be discounted using the same DF. Taxation is another important aspect to consider, because companies are only interested in after tax returns. The amount of initial investment and the life of the project also matter. However, the most important factors in assessing the contribution of a project to value creation are risk and taxes.

To explain the relevance of risk and taxes in estimating the NPV and return of a proposal, consider the case of a U.S. trader pondering the acquisition of a shipment of coffee from Brazil, at a cost of $5 million, to be paid now, for delivery in one year. To finance this transaction, the trader can use funds from a New York bank account earning 8% annual interest. Upon delivery of the shipment, the U.S. trader can sell it with no risk of defaulting, to a large U.S. retailing firm for $5.5 million. Both interest revenues and import profits are tax-exempt. Should the U.S. trader buy the Brazilian shipment? Is the project worth taking?

Prior to answering these questions, it is necessary to test the comparability of the two investment options implicit in the problem. These are either leaving the cash (or principal) in the bank or closing the bank account and using the proceeds to import Brazilian coffee.

A quick glance reveals that the two projects belong to the same risk category. This is because both of them require the same amount of initial investment ($5 million), have the same life span (one year), and similar tax rates. In addition, both options guarantee a return over the year period and certainty in the repayment of the principal.

THE RATE OF RETURN RULE

If the U.S. trader keeps the bank account for a year, at the end of the period he will have the initial deposit ($5 million) plus the interest earned ($400,000). Both items total $5.4 million. In contrast, if he decides to import the Brazilian coffee, at the end of the year, his revenue will amount to $5.5 million with profit on this project of $500,000. Given these facts, the U.S. trader will be better off importing the coffee.

Bank account return = – Initial deposit + initial deposit × (one plus the interest rate)
= – $5 million + $5 million × (1 + 8%)
= – $5 million + $5.4 million
= $0.4 million
= $400,000

Bank account rate of return = (Return/initial deposit) × 100
= ($0.4 million/$5 million) × 100
= (0.4/5) × 100
= 0.08 × 100
= 8%

Profit on coffee imports = –Initial investment + import revenue
= – $5 million + $5.5 million
= $0.5 million
= $500,000

Rate of return on coffee imports = (profit/initial investment) × 100
= ($0.5 million/$5 million) × 100
= (0.5/5) × 100
= 0.1 × 100
= 10%

If the trader undertakes the import project, the loss in interest revenue is the opportunity cost of capital (8%) and the import profit is the return on the investment (10%). These two facts confirm that the U.S. importer will be better off if he accepts the import project because his equity will be raised 2% ($100,000).[2] This result explains a very important investment decision rule: *Accept an investment when the rate of return of the project exceeds the opportunity cost of capital.* This is known as the *rate of return rule*.

THE NPV RULE

It is already known that the sale of coffee imports yields $5.5 million in revenues. Knowing this, how much does the importer need to deposit now in a New York bank account, paying 8% interest, to receive $5.5 million in one year? The answer is $5,092,593. If the U.S. importer deposits this amount in a bank account at 8% per year, at the end of the period he will have $5.5 million, which will be the sum of the initial deposit ($5,092,593) plus the interest earned in one year ($407,407).

$5,500,000 = $5,092,593 + ($5,092,593 × 8%)
= $5,092,593 + $407,407

This relationship can also be expressed as:

$5,500,000= $5,092,593 + ($5,092,593 × 8%)
= $5,092,593 × (1 + 0.08)

The last equation indicates that the *future value* of $5,092,593 compounded at 8% for one year is $5,500,000. The expression (1+ 0.08) is called the one-year *compound factor* at 8%. The initial deposit ($5,092,593) was estimated by dividing the future cash flow ($5,500,000) by the compound factor (1 + 0.08), where

Initial deposit = $5,500,000/(1 + 0.08)
= $5,500,000 × (1/1.08)
= $5,500,000 × (0.92593)
= $5,092,593

The *present value* of $5.5 million discounted at 8%, in one year is $5,092,593. The expression (1/1.08) is called the one-year DF at 8% and is equal to 0.925926. Which means that the present value of one dollar to be received a year later, discounted at 8% is roughly equal to 92 cents today. Discounting reduces the dollar value by almost 8 cents.

One-Year Investment

To illustrate the process of *compounding,* suppose that you have a $1 deposit in a savings account paying 10% interest compounded annually. If the dollar is left in that account for the entire year, the investor collects $1.10 at year's end. This dollar amount is the one-year future value of one dollar held today. This one-year future value can be expressed as follows:

(4.1) $FV = PV + k$

In equation 4.1, *FV* is the *future value* of money. *PV* is the initial deposit, present value, or principal. *k* is the dollar value of one year's interest paid on the one-dollar deposit at the end of the period. The future value of a deposit left in a savings account for one year can also be represented as:

$FV = PV + [PV × (k)]$
$= PV × (1 + k).$
$= $1 × (1 + 0.1)$
$= 1.1

Two-Year Investment

If a one-dollar deposit is left in a savings account for two years, the future value is $1.21.

$FV = PV × (1 + k)^2$
$= $1 × (1.1)^2$

$= \$1 \times 1.21$

$= \$1.21$

If the one-dollar deposit is left in the savings account for several years, the future value is:

(4.2) $FV = PV + PV(1 + k) + PV(1 + k) \times (1 + k) + ...+$

$= \Sigma\, PV(1 + k)^n$

In expression 4.2, the Greek letter sigma (Σ) symbolizes the sum of the terms $PV*(1 + k)^I$; FV and *PV* are as before; k is the interest earned on the deposit; and n is the number of periods left in the account earning interest.

PRESENT VALUE

The present value is the inverse of the future value. It is a *principal* that if held today grows to match a future stream of cash flow (CF) payments due over n periods. Alternatively, it can be viewed as the value today of a stream of payments discounted at the k rate. Since the present value is the mirror image of the future value, then Equation 4.2 can be transformed into a present value expression.

(4.3) $PV = \Sigma\, FV/(1 + k)^n$

$= \Sigma CF_i /(1 + k)^n$

$= \Sigma CF_i \times [1/(1 + k)^n\,]$

$= \Sigma CF_i \times (DF)^n$

$= \Sigma CF_i \times (DF)^{\,n}$

In Equation 4.3 the Greek letter sigma (Σ), *PV,* and *FV* hold the same meaning as before, except that k now plays the role of a discount rate used to estimate the discount factor [$1/(1 + k)$]. CF is the cash flow in period i. The periods run from i to n, for example, from 0 (initial period) to 10. The initial deposit to open a savings bank account is a typical case of a negative cash flow in period 0 ($-CF_0$).

The Present Value of a One-Year Investment

If a company is due to receive $100 a year from now, the present value of the receivable is $90.9 if the discount rate is 10%.

$PV= CF_1 \times (DF)$

$= \$100 \times (1/1.1)$

$= \$100 \times 0.909$

$= \$90.9$

The Present Value of a Two-Year Investment

A firm holds a $500 account payable due in two years. If the appropriate discount rate is 12%, the present value of the payable is $398.6.

$PV = CF_2 \times (DF)^2$

$= \$500 \times (1/1.12)^2$

$= \$500 \times 0.797194$
$= \$398.6$

The present value can also be estimated as follows:

$PV = CF_2 /(1 + k)^2$
$= \$500/(1.12)^2$
$= \$398.6$

This result indicates that $398.6 today is worth $500 two years from now, if the discount rate is 12%. It also means that the holder of the $500 payable is indifferent between waiting two years to collect $500, or trading the two-year $500 payable for $398.6 today.

NPV OF A PROJECT LASTING THREE YEARS

Normally, an investor is confronted with an infinite number of possibilities when deciding how to allocate current wealth in exchange for a future stream of cash flows. To decide whether to accept or reject a new business proposal, the investor needs to estimate the NPV of the project. NPV is equal to the present value of future cash flows less the initial investment.

$NPV = -CF_0 + CF_1 \times (DF)^1 + CF_2 \times (DF)^2 \ldots\ldots + CF_n \times (DF)^n$

This expression can also be expressed as follows:

$NPV = -CF_0 + CF_1 /(1 + k)^1 + CF_2 /(1 + k)^2 \ldots\ldots + CF_n (1 + k)^n$

For example, consider the case of an investor willing to purchase a $10,000 machine able to generate $3,000 profit each year for three years. If the market value of the machine at the end of the life of the project is $4,500 and the discount rate is 10% per year, is this project worth taking? The answer is yes because the project has a positive NPV of $841.

This result indicates the three-year project is worth $841 more that it costs. Therefore, this investment will increase the equity of the investor by $841 if the transaction is executed. This example also suggests that investors should always accept investment opportunities having positive NPVs. This rule is known as the NPV rule. A description of the method used to estimate this project is presented in Table 4.1.

PRESENT VALUE OF AN UNEVEN SERIES OF PAYMENTS

In many cases, the sequential payments of a stream of benefits are not always evenly distributed. For example, consider the case of a firm deciding whether to invest $10,000, in a three-year project offering future cash inflows of $2,000, $2,000, and $7,000 at the end of Years 1, 2, and 3, respectively. If the discount rate for this project is 10%, does the project have a positive NPV? Does it increase the firm's equity? In both instances the answer is no. The proposal generates a negative present value of $1,270. As such, it should be rejected to avoid a loss in equity (see Table 4.2).

Table 4.1
Present Value of a Project Lasting Three Years

Present value of CF_0	$-10,000 \times (1/(1.1)^0$	$-\$10,000 \times 1$	$-\$10,000$
Present value of CF_1	$\$3,000 \times *(1/1.1)^1$	$\$3,000 \times 0.90909$	$\$2,727$
Present value of CF_2	$\$3,000 \times (1/1.1)^2$	$\$ 3,000 \times 0.8264$	$\$2,479$
Present value of CF_3	$\$3,000 \times (1/1.1)^3$	$\$3,000 \times 0.75131$	$\$2,254$
Present value of CF_3	$\$4,500 \times *(1/1.1)^3$	$\$4,500 \times 0.75131$	$\$3,381$
Total present value @ 10%			$\$ 841$

Table 4.2
Net Present Value, Uneven Series of Payments

Present value of CF_0	$-\$10,000 \times (1/(1.1)^0$	$-\$10,000 \times 1$	$-\$10,000$
Present value of CF_1	$\$2,000 \times (1/1.1)^1$	$\$2,000 \times 0.90909$	$\$1,818$
Present value of CF_2	$\$2,000 \times (1/1.1)^2$	$\$2,000 \times 0.8264$	$\$1,653$
Present value of CF_3	$\$7,000 \times (1/1.1)^3$	$\$7,000 \times 0.75131$	$\$5,259$
Total present value @ 10%			$-\$1,270$

SPECIAL CASES OF CAPITAL BUDGETING

Until now, this chapter has provided the finance tools required to let business executives choose between competing proposals requiring the same amount of initial investment, similar life spans, and similar risk classes. Also, it has provided guidance on how to decide between projects belonging to the same risk family but lasting multiple years.

Unfortunately, the tools developed so far do not cover the whole range of challenges posed by the practice of business. This difficulty often confronts the owners of a firm with the task of selecting between projects dissimilar in size, or life span. To meet this challenge, the following sections present methodologies that allow the business executive to compare proposals differentiated by size or time to maturity.

CONTRASTING PROJECTS OF UNEQUAL SIZE

Suppose that a company has $6 million to invest and is considering Projects A, B, and C. The three projects last two years, and require initial capital expenditures of $2, $3 and $4 million, respectively. The discount year for each project is 8%, and the cash flows for each alternative are listed in Table 4.3.

All the proposals have positive NPV. Therefore, each one can contribute to increase equity. Implementing all the proposals is not possible due to budgetary constraints. Consequently, the firm has to choose either combination (A, B) or combination (A, C). Combination (B, C) is not feasible because it exceeds the budget constraint.

To choose between two feasible combinations, the firm needs to rank projects in terms of their profitability index, the ratio of present value to initial investment, and pick projects in a descending order of importance. Using this procedure, the firm should pick Project B first and then Project A. Both proposals require an initial investment of $5 million ($2 million expenditure on project A, plus $3 million expenditure on Project B). This combination generates a total NPV of $356,653. By contrast, combination (A and C) offers a smaller return of $282,579 and requires a larger amount of investment of $6 million.

Total NPV combination (A, B) = NPV (A) + NPV (B)
= $105,624 + $251,029
= $ 356,653

Total NPV combination (A, C) = NPV (A) + NPV (C)
= $105,624 + $176,955
= $ 282,579

In conclusion, if a firm is confronted with capital rationing and has to choose projects from a family of unequal size proposals, the best method to allocate funds is to rank the projects in term of the profitability index and choose proposals in descending order of importance up the point where the capital is fully optimized (see Table 4.3).

Profitability index (B) = present value/initial investment
= $3,251,029 /$3,000,000 = 1.08

Profitability index (A) = $2,105,624 /$2,000,000 = 1.05

Profitability index (C) = $4,176,955 /$4,000,000 = 1.04

An alternative method to ranking the three projects is to estimate the NPV of each project and choose the combination of proposals generating the highest total NPV, provided that this combination exhaust the funds and affords an equal or higher rate return than the method previously described.

Risk and Return

Before now, the returns on new investment opportunities have been considered certain. In reality, investment decisions are often based on *expected* rather than *secured* payoffs. For instance, consider the case of a U.S. merchant who pays $100,000 for a load of grain that can be sold for $132,000 if the conditions of the economy are good. However, if the state of the economy is fair, the selling price will be only $107,000. A third possibility is a bad state of economy, where the expected selling price drops to only $88,000. If all states of the economy are equally likely, the payoff for this transaction is estimated and summarized in Table 4.4.

Table 4.3
Present Value and Profitability Index for Unequal Size Projects

		Project A	Project B	Project C
1	Initial investment (CF$_0$)	-$2,000,000	-$3,000,000	-$4,000,000
2	Cash flow in year 1 (CF$_1$)	$ 700,000	$2,400,000	$ 900,000
3	Cash flow in year 2 (CF$_2$)	$1,700,000	$1,200,000	$3,900,000
4	Present value (CF$_1$, CF$_2$)	$2,105,624	$3,251,029	$4,176,955
5	Net present value (row 4 - row 1)	$ 105,624	$ 251,029	$ 176,955
6	Profitability index (row 4/row1)	1.05	1.08	1.04

Table 4.4
Risk and Return

State of Nature	Probability (1)	Selling Price (2)	Expected price (1 × 2)
Good	0.33	$132,000	$43,560
Fair	0.33	$107,000	$35,310
Bad	0.33	$88,000	$29,040
Expected payoff			**$107,910**

The anticipated profit on this transaction is (107,910 − 100,000) = $7,910. The expected return is = $7,910/100,000 = 0.0791 = 7.91%.

If the cost of borrowing is less than 7.91%, then the project is worth undertaking, since the expected rate of return will be higher than the cost of capital. Otherwise, the project should be rejected.

SUMMARY

The ability of a firm to find and implement profitable business opportunities is a factor commonly associated with sustained corporate success. Once a new venture is identified, the next step is to evaluate it from a finance perspective and decide whether the project can increase the firm's equity. The tool commonly used to evaluate new business ventures is NPV. To apply this concept, a corporation needs to know the amount of initial investment required to implement a new project, the dollar value of future cash flows to be generated by the proposal, and the discount rate that applies to the type of project being proposed. All these elements are integrated into a conceptual framework identified as discounted cash flow model. The discounted cash flow model lets investors estimate the NPV of a project, identify and rank proposals, and make decisions, which efficiently allocate venture capital.

A project is deemed acceptable when the NPV of the project is positive. Otherwise, the project should be ignored or rejected. If investors are confronted with several projects to choose from, they can estimate the NPV of each option, rank the options in descending order of importance, and choose first the project showing the highest NPV. This method of choosing projects is valid when all the proposals ranked belong to the same risk class.

Projects belong to the same risk family when they require the same amount of initial investment, have the same life span, and are subject to the same tax rate. If the projects fail to meet this standard they are classified as special projects. This chapter provided suitable methodologies to rank and choose from projects requiring varying amounts of initial investment. It also offered guidance to incorporate risk in NPV models.

PROBLEMS

1. What is the present value of $500 to be received three years from now if the discount rate is 9% per year?

2. What is the future value of $300 compounded semiannually at an interest rate of 12% over a two years?

3. Over what period of time will $100 turn into $153.90, if the initial investment is compounded at 9% per year?

4. Banca Confía offers a 12% interest rate compounded every six months on its savings accounts. If an investor opens an $8,000, two-year savings account today, how much money will he have at the end of the two-year period?

5. Consider the following information:

Period	0	1	2	3
Cash flow	−100	0	78	75

If the discount rate is 8 %, what is the NPV of the stream of payments?

6. A U.S. importer can purchase a container of computer parts in Taiwan for $8 million to be paid up front. The cargo can be delivered in six months. The net cash flows from selling this product are very sensitive to technological change, and they are listed below. The discount rate is 8%.

State of Technological Change	Probability	Net Cash Flow
No change	0.2	$16 million
Mild change	0.6	$10 million
Drastic change	0.2	$5 million

What are the NPV and the rate of return on this transaction?

7. A firm is confronted with three projects requiring varying amounts of initial investment, and lasting two years each. If the discount rate is 8%, what are the best and worse projects when applying the profitability index?

	Project 1	Project 2	Project 3
Initial investment	−$1,000,000	−$2,500,000	−$4,000,000
Cash flow in year 1	$700,000	$1,400,000	$900,000
Cash flow in year 2	$600,000	$1,200,000	$3,900,000

NOTES

1. G. Hawawini and C. Viallet, *Finance for Executives, Managing for Value Creation,* 2nd ed. Cincinnati, OH: South Western, 2001, p. 186.
2. This is the profit at the end of the life of the project. As such is stated in terms of future value. The present value of this profit is $100,000/(1 + 8%) = $92,593.

SUGGESTED ADDITIONAL READINGS

Eiteman, D., et al. *Multinational Business Finance*. 9th ed. Reading, MA: Addison Wesley Longman, 2001.

Federal Reserve System, The Bank of New York. "Depositary Receipts." http://www.adrbny.com/. (Accessed January 5, 2002).

Levich, R. *International Financial Markets: Prices and Policies*. 2nd ed. New York, NY: McGraw-Hill/Irwin.

Luca, C. *Trading in the Global Currency Market*. 2nd ed. New York, NY: NYIF, 2000 http://www.liffe.com/ (Accessed January 5, 2002).

Shapiro, A. *Foundations of Multinational Financial Management*. 4th ed. New York, NY: John Wiley, 2001.

Shapiro, A. *Multinational Financial Management*. 6th ed. New York, NY: John Wiley, 1999.

Solnik, B. *International Investments*. 4th ed. Reading, MA: Addison-Wesley, 2000.

U.S. Securities and Exchange Commission. "International Investing." http://www.sec.gov/answers/intinvs.htm. (Accessed January 5, 2002).

5

Inflation, Interest Rates, and the Exchange Rate

The advent of the digital economy has increased the efficiency and competitiveness of financial markets. This event has spurred the growth of buyers and sellers trading in the market, lowered the cost of obtaining information, standardized the quality of the products traded, and equalized the price of the financial products across national boundaries. Price equalization is known as the *law of one price*. Price equalization is the result of international arbitrage, which is conceptualized through several theories including:

- Purchasing power parity (PPP)
- Fisher effect
- International Fisher effect
- Interest parity

PPP focuses on the relationship between anticipated inflation rates and the exchange rate. The remaining frameworks emphasize the relationship between interest rate differentials across countries and exchange rates.

A common theme among the four theories of exchange rate determination is the relationship among money supply, inflation, interest rates, and the exchange rate. According to a widely held view, inflation occurs when money supply growth exceeds real output expansion. If too many dollars are chasing too few goods, then the purchasing power of money (the exchange rate between money and goods) will decline. The same analogy applies to currencies in the foreign exchange market. If the European Central Bank increases the supply of euros in excess of existing demand conditions, then the residents of the European Union, in an effort to reduce their cash holdings of euros, increase spending on both domestic and foreign imports. Their excess demand for imports will flood the foreign exchange market with euros, which eventually will cause the decline in the price of the euro relative to other currencies.

The goal of this chapter is to provide the business executive with the analytical tools required to examine the relationship among monetary policy, inflation, interest rates, and the exchange rate. This chapter will also show how variations in the parity of a currency in the foreign exchange market will change the rate of return on foreign currency investments. Toward those ends, this chapter presents:

- The absolute and relative versions of the theory of exchange rate determination otherwise known as purchasing power parity
- An analysis of the factors determining the demand for foreign currency assets
- Several of the theories of exchange rate determination, which link monetary policy and interest rates to currency pricing in the foreign exchange market

PURCHASING POWER PARITY

The global financial market owes credit for the theory of exchange rate determination to the Swedish economist Gustav Casel. He introduced it in 1918 to justify some of his policy recommendations aimed at restoring international trade relations after World War I. Since then, the theory has been widely used. Central Banks use it to monitor the parity of their currencies in the foreign exchange market. Multinational corporations employ this theory to estimate the rate of return on foreign direct investment and to assess the dollar value of cross border investment projects. This theory can be based on market anticipations about future domestic and foreign prices or in terms of expectations about inflation differences between countries. These instances are known as the *absolute* and *relative* versions of the PPP.

Absolute Purchasing Power Parity

Absolute PPP based on the *law of one price,* states that *in a competitive market identical goods traded in different countries must sell for the same price when they are expressed in terms of a common currency.* This equality holds true only if the goods traded are identical or not facing trade barriers and transportation costs.

To provide an example of how absolute purchasing power works, consider the case of a cordless telephone selling for \$30 in the United States, ¥2,700 in Japan, and £20 in Britain. Given these prices, purchasing parity will hold only if the dollars to yen and dollars to pound rates are ¥90/\$1 and \$1.5/£1.

Dollar price of Japanese phone = local price × (the dollar-yen spot rate)
= ¥2,700 × (\$1/¥90)
= ¥2,700/90¥ × (\$1)
= 30 × \$1
= \$30

Dollar price of British phone = Local price × (the dollar-pound spot rate)
= £20 × ($1.5/£1)
= (20£/1£) × ($1.5)
= 20 × $1.5
= $30

In practice, we do not use the price of two goods to estimate the exchange rate. We instead use the ratio of the prices of two baskets of goods. For example if the U.S. basket of goods is priced at $80 and the basket of the European Union is worth €100. Then, the exchange rate that maintains the purchasing power of the two currencies is $0.8/€1.

PPP exchange rate = (P$/P€)
= $80/€100
= $0.8/€1.

Alternatively, this relationship can be expressed simply as an index whose value, set at 100 in the initial period, varies as the price of the two baskets change. For example, if anticipated that the value of the U.S. basket of goods will change from $80 to $88, while the euro basket is expected to grow to €105, then the absolute purchasing power parity initially set at 100 is expected to increase to 104.76. This change signals a 4.76% dollar discount in the forward market. It is also a forewarning of a 4.76% increase in the interest rate of U.S. securities.

The initial exchange rate index
Dollar price of U.S. basket/Euro price of EC basket = $(P_\$/P_\epsilon)$
= ($80 /€100)
= ($0.8/€1)
= ($0.8/$0.8) × 100
= 100

The future or anticipated exchange rate index a year later
$(P_\$/P_\epsilon)$ = ($88/€105)
= (0.838095/€1)
= ($0.838095/$0.8) × 100
= 104.76

The anticipated percentage change and the purchasing power parity index
Anticipated change = [(expected index/current index) − 1] ×100
= [(104.76/100) − 1] ×100
= 0.0476 × 100
= 4.76%

Relative Purchasing Power Parity

The relative version of PPP which is used more often than the absolute version, states that exchange parities adjust to reflect the inflation differential between the two currencies.

To provide an explanation for this relationship, imagine that a U.S. resident living in Nogales, Arizona on the U.S. and Mexican border is planning to marry and wants to purchase all the items needed to furnish a new home. This person has the option of walking to stores located in both the United States and Mexico. He finds that the price of all the items required to furnishing the new home in Mexican stores is worth 200,000 pesos. In the United States, it costs $20,000 for items of similar quality. If the exchange rate is 10 Mexican pesos per dollar (MxP$10/$1), then the buyer should be indifferent between buying the items on either side of the border. The reason is obvious. The customer can purchase the home items in U.S. shopping centers for $20,000. Alternatively, he can trade the $20,000 dollars in a local bank for 200,000 Mexican pesos, cross the border, and buy the furnishing goods in Mexico. In this instance, the exchange rate of 10 Mexican pesos per one dollar (MxP$10/$1) is properly reflecting the PPP of the two currencies.

Over time, the domestic and foreign prices of the basket of goods can change due to inflation. For instance, if the rate of inflation is 4% in the United States and 8% in Mexico, then under this new scenario, the exchange rate of MxP$10/$1 will no longer reflect the same PPP for the two currencies in both market. Purchasing power parity will hold if the exchange rate changes to MxP$10.5/$1.

The relationship previously described suggests that in the absence of market imperfections, the home furnishing items will sell for the same price.[1]

Formally, relative purchasing power parity can be expressed as the ratio of expected (e_t) to current (e_0) exchange rates as follows:

(5.1) $e_t/e_0 = [(1 + i_d)^t/(1 + i_f)^t]$

In Equation 5.1, e_t is the purchasing power parity anticipated in period t, e_0 is the dollar value of one unit of foreign exchange at the beginning of the period. And i_d and i_f are the domestic and foreign rates of inflation. If PPP holds, Equation 5.1 can be restated as follows:

(5.2) $e_t = e_0 \times [(1 + i_d)^t/(1 + i_f)^t]$

To provide an example of how to estimate the PPP exchange rate, consider the case where the rates of inflation in the United States and the European Union are 4% and 2% respectively, and the spot rate is $0.80 per one euro ($0.8/€1). The application of this information into Equation 5.2 results in a two-year PPP rate, which is estimated at $0.831/€1.

$e_2 = $0.8 \times [(1 + 4\%)^2/(1 + 2\%)^2]$
$= $0.8 \times [(1.04)^2/(1.02)^2]$
$= $0.8 \times (1.0816/1.0404)$
$= 0.8×1.0396
$= 0.831

If the spot rate is higher at $0.85/€1, then the dollar is undervalued. If the exchange is less at $0.81/€1, then the dollar is overvalued.

The two-year exchange rate estimate (e_2) is an equilibrium exchange rate only if the initial rate (e_0) is in equilibrium and if the inflation rates used to perform the calculations are the appropriate ones.[2]

The numerical result of the previous exercise implies a very important principle in exchange rate determination. This is that *currencies experiencing a high rate of inflation devaluate against currencies displaying lower rates of inflation.*

Purchasing Power Parity in Practice

When applying PPP as a measure of the long-term relationship between two currencies, one must consider the following points. First, the estimation of PPP requires the careful selection of periods with trade parity. To select it, central banks and multinational corporations review trade balance tendencies and identify intervals showing a stable parity or periods where imports are equal to exports.

Another important aspect to consider in the application of this theory is the choice of a price index. There are many types of indices including consumer, wholesale, tradable, and nontradable goods.

The tradable goods index includes the price of domestic goods considered exportable. The basket price of nontradable goods incorporates the price of local goods that due to high transportation costs or technical standards cannot compete internationally.

The index on tradable goods is the ideal price to be used to estimate the PPP rate. However, this is not always available. A second choice is the wholesale price index. This index has several advantages. The basket on which it is based contains a large tradable component. This tradable component is easy to find and reflects long-term price relations.

Many important international institutions, such as the International Monetary Fund (IMF), use PPP extensively to calculate real exchange rates for various countries. While popular, PPP has several major shortcomings. Contrary to the assumptions implicit in the law of one price, transport costs and restrictions on trade do exist. Another inconvenience of PPP is related to the composition of the basket of goods. The items included in the basket of one country do not necessarily reflect the composition of the basket in another region. As such, their ratio may not reflect PPP properly.

INTEREST RATES IN THE MONEY MARKET

Modern financial markets offer the contemporary investor a large variety of investing and lending opportunities. In the U.S. *money market*, a corporation can place short-term debt instruments at prime, federal funds, or commercial paper rates. Financial entities can issue finance paper, certificates of deposit, or bankers acceptances. Government owned financial institutions sell treasury bills (T-bills).

The international financial market is equally rich in terms of the quantity and quality of financial products. There are euro deposits stated in a wide range of currencies, which are quoted at the London Inter-bank Offered Rate (LIBOR). There are also London Late Eurodollar loans at LIBOR plus a mark-up.

All these interest rates listed in Table 5.1 are quoted in nominal terms. This means that they are expressed as the rate of exchange between current and future values. For example, a $1, one-year loan at 6% nominal rate generates a $1.06 return that must be repaid in one year. However, the parties to a loan agreement do not care about nominal returns, but they are interested only in real interest rates. They measure the rate at which current goods are being converted into future goods.[3] In practice, however, the relationship between lenders and borrowers is dominated by contractual obligations stated in nominal interest rates.

Nominal rates have two components, a real rate of return and an inflation premium equivalent to the expected level of inflation. This approach to interest rate determination is known as the *Fisher effect*. This principle suggests that if the real rate of return is 2%, and the expected rate of inflation is 4%, then the nominal rate should be roughly 6%.[4]

The nominal interest rate = real interest rate return + expected rate of inflation = 2% + 4% = 6%

The logic behind the Fisher effect is based on fairness. The future cash flow of a loan repayment has to be large enough to compensate the lender for the loss in the value of the initial investment due to inflation (4%) and to provide him with a real return (2%). For example, an investor will be willing to lend $0.961538 in exchange for a future cash flow of $1.02, because this cash flow is large enough to meet the inflation premium and provide a 2% real return as shown below.

Nominal return = $0.961538 × (1 + 4%) × (1 + 2%)
= $0.961538 × (1.04) × (1.02)
= $1.02

The generalized version of the Fisher Effect asserts that arbitrage equalizes the return on securities of similar risk across countries. Arbitrage sets in motion capital movements across countries, which help to restore currency equality worldwide.

To illustrate the role of arbitrage, consider the case of a return differential between the United States and the European Union. If the real returns are higher in dollars compared to returns in euros then the capital will shift from the second currency to the first. This process of arbitrage will continue until the real return in the two currencies is evened.

In equilibrium, the Fisher effect states that the nominal interest difference between local (r_h) and foreign (r_f) currencies will be approximately equal to the inflation differential between countries ($i_h - i_f$):

(5.3) $r_h - r_f = i_h - i_f$

Equation 5.3 describes a very important global finance principle. It asserts that *securities stated in terms of currencies experiencing a high rate of inflation offer the investor a higher rate of return than the one provided by securities stated in currencies with lower rates of inflation.* According to this principle, if the rates of inflation for euro and dollar are 2% and 4%, then, the dollar rate of return is anticipated to be 2% higher than the euro rate.

Table 5.1
Money Market Interest Rates

Prime rate	Base rate on corporate loans posted by at least 75% of the nation's 30 largest banks	
Federal funds	Reserve traded among commercial banks in amounts of $1 million or more	Overnight
Discount rate	The charge on loans to depository institutions by the Federal Reserve banks	
Call money	The charge on loans to brokers on stock exchange collateral	
Commercial paper	Unsecured notes sold through dealers by major corporations	30-90 days
Certificates of deposit	Rates paid by major New York Banks on primary new issues of negotiable CDs, usually in amounts of $1 million and more	30-180 days
Bankers acceptances	Offered rates of negotiable bank-backed business credit instruments, typically financing an import order with a minimum amount of $100,000	30-180 days
LIBOR	The average of Inter bank offered rates for dollar deposits in the London market based on quotations at five major banks	30-365 days
Treasury Bills	Short-term government bills sold at a discount from face value in units of $10,000 to $1 million	13-26 weeks
Foreign Prime Rates	These rates are not directly comparable; lending practices vary widely by location	

Source: *Wall Street Journal*, June 7, 2001.

THE INTERNATIONAL FISHER EFFECT

The exchange rate is the price of one currency in terms of another currency. For instance, on July 3, 2001, a Japanese resident needs 124 yen to buy one dollar. On the same day, a U.S. resident pays $1.40 to buy one British pound. These two quotations imply that the yen/dollar exchange rate is ¥124/$1, and that the dollar/pound rate is $1.40/£1.

The exchange rate is the price of the monetary unit of a country in terms of another currency and it is also the asset price. Acquiring an asset is a procedure used by the investors to transfer purchasing power from the present to the future. Therefore, the current price of an asset is directly related to the future return of the asset measured in terms of goods and services. Regarding currencies, their return is linked directly to the future value of the exchange rate.

A change in the exchange rate is described either as *depreciation* or *appreciation*. Depreciation of the dollar against the pound is an increase in the dollar price of pounds. For example, a variation in the exchange rate from $1.40/£1 to $1.50/£1 reflects a depreciation of the dollar. In contrast, a change in the exchange rate from $1.40 to $1.35 per pound reflects a decrease in the dollar price of the pound, or a dollar appreciation.

Dollar depreciation generates a negative return for non-U.S. residents holding this currency. For example a change in the spot value of the dollar from $1.40 to $1.50 yields a return of −6.67%. In contrast the dollar change from $1.40 to $1.30 generates a positive return of similar magnitude.

Return on dollar depreciation = [(new exchange rate/initial exchange rate) − 1] × 100 = [(1/$.150)/(1/$1.40) − 1] × 100

= −0.0666 × 100

= −6.67%

THE DEMAND FOR FOREIGN CURRENCY ASSETS

Exchange rate determination is a process shaped by the factors influencing the demand for foreign currency assets, such as bank accounts held in a foreign bank. To better understand exchange rate determination, it is necessary to learn what influences the demand for foreign currency-denominated assets.

The conventional view is that the demand for foreign currency-denominated bank accounts depends on the asset's rate of return and the expected appreciation or depreciation of the currency on which the asset is stated. For instance, the demand for a bank account deposit in Japan depends on the rate of return in the Japanese bank account and whether the yen will appreciate or depreciate against the dollar.

To estimate the profitability of a foreign currency-denominated bank account, investors need to consider the rate of return on foreign currency denominated bank accounts and to estimate the direction and magnitude of the change in the exchange rate over the investment period. With these two pieces of information, investors can estimate the profitability of the different investment opportunities in various countries.

To illustrate the estimation of a foreign bank account return, suppose that the dollar and British interest rates are 6% and 8% per year, respectively. A $1 deposit pays $1.06 after a year, while a one-pound deposit pays £1.08 over the same period. To determine which bank account generates the highest return, the investor has to estimate the amount of dollars that he will receive at the end of one year on each alternative. Estimating the return on a foreign currency-asset requires a three-step procedure.

Step 1

In the first step, investors estimate the dollar price of one British pound deposit. If the dollar price of a British pound is $1.40, then the current dollar price of one British pound deposit is just $1.40.

Step 2

In the second step, they determine the pound return on a British bank account. We know that the interest rate on British pounds is 8% so at the end of one year the British deposit is worth £1.08.

Step 3

If the dollar appreciates to \$1.35 dollars per British pound, then the dollar value of the British pound deposit is \$1.458. In the third step, they calculate the dollar value of the British pound return at the end of the year.

Dollar value of pound investment = (£1.08) × (\$1.35/£1)]
= (£1.08/£1) × \$1.35
= 1.08 × \$1.35
= \$1.458

The percentage rate of return on the British bank account is given as follows:

Pound return = [(dollar return on pound deposit/initial dollar deposit) −1] times 100
= [(\$1.458/\$1.40) − 1] × 100
= (0.0414] × 100 = 4.14%

The previous result indicates that a one-year pound bank account offering an 8% return generates only 4.14% when it is measured in dollar terms. A comparison of the rates of return between British and US banks indicates that the investors from both countries will be better off holding dollar deposits. The return differential opens arbitrage opportunities that encourage the transfer of funds from the European country to the U.S. The shift of funds will cease at the equalization of return across countries.

A simplified procedure to assess returns on foreign currency deposits is the following:

Dollar return on pound deposit = foreign return − the anticipated rate of depreciation of foreign currency[5]
= 8% − [\$1.35/\$1.4) − 1] × 100
= 8% − 3.57%
= 4.43% (rough estimate)

This approach is identified as interest parity condition or International Fisher Effect. Its application provides traders only with a rough estimate of the rate of return on a foreign currency deposit. The reader interested in more precise estimates should apply steps 1 to 3. Interest parity can be stated in more formal terms as follows:

(5.4) $r_\$ = r_f + [e_1(f/\$)/e_0(f/\$) - 1] \times 100$

where: $r_\$$ = interest rate on one-year dollar deposits;

r_f = interest rate on one-year foreign currency deposit

$e_1(f/\$)$ = expected foreign currency/dollar exchange rate at the end of one year

$e_0(f/\$)$ = current foreign currency/dollar exchange rate

Equation 5.4 can be rearranged as follows:

(5.5) $r_\$ - r_f = \{[e_1(f/\$)/e_0(f/\$)] - 1\} \times 100$

Equation 5.5 describes another important global financial principle. It asserts that *currencies with low interest rates appreciate against currencies having high interest rates.*

To apply the principle stated in Equation 5.5, consider that on July 3, 2001, the interest is 6% in the United States and 10% in Mexico. Given this information, the dollar is expected to appreciate approximately 4% against the Mexican peso over a year. Consider that for the same date, the interest rate in Switzerland is only 3%. In this instance, the interest rate in the United States is 3% higher than in Switzerland. Therefore, the Swiss franc will sell at a 3% forward premium against the dollar.

The right side of equation 5.5 is also known as the foreign currency forward premium (or discount). This equation can also be arranged to describe the annualized forward premium of quotations stated in less than a one-year period, such as 90 or 180 days.

Dollar premium = $[e_f(\$/f)/e_s(\$/f) - 1] \times 100 \times (360/n)$

where: $e_f(\$/f)$ = forward quote (dollars per one unit of foreign exchange)

$e_s(\$/f)$ = spot quote (dollars per one unit of foreign exchange) spot quote

n = days to maturity

To explain the concept of a dollar forward premium, consider the information provided by the Bank of Montreal on July 3, 2001.[6] The 180-day forward rate is \$0.8456/€1 per euro, while the spot rate for the same currencies is \$0.8479/€1. This information indicates that the dollar is selling at annualized forward premium of 0.54% against the euro. This result implies that a trader needs a lesser amount of dollars to buy euros in the forward market than in the spot.

Dollar premium = (180-day forward/spot) − 1] × 100 × (360/180)

= [(\$0.8456/\$0.8479) − 1] × 100 × (2)

= [(0.9973) − 1] × 100 × 2

= −0.0027 × 100 × 2

= −0.27% × 2

= −0.54%

INTEREST RATE PARITY AND THE EXCHANGE RATE

Interest parity is another a method widely used to forecast exchange rates. A popular version of this approach as follows:

(5.6) $e_t/e_0 = [(1 + r_d)^t/(1 + r_f)^t]$

In Equation 5.6, r_d and r_f are the domestic and foreign interest rates. e_0 the dollar value of one unit of foreign exchange at the beginning of the period and e_t is the spot rate in period t. If interest rate parity holds, then equation 5.6 can be transformed into equation 5.7.

(5.7) $e_t = e_0 \times [(1 + r_d)^t/(1 + r_f)^t]$

The value of e_t presented in equation 5.7 is known as the interest rate parity exchange rate. To provide an example of how to apply this concept to exchange rate determination, consider the case where the interest rates expected to prevail in the United States and the European Union during the next three years are 6% and 4% respectively, and the dollar/euro spot rate is \$0.80/€1. Applying this information to equation 5.6 generates an estimate for the future spot rate at the end of year three, which is equivalent to \$0.847/€1.

$e_2 = \$0.8 \times [(1 \times 6\%)^2/(1 \times 4\%)^3$
$= \$0.8 \times [(1.06)^3/(1.04)^3$
$= \$0.8 \times (1.191016/1.124864)$
$= \$0.8 \times 1.058809$
$= \$0.847/€1$

SUMMARY

This chapter examines the determination of the exchange rate from several perspectives, including absolute PPP, relative PPP, and the International Fisher effect. All these conceptions stem from the law of one price, or the notion that under free trade, arbitrage ensures that the exchange rate adjusted price of identical goods and financial assets traded in various markets is the same.

The technical specification for each one of the exchange rate approaches to exchange determination examined is as follows:

Absolute PPP

$\quad e_t = (P_\$/P_f)$

where:

$\quad\quad e_t$ = the dollar value of one unit of foreign exchange in period t
$\quad\quad P_\$$ = the dollar value of a U.S. basket of goods
$\quad\quad P_f$ = the foreign currency value of a basket of goods overseas

Relative PPP

$\quad e_t/e_0 = [(1 + i_d)^t/(1 + i_f)^t]$

where:

$\quad\quad e_t$ = the dollar value of one unit of foreign exchange in period t.
$\quad\quad e_t$ = current dollar value of one unit of foreign exchange
$\quad\quad i_d$ = the domestic rate of inflation
$\quad\quad i_f$ = the foreign rate of inflation

The International Fisher Effect

$\quad e_t/e_0 = [(1 + r_d)^t/(1 + r_f)^t]$

where:

$\quad\quad e_t$ = the dollar value of one unit of foreign exchange in period t.
$\quad\quad e_0$ = current dollar value of one unit of foreign exchange
$\quad\quad r_d$ = the domestic interest rate in period t
$\quad\quad r_f$ = the foreign interest rate in period t

In spite of the mathematical sophistication shown by the formulas, these are simply close approximations to exchange rate determination. A variety of factors can lead to exchange rate estimates showing sustained and wide disparities from exchange rate equilibrium.

Another problem often encountered in the practical applications of these theories is the fact that the different approaches can generate empirical result providing conflicting evidence. For example, PPP can point to currency appreciation. Interest parity, in turn, may produce a contrasting result suggesting currency depreciation.

In spite of these shortcomings, the parity theories remain as valuable tools widely used by central banks and international institutions, such as the IMF and the World Bank, to monitor the exchange rate equilibrium of a variety of currencies. Multinational corporations also apply them to a wide assortment of business situations, such as determining country risk, estimating cross-border transactions, and discounting future cash flows stated in terms of foreign monetary units.

The parity conditions provide the foundation for much of the material that is presented in the reminder of this book. For this reason, they should be well understood by the reader before proceeding to later chapters.

PROBLEMS

1. The wholesale price index of a British basket of goods is £1,000. In the United States a similar basket sells for $1,400. Given this information, what should be the PPP exchange rate of the British pound per one dollar?

2. If the inflation rate in the United States is 5% and in Britain only 3%, what should the one-year forward (pounds per one dollar) exchange rate be?

3. Considering the information provided in Questions 1 and 2, which country should have the highest rate of return? How much should the interest rate differential between the United States and Britain be?

4. If the euro spot rate is €1.10/$1 and the 90-day forward rate is €1.06/$1, is the euro selling at a forward premium or discount against the dollar?

5. If Swiss and U.S. investors require a real rate of return of 3% and the Swiss and U.S. interest rates are 6% and 4% (annually), what is the numerical value of the Swiss franc premium or discount against the dollar, assuming that interest rate parity holds?

6. The larger the degree by which the U.S. interest rate exceeds foreign exchange rates, the smaller will be the forward premium of foreign currencies against the U.S. dollar. Is this true? Please comment.

7. If the spot rate is $0.1208 per one rand and the rates of inflation in South Africa and the United States are 3% and 9% respectively, what is the expected rate of dollars per rand three years later?

NOTES

1. If PPP does not hold, then there is an arbitrage opportunity.

2. Otherwise, e_2 will not represent the equilibrium- exchange rate at the end of the second period.

3. A. Shapiro, *Multinational Financial Management* 6th ed. Englewood Cliffs, NJ: Prentice-Hall, 1999, p. 219.

4. The nominal rate of return is equivalent to the real rate, plus inflation, plus the real rate of return times the inflation rate, that is $2\% + 4\% + 2\% \times 4\% = 6.08\%$.

5. If it is the case of a foreign exchange appreciation against the dollar, then it is necessary to add the appreciation to the foreign currency return.

6. http://www.bmo.com/economic/regular/fxrates.html.

SUGGESTED ADDITIONAL READINGS

Caves, R., Frankel, J., and Jones, R. *World Trade and Payments*. 9th ed. Boston, MA: Addison Wesley 2002. See Chapter 26.

Bureau of the Public Debt Online. "Inflation Indexed Securities." http://www.publicdebt.treas.gov/of/ofinflin.htm. (Accessed November 7, 2001).

Federal Reserve Bank of New York. "Foreign Exchange Rates." http://www.ny.frb.org/pihome/statistics/forex12.shtml. (Accessed November 14, 2001).

Fisher, S. "Exchange Rate Regimes: Is the Bipolar View Correct?," New Orleans, January 6, 2001, http://www.imf.org/external/np/speeches/2001/010601a.htm. (Accessed November 29, 2001).

Shapiro, A. *Multinational Financial Management*. 6th ed. New York, NY: John Wiley, 1999. See Chapter 7.

6

Global Arbitrage

The foreign exchange market is one of the most competitive markets in the world. As such, it is ruled most of the time by the law of one price. This simply means that the quote for a currency should be the same in all markets, if the exchange rate is stated in terms of a single currency, for example, the number of Japanese yens per one dollar. Exchange rate equalization is the result of *arbitrage*, which can be defined as profiting from short-term distortions in the foreign exchange market. An arbitrage transaction is executed when a trader buys a currency cheap and sells it expensive. This type of trading is a risk-free activity because a trader acts simultaneously on both ends of the market with full price information.

Traders who specialize in arbitrage (also known as *arbitrageurs*) create an excess demand in the section of the market where the quotation for a currency is low and excess supply in the segment where the price for the same currency is high. The excess demand in the sector where the currency is selling low will raise the price of the currency. The opposite happens in the location where the currency is expensive. These two trends will bring currency prices back to equilibrium within and across regional foreign exchange markets.

The aim of this chapter is to provide the business executive with the financial tools required to identify and manage arbitrage opportunities. To meet this objective, this chapter:

- Describes the different variants of arbitrage
- Explains how to identify arbitrage opportunities
- Illustrates how to implement arbitrage transactions

FORMS OF ARBITRAGE

The type of arbitrage discussed in this chapter is primarily global in scope. It is applied to foreign exchange and international money market transactions and adopts a form related to any one of the following variants:

- Locational arbitrage
- Triangular arbitrage
- Covered interest arbitrage

Locational Arbitrage

This form of international arbitrage is the result of existing price distortions in two or more foreign exchange locations. An arbitrageur can capitalize on the quote differences between sites when the *offer price* in one location is lower than the *bid price* in another site. To profit from this discrepancy foreign exchange market participants buy currencies at the offer price and sell them at the bid price. For example, in Table 6.1, the bank in one location is quoting bid and offer exchange rates at €0.8355/$1, and €0.84$1 respectively. In contrast, the bank in the second site is quoting the same rates at €0.8455/$1, and €0.8477/$1.

Given this information, a trader will gain a profit buying dollars (cheap) at €0.84 (offer price at bank 1) and selling them (expensively) at €0.8455 (bid price at bank 2). The profit from this operation is €0.0055 per dollar traded.

Triangular Arbitrage

Triangular arbitrage refers to the simultaneous selling expensive currency previously purchased cheaply in another location. To identify triangular arbitrage opportunities, the traders compare cross rates across regional foreign exchange markets. If the two quotes differ, then there are triangular arbitrage opportunities.

For example, if in New York the Euro and pound are quoted in the spot market at $1.2/€1 and $1.4/£1, the cross rate is €1.166/£1. This cross rate quotation was obtained by applying the *chain rule*. By comparison, the same cross rate in London is quoted at €1.18/£1 (Table 6.2).

Table 6.1
Bid and Offer Exchange Rate Quotations (€/$)

Bank, location 1		Bank, location 2	
Bid	Offer	Bid	Offer
€0.8355/$1	€0.84/$1	€0.8455/$1	€0.8477/$1

Table 6.2
Cross Rates and Triangular Arbitrage

	New York	London
Spot rates	$1.2/€ 1	
	$1.4/£1	
Cross rates	€1.166/£1	€1.18/£1

Cross Rate Estimation Applying the Chain Rule (New York Spot Quotes)

Cross rate (Euro per one pound) = (€/$) × ($/£)
= (€1/$1.2) × ($1.4/£1)
= ($1.4/$1.2) × (€1/£1)
= 1.166 × (€1/£1)
= €1.166/£1

    The observed discrepancy between the cross rates in New York and London is a market distortion permitting triangular arbitrage. According to the law of one price, the euro should have the same price in terms of pounds in both locations.

    To take advantage of this opportunity, traders can purchase euro cheaply in London at €1.18/£1 and sell it in New York for considerable more at €1.166/£1.

    The execution of a £1,000 triangular arbitrage would result in a £11.43 profit. This transaction is described in Figure 6.1, and the calculations used to arrive at this figure are presented in detail.

    To implement the £1000 transaction, the trader has to invest £1000 in London to purchase euro cheaply at €1.18/£1. This transaction nets €1,180.

£1,000 = £1,000 × spot rate
= £1,000 × (€1.18/£1)
= (£1,000/£1) × €1.18
= 1,000 × €1.18
= €1,180

Second, the arbitrageur has to invest the euros in New York to purchase dollars at $1.2/€1. This transaction generates an inflow of $1,416.

€1,180 = €1,180 × spot rate
= €1,180 × ($1.2/€1)
= (€1,180/ €1) × $1.2
= 1,180 × $1.2
= $1,416

    In a third and final step, the arbitrageur trades dollars per pound at $1.4/£1, which yields £1,011.43:

$1,416 = $1,416 × spot rate
= $1,416 × (£1/$1.4)
= ($1,416/$1.4) × £1
= 1,011.43 × £1
= £1,011.43

Figure 6.1
Triangular Arbitrage

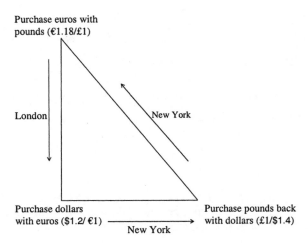

Purchase euros with
pounds (€1.18/£1)

London

New York

Purchase dollars
with euros ($1.2/ €1) ———————→
New York

Purchase pounds back
with dollars (£1/$1.4)

The opportunity to profit from cross-rate discrepancies does not last very long because traders all over the world will execute triangular arbitrage that will increase the demand for euros in London and will raise the supply of pounds in New York. This process, which lasts a few minutes, will return the cross rate parities to equilibrium in both London and New York.

Triangular arbitrage normally does not occur within a single bank. Usually, the three transactions previously described will involve three separate banks.

The identification and execution of both local and triangular arbitrage is not within the control of individuals or institution lacking the technology and expertise that is required to implement an arbitrage strategy. These transactions are only executed by highly specialized foreign exchange dealers having the computer facilities required to detect misalignment in spot and cross exchange rates.

The institutions engaged in arbitrage enjoy the benefits of being involved in transactions, which do not tie corporate funds, and are risk free. Arbitrage lets traders operate simultaneously on both ends of the market with full exchange rate information. As such, there is no uncertainty or risk involved in executing arbitrage transactions.

Covered Interest Arbitrage

Covered interest arbitrage involves investing local funds in terms of a foreign currency at higher rates of return and without exchange rate risk. Covered interest arbitrage is implemented only when a return in foreign exchange, measured in terms of local currency, is higher than returns offered by investment opportunities at home.

A return differential between local and foreign investment opportunities violates the law of one price and constitutes a market distortion offering profit opportunities. Covered interest arbitrage is a risk-free transaction because investors lock in, from the beginning, forward contracts; the proceeds to be obtained from investing overseas.

To identify covered interest arbitrage opportunities, investors apply the *interest rate parity principle*. Under this principle, there are incentives for covered interest arbitrage when the interest rate difference between two currencies differs from the forward premium (or discount) observed in foreign exchange markets. However, if the interest rate differential is equal to the forward premium, then interest parity holds and arbitrage opportunities do not exist.

Identifying Covered Interest Arbitrage Opportunities

The calculations shown in Table 6.4, which are based on the information provided in Table 6.3, indicate that it is profitable for U.S. residents to transfer funds from the United States to Switzerland and invest them in the European country. This transfer will gain a rate of return 0.4% higher than rates on similar investment opportunities in the United States. This happens because the annualized Swiss franc forward premium (1%) is large enough to offset the 90-day interest rate differential in favor of U.S. money market instruments (0.6%), as shown in Table 6.4.

Table 6.3
U.S. and Swiss Interest, Spot, and Forward Rates

Rates	United States	Switzerland
Spot rate	$1.7995/Swf 1	
90-day forward rate	$1.804/Swf 1	
90-day interest rate	3.75%	3.15%
Transaction size	$2,000,000	

Table 6.4
Interest Rate Parity

Interest Rate Differential	Dollar Premium (or Discount)
(U.S. – Swiss interest rate)	[(forward rate/spot rate) – 1]× 100 * 360/90
(3.75% – 3.15%) = 0.6%	[($1.804/$1.7995) – 1]× 100 * 4
	[(1.0025) – 1] × 4
	(0.0025) × 4
0.6%	1%

Covering a Swiss Franc Investment

To take advantage of the market distortion exhibited by the 90-day forward rate (dollars per one Swiss franc), an investor must take the following actions. She should trade the $2,000,000 in the spot market at $1.7995/Swf1. This transaction yields Swf1,111,420 that can be used as an initial investment to open a Swiss bank account.

Initial investment = $2,000,000 × (spot rate)
= $2,000,000 × (Swf1/$1.7995)
= $2,000,000/$1.7995) × Swf1
= 1,111,420 × Swf1
= Swf1,111,420

Next, the investor must open a 90-day Swiss francs account paying 3.15% per year. At the end of the 90-day period, the total return on this investment is equal to Swf1,120,172.

Future value of cash flows = initial investment times (1 + Swf interest rate/4)
= Swf 1,111,420 × (1 + 3.15%/4)
= Swf 1,111,420 × (1 + 0.007875)
= Swf 1,120,172

Lastly, the arbitrageur has to eliminate exchange rate risk. She can do so by locking in a 90-day forward exchange rate. This can be accomplished by purchasing a 90-day forward contract at the forward rate of $1.804/Swf1. Hedging the Swiss franc cash flow generates $2,020,79.

Future value of cash flows ($) = (Swf future cash flow) × forward rate
= (Swf 1,120,172) × ($1.804/Swf1)
= (Swf 1,120,172/Swf1) × $1.804
= 1,120,172 ×$1.804
= $2,020,79

The percentage return on the Swiss investment measured in dollars is equal to 4.16%, which is 0.41% higher than the U.S. return.

Swiss franc return ($) = [(dollar return on Swf investment/initial dollar investment) – 1] × 100 × 4
= [($2,020,791/$2,000,000) – 1] × 100 × 4
= [1.0103 – 1] × 100 × 4
= 0.0103 × 400
= 4.16%

IMPLEMENTING COVERED INTEREST ARBITRAGE

Another example of how to apply covered interest arbitrage technique is provided by the case of a multinational corporation holding $2.8 million in cash available to redeem (buy back) a 90-day dollar payable.

As a result of the discrepancy between cash availability and the maturity of the short-term debt, the corporation has $2.8 million cash available for a 90-day investment in the U.S. or British money markets.

In principle, the firm prefers to invest in the United States at 7% because there is no exchange rate risk involved. However, the higher British rate of return (12%) is an incentive to invest in that market if there is a forward cover to eliminate exchange rate risk.

To cover this risk, the company executive needs to implement several actions. Initially, she must buy British pounds in the spot market. Simultaneously, she must invest the pounds for 90 days at 12% in the British money market and sell the investment's proceeds in the forward market at the best forward rate. At maturity, she will deliver pounds to fulfill its forward contract commitment and settle the dollar payable. The actions needed to implement covered interest rate arbitrage are presented below:

Performing Covered Interest Arbitrage

Initial Date

Transaction 1: Company executive sells the $2,800,000 in the spot market (the corporation obtains £2,000,000).

Transaction 2: She invests £2,000,000 for three months in the British money market at 12% (annual rate). Total return after 90 days is £2,060,000 = £2,000,000*[1 + 0.12/4)]

Transaction 3: She sells £2,060,000 forward three months at $1.3860/£. The amount to be sold forward includes both the principal (£2,000,000) and the three months' interest generated by the investment in Britain (£60,000)

At Maturity, Three Months Later

Transaction 4: The company executive fulfills the forward contract by delivering £2,060,000 at $1.3860/£1 in exchange for $2,855,160 to be received the same day.

Transaction 5: She settles the $2,800,000 payable outstanding.

The profits from the covered interest arbitrage operation, which are equivalent to $6,160. They include the proceeds received from forward contracts (step 4, $2,855,160), less the principal initially invested ($2,800,000), less the opportunity cost of money in the U.S. money market ($2,800,000 × 0.07/4 = $49,000):

Profit = $2,855,160 - $2,800,000 - $49,000 = $6,160

SUMMARY

This chapter described the various forms of arbitrage and explained the techniques used by foreign exchange dealers to identify and implement arbitrage opportunities.

Arbitrage in any form is due to the profit opportunities opened by foreign exchange market distortions related to asset prices deviating from the law of one price.

Locational arbitrage is related to market distortions in the spot market where the exchange rate quoted by a bank to purchase foreign exchange in one place is less that the rate quoted by another bank selling the same currency in another location.

Triangular arbitrage is used to profit from cross rate differentials across locations. Its implementation requires three steps, which are likely to be executed by the dealer in various financial institutions.

Covered interest arbitrage, which is the most widely used form of arbitrage, is the result of profit opportunities opened by violations to interest rate parity.

If an interest rate differential exceeds a forward discount, firms should invest in the currency with the highest rate of return. However, if a forward discount is higher than interest rate differential, then it is better to invest in the currency with the lower rate of return to take advantage of the high forward premium on this currency.

To evaluate a covered arbitrage opportunity, firms have to take into consideration additional factors that may limit the benefits of a covered interest transaction, such as spreads between bid and offer exchange rates, transaction costs, taxes, and exchange rate controls.

PROBLEMS

1. Assume the following bid and ask rates of the pound for the two banks

Institution	Bid rate	Offer rate
Bank 1	$1.41/£1	$1.42/£1
	$1.39/£1	$1.4/£1

   a.   Is locational arbitrage possible?

   b.   What are the profits per unit of currency traded?

2. Assume the following information:

Rate	Toronto	London
Spot	Can$1.5807/$1	
Spot	£0.7003/$1	
Cross		Can$2.2401/£1

   a.   Is triangular arbitrage possible? If it is possible, indicate the net return on a £1 million investment.

3. You have $1 million to invest and you are given the following information:

Rates	United States	Britain
Interest	2% annual	3.6% annual
Spot	$1.428/£1	
180-day forward	$1.41/£1	

   a.   Is there an opportunity for covered interest arbitrage?

   b.   If so, what is the numerical value of profits?

4. You are provided with the following information:

Rates	United States	Japan
Interest	4.5%	1.5%
Spot	$0.00758	
180-day forward	$0.007673	

    a.   Is covered interest arbitrage possible?

    b.   If covered arbitrage is possible, indicate the return (%) on the investment.

5.   The following quotations on South African rand and Portuguese escudo are offered on March 25, 2002, in Montreal and in Pretoria.

Montreal	Pretoria
Can$0.1386/Rnd1	
Can$1.3889/Esc1	
	Esc0.098/Rnd1

    a.   Are opportunities for triangular arbitrage?

    b.   If so, what is the potential profit on a one million escudo transaction?

Case: SKF in Poland

Tore Bertilsson, finance director of the Swedish manufacturing firm SKF, was thinking about all the changes that he had introduced into the company's finance reporting over the last five years. From being a local manufacturer with some experience in other European countries such as Italy, the company had turned into a global player by expanding heavily into Asia, America, and eastern Europe.

To cope with problems posed by globalization, namely a greater reliance on foreign security markets to fund the company's activities and the increasing complexity of the finance function, Tore introduced a financial reporting structure that closely scrutinized costs and investments worldwide without hampering operational management or strangling local plant innovation. He called this new system the Twin Track Approach. It was aimed at providing SKF production managers in different parts of the world (Sweden, Malaysia, Brazil, or Mexico) with relative freedom to make capital investment expenditure decisions.

The factors prompting implementation of the Twin Track Approach were the difficulties initially faced by country managers in getting approval of small and large capital expenses. In the initial phase of global expansion, the old approval system created complicated bottlenecks around the world because every capital expenditure, regardless of its importance, had to be referred to headquarters in Gothenburg for approval. The most damaging aspect of the old approval procedure was not the delay caused by referring all capital expenditures to headquarters. Rather, it was the lack of awareness associated with compliance. Headquarters had the responsibility of approving capital expenditures for which the authorizing executive had little or no knowledge of the reasons for the request. The intent of the Twin Track Approach was to speed up the approval process and to eliminate bottlenecks.

Under the Twin Track Approach, the only spending subject to headquarters approval were large investment expenditures where the final approval came from the office of Mr. Bertilsson. Before these proposals reached his desk, they had to have the approval of both the Country Manager and the regional treasurer. These two executives, as a rule, considered and approved only carefully crafted proposals currently showing a positive net present value.

The role of a regional treasurer, which may be based in any one of the large company markets such as Germany, France, Italy, Singapore, or the United States, was to calculate the expected return on the proposed investment and to find the most suitable sources of capital funding in a particular territory. There were two exceptions to this approach, Asia and South America. The treasuries in these two regions, were centrally administrated from Gothenburg.

At the regional offices of the treasury, the analysis of how and where to fund a project started with an analysis of the relationship between local and foreign interest rates, and spot and forward rates. This exercise would lead to the identification of possible foreign exchange market distortions including low interest rate costs exchange rate instabilities. This analysis of both interest rate and the foreign exchange market was also useful in relocating the capital surplus of different subsidiaries to invest them in countries offering the best returns.

There was tremendous pressure at SKF to expand into the emerging markets because the firm wanted to reduce its dependence on slow growing western European markets, which accounted for 65% of the firm's manufacturing base. One of the countries targeted for expansion was Poland, where the demand for the company's products were growing at rates reaching 40% per year. To tap the potential of this market, SKF considered a six-month, $10 million investment to lay the financial groundwork for the operation of a new Polish plant.

To obtain these funds, the company considered borrowing from foreign markets, especially the New York. To facilitate funding from the United States, the company adjusted its financial reporting to meet the U.S. Generally Accepted Accounting Principles. This form of reporting provided global investors better quality information about the company in which they would invest. Also, SKF incorporated geographic subtleties in their annual report. They wanted to address U.S. investors' concerns about operational matters while keeping their European investors informed on cost cutting programs and the value of advertising budgets.

Andreas Erickson, a financial manager at SKF in Gothenburg, has been scanning the foreign exchange and interest rate information to determine the most convenient way to finance the $10 million loan to fund the Polish project. He also was trying to determine the potential foreign change risk involved with that loan over the six-month period and considering the possibility of covered interest arbitrage.

Andreas Erickson identified covered interest rate opportunities using the interest rate parity approach. According to this principle, there are covered arbitrage opportunities when the interest rate difference between two currencies is dissimilar to their forward premium (or discount). This happens, for example, when the interest rate between dollars and euros ($R_{us} - R_{\epsilon}$) does not match the dollar forward premium (or discount) against the euro.

If the interest rate differential and the forward premium are not equal, then SKF can use this information to invest at high rates of return in foreign countries or to borrow in foreign markets at interest rates lower than the ones prevailing in the home market.

Estimating the interest rate differential is an easy task. Estimating a forward premium is more cumbersome. To estimate the forward premium Mr. Erickson uses the following expression:

Forward premium = [n-day forward/spot – 1] × 100 × (360/n),

In this expression, n is the number of days the forward contract is due. Typical due dates are 30, 90, and 180 days. If the forward and spot rates are stated in terms of the number of dollars per unit of foreign exchange, then the numerical result of this exercise provides the dollar premium against a foreign currency.

The dollar is at a forward premium against a foreign monetary unit when the numerical value of a premium estimate is negative. A premium bearing a negative sign indicates that the dollar price of a foreign currency is less in the forward than the spot market. In contrast, if the sign is positive, it indicates that a unit of foreign exchange sells at a higher dollar price in the forward than the spot market.

To find out cheap sources of corporate funding, Andreas Erickson defines the amount of principal that the company wants to borrow. For example, in the case of the Polish investment, the principal is $10 million or its equivalent in foreign exchange. Then, he collects interest rate information that he uses to estimate the future value of the prospective loan in terms of various foreign currencies, for example dollars, euros, pounds, yens, and so on. Finally, he inquires about forward rate quotations from different money centers, and uses the best forward rates to lock in dollar or Euro cash flows for each funding alternative. For example, if he borrows in Swiss francs, he may lock in the cost of the Swiss franc debt in dollars or euro purchasing a forward contract. He often uses futures or options contracts as well.

Case Table 6.1
Interest and Exchange Rate Information (New York)

Country	Currency	Forward rate	Spot $/foreign	Interest rate (%) 30-day	90-day	180-day
Argentina	Peso		1.0006			
Britain	Pound		1.4108	4.83	4.84	4.67
		1-month	1.4092			
		3-month	1.4059			
		6-month	1.4008			
Canada	Dollar		0.658	4.08	4.06	4.01
		1-month	0.6576			
		3-month	0.657			
		6-month	0.6561			
Europe	Euro		0.8466	4.33	4.18	4.04
		1-month	0.846			
		3-month	0.845			
		6-month	0.844			
Japan	Yen		0.007948	0.47	0.47	0.46
		1-month	0.007974			
		3-month	0.008024			
		6-month	0.0081			
Mexico	Peso		0.1093			
Poland	Zloty		0.2381			
Sweden	Krona		0.0914			
Switzerland	Franc		0.5574	2.68	2.69	2.63
		1-month	0.5498			
		3-month	0.5504			
		6-month	0.5514			
United States	Dollar			4.47	4.24	4.08

Source: http://www.bmo.com/economic/regular/fxrates.html. (Accessed July 6, 2001).

Case Table 6.2
Key Cross-Currency Rates (Montreal, Canada)

	Canada dollar	U.S. dollar	British pound	Japan yen	Swiss franc	Euro
Canada dollar	1	1.5198	2.1442	0.01208	0.8472	1.2867
U.S. dollar	0.658	1	1.4108	0.007948	0.5574	0.8466
British pound	0.4664	0.7088	1	0.005634	0.3951	0.6001
Japan yen	82.78	125.81	177.5	1	70.13	106.51
Swiss franc	1.1804	1.7939	2.5309	0.014259	1	1.5188
Euro	0.7772	1.1812	1.6664	0.009388	0.6584	1

Source: The Bank of Montreal, www.bmo.com/economic/regular/fxrates.html. (Accessed July 6, 2001).

CASE PROBLEMS

1. Are there 180-day covered interest arbitrage opportunities for SKF in the spot and forward markets?

2. Are there opportunities for triangular arbitrage?

3. What is the cheapest source of funding for the 180-day $10 million loan?

SUGGESTED ADDITIONAL READINGS

Contigency Analisis. "Arbitrage." http://www.contingencyanalysis.com/glossary arbitrage.htm. (Accessed March 25, 2002).

Investopedia. Arbitrage. What Does it Mean?" http://www.investopedia.com/terms/a/arbitrage.asp. (Accessed March 25, 2002).

The Securities Lawyer's Deskbook. "Arbitrage Transactions." http://www.law.uc.edu/CCL/34ActRls/reg16E.html. (Accessed March 20, 2002).

7

Globalization and the Balance of Payments

The information provided in the balance of payments is widely used by governments and multinational corporations for a variety of applications that range from designing monetary, fiscal, and trade policies to managing country risk, global portfolios, and foreign direct investment.

This information is also used to identify international trade linkages, to recognize country structural strengths and weaknesses, and to rate the financial performance of a country.

In a similar fashion as to what happens to the financial statements of a multinational corporation, the balance of payments information is also subject to speculation. It is not unusual to find highly trained experts arriving at opposing conclusions, based on the analysis of similar balance of payments data.

To judge the quality of the conclusions reached and the subsequent policy recommendations arising from a balance of payments analysis, every government official and global executive should understand and know how to apply and interpret balance of payments information.

The purpose of this chapter is to provide the reader with the tools required to analyze the financial and trade relationships of one country with the rest of the world. To meet this goal, this chapter:

- Describes the balance of payments, its components, and how they are applied to determine the financial position of a country in the world market
- Examines how the balance of payments linkages affect ongoing business activities and the viability of a new business venture
- Identifies the basic forces underlying the flow of goods, services, and capital between countries

- Identifies the relationship that exists between the different balance of payments flows and key political and economic factors

STRUCTURE OF THE BALANCE OF PAYMENTS

The balance of payments is a statement of a country's international transactions over a quarter or a year. It describes all the transactions, that have taken place between residents, businesses, and government agencies of a country and the rest of the world. The balance of payments includes imports, exports, money spent by residents traveling abroad, and disbursements made by visiting foreigners in the home country.

Every international transaction requires two entries. The initial entry can be recorded as a credit in one location and later as a debit elsewhere. To decide whether the initial entry should be credited or debited, it is necessary to look into the nature of the transaction. In general, business transactions causing money to flow into a country are registered as *credits*. In contrast, *debits* are contractual agreements causing money to leave a country. For instance, U.S. software exports to China cause a credit in the U.S. trade balance and a debit entry in China.

To keep track of all international transactions, the balance of payments classifies and organizes them into two major accounts, the *current account* and the *capital account*. The current account keeps records of payments related to the exchange of goods, services, and investment revenues. The capital account records flows of financial and non financial capital. Both accounts are further divided into various sub accounts. The current account includes merchandise trade, service, income receipts, and transfer balances. The capital account includes foreign direct investments, portfolio investments, bank-related flows, and official reserve transactions.

The Current Account

The current account comprises the following:

- The *merchandise or trade balance* is a display of all the transfers of goods between domestic and foreign residents. It consists of all raw materials and manufactured goods bought or sold. A *resident* is defined as an individual or a business firm engaged in the export or import of "movable" or "visible" goods

- The *service or "invisibles" balance* includes payments made or received from tourism, transportation, freight, insurance, travel, and professional services like management, engineering, computer, economics, and accounting consultancy

- The *income balance* includes payments and receipts derived from the ownership of assets, such as dividends on holding of stock and interest on securities. Upon first exposure to balance of payments accounting, the readers are inclined to believe that interest payments and receipts are part of the capital account, but they are not. Interest payments are included in the income balance, because they are considered payments for "service" rendered by foreign investors. The repatriation of profits by a subsidiary is also considered a payment for services rendered by the capital used in the factory owned by a subsidiary

- *Unilateral transfers balance* includes only one-way transfers of money, such as workers' remittances from abroad and direct foreign aid. Unilateral transfers consist of government and private donations sent or received, remittances by migrant workers to their family members back home, interpersonal and institutional gifts, and government grants. These transfers, unlike loans, do not create a liability on the recipient.

The current account results are considered an indication of the international competitiveness of a country. The degree of competition of a nation is made more obvious if the transfer balance is excluded and the analysis focuses on the remaining accounts. They show the extent of a country's ability to earn its consumption of foreign goods and services.

A current account deficit occurs when the country is not exporting enough to pay for its imports of goods and services. To offset this deficit, the country needs to run a surplus in the capital account. If this is not the case, then the central bank has to sell foreign exchange reserves to erase the deficit. This activity is recorded in the settlement balance.

In contrast, a current account surplus exists when a country is selling in excess of what is needed to meet the goods and services import bill. To counterbalance a surplus, countries can run a capital account deficit. Otherwise, the central bank can offset the surplus acquiring foreign exchange reserves.

The Capital Account

The capital account records all transactions related to the purchase and sale of foreign assets, such as, trading corporations, subsidiaries, plant and equipment, stocks, bonds, and real state. Similar to the current account, the capital account also has four sub-accounts:

- *Foreign direct investment* occurs when residents acquire control of a company overseas or establish a new business in another country. The transaction may involve the acquisition of corporate assets such as real estate, equipment, or stock.

- *Portfolio investment* records international transfers of financial assets, such as small purchases of stock, and any amount of bonds. Portfolio transactions can be short-term or long-term. The purchase of foreign securities with a term to maturity of less than twelve months is a short-term portfolio investment. The acquisition of foreign bonds and long-term deposits represent examples of long-term portfolio investments. An issue related to the capital account is the determination of what constitutes foreign direct investment as opposed to a portfolio transaction when the transaction is related to stock purchases. In general, an investment is categorized as a portfolio transaction if it involves the acquisition of less than 10% of a company's stock. In contrast, purchasing shares is considered foreign direct investment if it is related to the acquisition of more than 10% of a company's stock.

- *Bank related flows* include loans granted by banks to countries or to foreign companies. It also includes the opening or closing of bank accounts. These transactions normally take place between international financial institutions that record these flows.

- The *balance on official reserve transactions or settlement balance* records the transfer of international reserves between central banks and international financial institutions, such as the IMF and the World Bank. It includes purchases and sales of central banks, international official reserves, and transfers of drawing rights between countries. Official reserves are holdings of "hard currencies" or highly liquid assets such as gold, securities, and foreign-currency checking accounts.

The net result in the capital account is often seen as a measure of the ability of a country to attract foreign funds that can help it to speed up its domestic capital formation.[1] However, a capital account surplus can be misleading. It may simply be the result of massive transfers of "hot money" in search of high yields. *Hot money* refers to wire transfers that are deposited in countries for very short periods of time lasting from several hours to few days.

THE UNDERLYING BALANCE OF PAYMENTS PRINCIPLE

In theory, the current account and the capital account should balance. That is, the addition of the various balance of payments credits should match the accumulated value of the debits. Therefore, the net result in the balance of payments should be zero.

In practice, this is not always the case. The globalization of capital markets and developments in telecommunications has facilitated the international transfer of funds. However, the collection of financial data on the part of the bureaus charged with this responsibility has led to information gaps that are often reflected in discrepancies between the balance of payments debits and credits. To eliminate these discrepancies, the balance of payments includes an *errors-and-omissions account* that erases the discrepancies.

Often, errors and omissions are merged with the short-term capital account. This action reflects the perception held by many international agencies, charged with the collection of national statistics, that the balance of payments discrepancies originate in short-term capital movements. However, in most instances, the two accounts are reported separately.

The Accounting System

Each transaction recorded in the balance of payments gives rise to two entries: a debit and a credit. A debit entry implies a use of foreign exchange, an outflow of funds, an import, or a payment. A credit entry is a source of foreign exchange, an inflow of funds, an export, or a receipt. If the convention of double-entry bookkeeping is followed, total debits will always equal total credits. In this trivial sense, the balance of payments always balances.

To make the accounting of the balance of payments useful for economic and business analysis, debits and credits have to be properly placed into the eight subcategories previously discussed. This task is accomplished in Table 7.1, which describes in detail, the taxonomy of the balance of payments.

Double Entry Bookkeeping

To familiarize the reader with double-entry bookkeeping and its use in creating a balance-of-payment statement, the following paragraphs describe some international transactions and the corresponding entries. Later, all transactions are entered into a U.S. balance of payment statement, described in Table 7.2.

Balance of Payments Entry Transactions

Transaction 1:   *A U.S. firm based in Phoenix, Arizona, exports computer equipment to Mexico, worth $10,000,000.* The importer settles the transaction with a check drawn from a bank account of the Mexican manufacturer in Mexico City.

The U.S. export is a source of funds. To reflect this fact, the transaction is recorded as a trade balance credit. This entry can also be viewed as a reduction in U.S. goods.

Transaction (1)	Debit (−)	Credit (+)
U.S. exports (trade balance)		$10,000,000
Private foreign assets (short-term capital account)	$10,000,000	

The fact that the U.S. exporter is paid with a Mexican check is equivalent to a U.S. acquisition of a foreign asset or a use of funds. To reflect a private capital outflow, a debit is entered in the short-term capital account.

Transaction 2:   *American tourists travel to France and spend $250,000 on food, lodging, and other goods.* The tourists pay the expenses with travelers checks acquired prior to departure from a U.S. bank.

The U.S. acquisition of French services (tourism) is a use of funds debited in the service account.

Paying the French residents with U.S. traveler checks is equivalent to selling U.S. assets to French residents, or a source of funds for the U.S. Therefore, a credit is recorded in the short-term capital to reflect a capital inflow.

Transaction (2)	Debit (−)	Credit (+)
Tourism (service account)	$250,000	
Private U.S. assets (short-term capital account)		$250,000

Table 7.1
The Balance of Payments

DEBITS (−)	CREDITS (+)
Use of Foreign Exchange	**Source of Foreign Exchange**
Merchandise imports	Merchandise exports
Transport service payments	Transport service receipts
Insurance payments from abroad	Insurance income from abroad
Travel expense by residents while abroad	Travel expenditures by non residents when visiting
Interest and dividends paid to foreigners on loans and investments made in the country	Interest and dividends received on foreign loans and investments abroad
Government and private aid to other countries	Government and private aid received from abroad
Direct investment by residents	Foreign direct investment in the home country
Portfolio investment by residents abroad	Foreign portfolio investment in the home country
Increase in domestic banks' loans to non residents	Foreign banks' increase in loans to residents
Increase in the commercial bank or central bank's holding of foreign exchange	Increase in foreign loans to domestic commercial banks or to the central bank

Transaction 3:   *An American importer purchases oil from Saudi Arabia for$7,000,000.* The transaction is settled with a check issued by the American importer from an account held in a Swiss bank.

The U.S. oil imports imply a use of funds. As such, the transaction is entered as a balance of payments debit.

Transaction (3)	Debit (−)	Credit (+)
Import (trade balance)	$7,000,000	
Private foreign assets (short-term capital account)		$7,000,000

The import settlement with a check drawn from a bank account held by the U.S. importer in Switzerland is equivalent to the sale of a U.S. held asset, a source of funds. Consequently, a credit is recorded in the short-term capital to reflect a capital inflow.

Transaction 4:   *U.S. investors holding Italian assets receive $2,000,000 in interest and dividends paid by an Italian bank with a check drawn from a U.S. bank.* The interest and dividends earned by U.S. investors represents a source of funds.

To reflect the inflow of capital, the transaction is credited in the income balance.

The Italian payment with a check drawn from a U.S. account held by the Italian bank is equivalent to the U.S. buying back U.S. assets held by a foreigner, a use of funds. To reflect the outflow of capital, this transaction is recorded as a debit in the short-term capital account.

Transaction (4)	Debit (−)	Credit (+)
Interest income (income balance)		$2,000,000
Private foreign assets (s-t capital account)	$2,000,000	

Transaction 5:   *Japanese residents purchase $200,000 of common stock on the New York Stock Exchange.* They issue checks from accounts held by Japanese residents in U.S. banks.

The sale of U.S. stock, representing less than 10% of the shares issued by a U.S. company, is a portfolio transaction or source of funds. To reflect the inflow of funds, the transaction is credited as a portfolio transaction in the capital account.

The payment with a U.S. check is equivalent to the U.S. acquisition of a foreign held asset, a use of funds. To reflect the outflow of capital, this transaction is recorded as a debit in the short-term capital account.

Transaction (5)	Debit (−)	Credit (+)
Private US assets (portfolio account)		$200,000
Private foreign assets (short-term capital account)	$200,000	

Transaction 6:   *Ford Motors ships a drill press worth $1,000,000 to Mexico for installation in the maquiladora plant held by Ford in Hermosillo, Mexico.*

The shipment of the drill is equivalent to a U.S. export, a source of funds. To record the inflow of funds, the transaction is entered as a credit in the trade balance.

The installation of the drill is equivalent to the U.S. acquisition of a foreign asset, a use of funds. To record this transaction, the outflow of funds is entered as a U.S. foreign direct investment in the capital (long-term) account.

Transaction (6)	Debit (−)	Credit (+)
Export (trade balance)		$1,000,000
Private foreign assets (l-t capital account)	$1,000.000	

Assembling the Balance of Payments

A hypothetical U.S. balance of payments is presented in Table 7.2. This statement brings together the information furnished by the transactions discussed in previous paragraphs. Each entry in the table is identified with a number that relates to the order in which the international transactions was discussed. For instance, the first entry in the merchandise line bears the number (3), which means that this entry corresponds to transaction number 3.

Table 7.2
U.S. Balance of Payments

Balance	Debits (–)	Credits (+)	Net
Goods and Services			
Merchandise	(3) 7,000,000	(1)+(6) 11,000,000	+4,000,000
Travel	(2) 250,000		-250,000
Investment Income		(4) 2,000,000	+2,000,000
Current Account	**7,250,000**	**13,000,000**	**+5,750,000**
Long-term Capital			
Direct Investment	(6) 1,000,000		-1,000,000
Portfolio		(5) 200,000	+200,000
Basic Balance	**8,250,000**	**13,200,000**	**+4,950,000**
Private short-term	(1) 10,000,000	(2) 250,000	9,750,000
	(4) 2,000,000	(3) 7,000,000	+5,000,000
	(5) 200,000		-200,000
Net	12,200,000	7,250,000	-4,950,000
TOTAL	**20,450,000**	**20,450,000**	**0**

ANALYZING THE BALANCE OF PAYMENTS

The information provided by the balance of payments has a wide variety of applications. Commercial banks use it to determine the risk involved in foreign lending. Multinational corporations use the information contained in the balance of payment to determine the risk and return associated with foreign direct investment. Government officials and monetary authorities employ it to forecast macroeconomic variables and to set commercial and exchange rate policies. Multinational financial institutions such as IMF and the World Bank often utilize balance of payments information to design adjustment programs for countries suffering from price instability and trade imbalances.

The information presented on Countries A and B in Table 7.3 is used to illustrate how the analysis of the balance of payments assists the decision-making process of either the corporate executive or the government official managing foreign affairs.

The balance of payments of Country A shows a large surplus in portfolio investment, which helps to finance both the current account and foreign direct investment deficits. Overall, the basic balance of Country A shows a surplus of $800, deficits in short-term capital movements, errors, and omissions. After adjustments made to consider the deficits, the settlement balance of Country A presents a $200 surplus, which is applied to increase the official reserves of the central bank of this country

Similarly to Country A, the balance of payments of Country B shows a basic balance surplus of $800. However, unlike Country A, the surplus in Country B is the result of a strong export performance.

Adjustments for short-term capital movements and errors and omissions in the balance of payments of Country B consume a portion of the basic balance surplus. Consequently, the net balance of payments surplus is reduced to $200. This surplus also ends up as an increase in the reserves of the central bank in Country B.

Table 7.3
Comparative Analysis of the Balance of Payments

Balance	Country A	Country B
Merchandise Trade	−1,000	+2,000
Services	−500	−1,200
Transfers	+ 900	−100
Current Account	**−600**	**+700**
Long-term Capital		
Portfolio Investment	+1,500	−200
Direct Investment	−100	+300
Basic Balance	**800**	**800**
Short-term capital	−400	−580
Errors and Omissions	−200	−20
Settlement Balance	**200**	**200**
Official Reserve Transactions	−200	−200

A financial analyst faced with the responsibility of recommending the site for a new subsidiary will notice that the balance of payments performance of Countries A and B, while similar in overall balance performance, have quite different meanings. Country B has earned its balance of payments surplus by exporting and creating a climate favorable to foreign direct investment, whereas Country A has borrowed it.

The government official responsible for approving long-term government loans to either country will notice that the result in the balance of payments of Country A depends on the competence of the country to negotiate external bank loans. In contrast, the accomplishment of Country B depends on its ability to export.

Both the financial analyst and the government official will conclude that Country A and Country B are experiencing very different circumstances, in spite of the similarities in the balance of payment results. Therefore, Country A, contingent upon further information, should be considered risky, whereas Country B should be assessed the rank of high profile.

NATIONAL INCOME AND THE BALANCE OF PAYMENTS

The level of domestic sales and the value of exports, measured in terms of local currency, determine the revenue of global corporations. Local earnings are a function of anticipations regarding the future level of real national income and real income growth. For example, corporate sales expectations are good in the United States, if there are anticipations of a strong U.S. economic growth.

Export proceeds are related to expectations concerning the growth of foreign real income and changes in the exchange rate. For instance, U.S. companies expect exports to increase if the Canadian economy is healthy and growing. Similarly, U.S. firms expect to increase their exports to Canada if a depreciation of the local currency against the monetary unit of Canada is anticipated.

The previous discussion suggests that there is a connection between the economic performance of a country and the transfer of goods, services, and capital across borders that need to be formalized. As such, the reminder of this chapter will be dedicated to developing a frame of reference linking the balance of payments to national income.

The Circular Flow

Every day countless market transactions occur, even in small countries. Individuals work and consume. The firms produce and invest. The governments collect taxes and implement social expenditure programs. Households, government, and firms export and import goods and services. It is conceivable to organize, classify, and aggregate all these transactions.

The expenditures of households on all kinds of goods and services, except housing, are classified as *consumption*. The acquisition of raw materials, parts, and capital goods by firms is aggregated under *investment*. The expenses incurred by the government are listed under *government expenditures*. The sale of domestic goods and services to foreigners is called *exports*. The acquisition of foreign goods by local residents is considered *imports*.

(7.1)   National spending = consumption (C) + investment (I) + government spending (G) + (exports (X) − imports (M))

In terms of the national accounting system, exports less imports are equal to the current account.

(7.2)   National spending = consumption + investment + government spending + current account (CA)

The expenditures of households, firms, government, and residents, represent an income for someone else. Therefore, the accumulation of all the income generating expenditures is known as the *level of national income*.

(7.3)   National spending = national income (or national product).

Once national income is generated, it is distributed to the different social groups integrating the national economy. For example, the government takes its portion first when it collects *taxes*. The amount of income left, after taxes, is known as *disposable income*.

(7.4)   Disposable income (Yd) = national income (Y) − taxes (Tx)

Disposable income is the proportion of national income left to the households, which they use to satisfy their needs and wants. The leftover is considered *savings*. This portion of national income is placed in the form of bank account deposits in financial institutions across the country.

(7.5)   Savings (S) = disposable income (Yd) − consumption (C)

The banks, identified as financial intermediaries, do not want to keep deposits idle, mainly because they have to pay interest on them. To avoid losses and generate profits, banks lend the savings to firms, which invest it.

At this point, the portion of national income received by the government, households, and firms, has been recycled back into a circular flow. This last transaction seals the circular flow that keeps the economy in motion. Figure 7.1 illustrates this circular flow.

(7.6)   National income = taxes + consumption + savings

Figure 7.1
Circular Flow Graphic

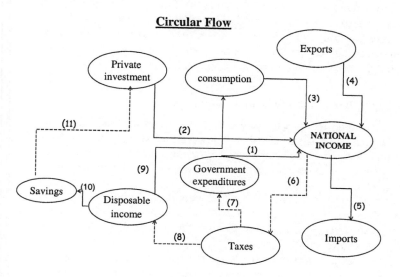

Circular Flow

From the description of how the economic system operates, it is possible to identify the critical connections that are vital to maintain the stability of the circular flow. This is the relationship between the current account with net savings (savings — investment), and the government budget (taxes — government spending).

This association can be explained by re-expressing Equation 7.3 as follows:

(7.7)   Investment + government. spending + current account = (taxes + savings)

Relating each allocation of national income with its associate spending provides the linkages between the balance of payments and the national economy that we are seeking.[2] For example, exports provide the revenue and imports are the spending counterpart.

Similarly, household savings provide the inflow of bank capital to fund private investment. Finally, taxes provide government revenues, which in turn are spent on social programs labeled with the generic name of government expenditures. Consequently, Equation 7.7 can be restated as:

(7.8)   Current account (CA) = (savings (S) − investment (I)) + (taxes (Tx) − government spending (G))

If taxes are assumed to be equal to government spending, then Equation 7.8 can be simplified as follows:

(7.9)   Current account = (savings — investment)

According to Equation 7.9, if the savings of a nation exceed its investment, that country is running a current account surplus. This equation explains why some Asian countries, like Japan, have very high rates of savings and record current account surpluses. Latin America is an opposite case. In this region, the countries save less than they invest and current account deficits are frequent.

The more comprehensive setting presented in Equation 7.8 indicates that if savings and taxes exceed investment and government expenditures, the nation can run a current account surplus. However, if the government deficit (taxes − government spending) exceeds net private savings (savings less investment), then the country can experience current account deficits.

Currency Depreciation and the Balance of Payments

A depreciation normally conveys good and bad news for the local economy. The good news of depreciation is that it lowers the world price of domestic goods and services, which helps to increase the quantity of exports and reduce the volume of imports. These adjustments in the current account are known as the *volume effect*.

The bad news of depreciation is that each export unit brings a lesser amount of foreign exchange. In addition, it forces local consumers to pay a larger quantity of local currency to purchase foreign goods. These two aspects of the depreciation are known as *value effect*.

If both the volume and value effects are measured in percentage terms, it is possible to relate the two for both imports and export transactions in terms of the price elasticity.

(7.10)   Price elasticity (for exports and imports) = volume effect/value effect

Equation 7.10 indicates that if the volume effect exceeds the value effect on both imports and exports, then the numerical value of elasticity for exports and the elasticity for imports will be greater than one, in absolute terms.[3] If this is the case, the nation that experiences devaluation will enjoy an improvement in the current account balance. However, if the addition of the two elasticities is less than one, the depreciation leads to a deterioration of the current account. This result is known as the *J effect*.

In short, a devaluation improves the current account only when the sum of the two elasticities, the price elasticity of exports and the price elasticity of imports, is greater than one, in absolute terms.[4]

SUMMARY

The balance of payments is an accounting statement of the international transactions of one country over a specific period. The statement shows the transactions of individuals, businesses and government agencies located in one country, with those located in the rest of the world.

The balance of payments is based on double-entry bookkeeping, where every transaction generates two entries: a debit and a credit. A debit shows a purchase of foreign assets and signals a use of foreign exchange. A credit is a sale of domestic assets. As such it is a source or inflow of foreign exchange.

The balance of payments separates the international transactions into two major blocks, the current account and the capital (or long-term capital) account. Each of these accounts is divided into four sub accounts. The current account, which records payments related to transfers of goods and services and to earnings on investment, includes the trade, service, income receipts, and unilateral transfer balances. The capital account, which records trade in assets such as companies, bonds, stocks, real state, and factories, integrates the direct foreign investment, portfolio investment, bank related flows, and official reserve balances.

Many countries in Latin America used to run current account deficits. The content of this chapter shows that these deficits were a macroeconomic phenomenon that could be traced back to the countries' investments exceeding national savings.

PROBLEMS

1. What are the appropriate entries (debit and credit) in the U.S. balance of payments for each of the following transactions?

    a. An Argentinean exporter ships $50,000 worth of leather to the United States and receives payment in the form of a dollar deposit in a U.S. bank.

    b. Chrysler ships auto equipment worth $1,000,000 to Mexico for installation in its branch factory in Saltillo, Mexico.

    c. A Japanese citizen purchases $500,000 worth of U.S. government bonds; the U.S. seller is paid with a check drawn from a bank in Tokyo.

    d. A U.S. citizen purchases $250,000 worth of German bonds; the German seller is paid with a check drawn from a U.S. bank.

2. Organize the information provided, into a balance of payments table for the United States. Attach the correct sign to each entry and incorporate an errors and omissions entry if the accounts do not balance.

    a. What is the numerical value of the current account, the basic balance, and the official settlement accounts?
        Current account   = $ _____
        Basic balance   = $ _____
        Short-term capital balance = $ _____

b. Use the relevant entries in your balance of payments table and some or all of the numbers below to calculate the level of gross national product GNP for the United States.

Consumption   300   Government purchases   1000
Savings   650   Investment   700
GNP = $ _____

Note: To calculate GNP you need the current account result of exercise "a."

Items	Value
Merchandise imports	400
Foreign direct investment by US firms	70
Profit remittances to foreigners	40
Merchandise exports	200
Foreign tourist expenditures in the United States	40
Foreign purchase of U.S. corporate securities	150

3. The following transactions took place in South Africa in the year 2002:

a. South African gold mine companies ship gold worth €8400 million to the Netherlands. 70% of this revenue is used to settle interest payments on private and government external debt owed to Switzerland. Thirty percent of the revenue is used to acquire machinery and equipment form different countries of the European Union.

b. Private South African investors received interest payments from a previous purchase of German government bonds. The coupon payment made by the German government to South Africa amount to €7.2 million. This interest payment is settled with a check issued by the German government from an account held with a German bank.

c. Tourists visiting South Africa spent €6 billion in this country. Most of these revenues are in the form of credit card vouchers.

d. Local South African companies pay fees to American Express, VISA, and Master Card equivalent to 7.5% of tourism revenue (0.075 × €6000 = €450 million). Payment is settled with checks drawn from U.S. banks.

e. The South African government has been providing financial assistant to other African nations in the form of gold deliveries. This aid amounts to €3.1 billion. However, 40% of this assistance is reimbursed to the South African government by the European Union in the form of checks drawn against the European Central Bank.

f. South African companies imported food and raw materials equivalent to €10.2 billion. The payment for these shipments is settled with checks drawn from banks operating in the European Union.

g. The Saudi Arabian government provided South Africa with a €6 billion loan to fund the training of South African Muslims in European and U.S. universities. Half of the payment is paid with checks drawn from accounts held by the Saudi government in the United States, and the remaining 50% with Saudi oil, delivered to the South African government.

Fill in the blanks in the South African balance of payments sheet.

South Africa, Balance of Payments

Balance	Debit (−)	Credit (+)	Net
Merchandise			
Exports			
Imports			
Service			
Interest earned			
Interest paid			
Export			
Imports			
Transfer			
Current Account			
Long-Term capital			
Portfolio			
Foreign Direct Investment			
Basic Balance			
Short-Term capital			

Case: The U.S. Balance of Payments

One of the most informative ways to learn about a country's balance of payments statistics is to take a careful look at them for a particular period. The information included in Case Table 7.1 presents balance of payments statistics for the United States covering four quarters in 1999 and the first quarter of the year 2001. The information is presented in terms of debits and credits.

The best way to explain these cash flows is by suggesting that any transaction that causes money to flow into the United States is a credit. Conversely, any transaction that causes money to flow out is a debit. For instance, consider the case of U.S. exports of goods to a foreign country. The settlement of an export transaction generates a cash inflow to be recorded as a credit. In contrast, a US import of foreign goods will cause a cash outflow. Therefore, this last transaction should be recorded as a debit.

According to the items included in Case Table 7.2, the balance of payments of the United States, and any other balance of payment from any country in the world, encompasses several main accounts, some of which have sub accounts of their own.

The key accounts are the current account and the capital account. The first one measures the net flow of goods and services. The value of the current account is determined, at a large extent, by the results of the trade, service, and transfer sub accounts. The trade balance is also known as merchandise balance. The trade balance measures import and export of goods flows. The service account contains many different items. However, the most important one is earning on investments. This last item is so important for some countries that often it is reported in a separate account.

The capital account consists of capital transfers and the acquisition and disposal of nonfinancial assets such as machinery and equipment and real state. There is also the financial account, which records investment flows, known as portfolio investment.

Overall, a current account surplus should have as a counterpart, a deficit in the capital account. Similarly, a deficit in the current account should be balanced with a capital account surplus. The United States shows a current account surplus, when the sale of U.S. goods and services to the rest o the world exceeds the U.S. acquisition of these items from other countries. The United States has a deficit in the capital account when U.S. corporations invest abroad in excess of what foreign multinationals invest in the United States.

In practice, a current account deficit is not always offset by a capital account surplus due to statistical discrepancies, accounting conventions, and exchange rate movements. To conduct the analysis of the U.S. balance of payments, notice that there is no information on errors, and omissions, therefore, this account should be considered with a zero balance.

Finally, remember that the net result in the U.S. balance of payments has to be zero. As such, if the basic balance shows a surplus, this has to be compensated with an outflow of international reserves—acquisition of foreign exchange by the Federal Reserve System. Conversely, if the basic balance is in deficit, this has to be counterbalanced with a cash inflow—sale of foreign exchange by the Federal Reserve System.

Case Table 7.1
U.S. Balance of Payments Information
(Quarterly, $ billions)

| Period | Goods | | Service | | Income | Payment | Transfers |
	exports	imports	exports	imports	assets	assets	net
1999.1	163	236	66	46	62	64	10
1999.2	166	249	67	47	66	68	11
1999.3	173	266	68	48	70	74	11
1999.4	180	276	69	49	74	78	14
2000.1	183	289	71	51	79	81	11

Period	US Assets Abroad	Foreign Assets in the United States
1999.1	121	102
1999.2	170	272
1999.3	122	194
1999.4	114	184
2000.1	143	215

Case Table 7.2
U. S. Balance of Payments

Balance	Debit (−)	Credit (+)	Net
Merchandise			
Export			
Imports			
Service			
Exports			
Imports			
Interest payments to foreigners			
Interest payments from foreigners			
Unilateral Transfers			
CURRENT ACCOUNT			
Capital Account			
Capital account transactions, net			
U.S.-owned assets abroad, net			
Foreign-owned assets in the United States, net			
BASIC BALANCE			
Errors and omissions			
Change in international reserves			
NET			

CASE PROBLEMS

1. Is the U.S. current account showing a surplus or a deficit?

2. If it is a deficit, how is the United States balancing the current account deficits? By borrowing or by selling more capital assets than it is buying?

3. What are the consequences for the US economy if the country runs a persistent current account deficit?

NOTES

1. As a matter of fact, attracting foreign direct investment has been turned into the centerpiece for various economic development strategies implemented at the turn of the 21st Century.

2. Notice that consumption has been eliminated from both sides of the equation. This action maintains the equality between national spending and uses of income.

3. Elasticity normally yields negative results.

4. This is known as the Marshall-Lerner condition, in honor of the two economists who developed this concept.

SUGGESTED ADDITIONAL READINGS

Caves, R., Frankel, J., and Jones, R. *World Trade and Payments*, 9th ed. Boston, MA: Addison Wesley 2002. See Chapter 15.

Federal Reserve Bank of New York. "Balance of Payments." http://www.ny.frb.org/pihome/fedpoint/fed40.html. (Accessed November 28, 2001).

International Monetary Fund, IMF Staff. "Globalization: Threat or Opportunity?" April 12, 2000, http://www.imf.org/external/np/exr/ib/2000/041200.htm. (Accessed November 28, 2001).

Krugman, P., and Obstfeld, M. *International Economics, Theory and Policy*. 5th ed. Boston, MA: Addison Wesley Longman, 2000. See Chapter 12.

Shapiro, A. *Multinational Financial Management*. 6th ed. New York, NY: John Wiley, 1999. See Chapter 4.

The World Bank Group, World Bank Briefing Papers. "Assessing Globalization." http://www.worldbank.org/html/extdr/pb/globalization/. (Accessed November 28, 2001).

8

Financing Global Trade and Foreign Direct Investment

Multinational corporations engage in sourcing, marketing, manufacturing, and organizing the development of new products across borders. To implement these activities, they have to trade across countries and invest overseas.

Sourcing occurs when companies import raw materials and parts for use in local manufacturing or when they operate foreign assembly plants to take advantage of relatively low labor costs. For example, the maquiladora plant operated by Zenith in Ciudad Juarez, Chihuahua, Mexico, is a form of sourcing set up to take advantage of lower wage rates in Mexico compared with those prevailing in the United States. Sourcing also happens when a multinational transfers the engineering and manufacturing of certain elements of a process to other firms. In Brazil, the German company Volkswagen has an auto plant integrated by four divisions. Each division, funded and managed by companies unrelated to Volkswagen, has the complete responsibility of producing one of four modules required to manufacture Golf and Audi automobiles.[1]

Global Marketing is a promotional tool used by multinational corporations to advertise the corporate image or to promote a product worldwide. This instrument can adopt at least two extreme variants: the global marketing plan can be planned totally at headquarters, or it can be designed on a peace meal basis, in a totally decentralized environment, by the different subsidiaries based on the guidance provided by headquarters. An example related to the first instance is the marketing program prepared for Vanilla Coke, which was conceived and planned in Atlanta. An illustration of the second variant is the case of Bacardi, the multinational from Puerto Rico, which operates with a decentralized marketing budget that let each subsidiary to plan and design its own marketing programs.

Global Manufacturing occurs when a multinational operates plant and equipment facilities in foreign countries to manufacture products for distribution and sales in local and foreign markets. For example, BMW, the German car producer has auto plants in South Carolina, in the United States, producing automobiles for U.S. and European markets.

Organizing the development of a global product happens when an entity of a multinational corporation engages in the process of creating new products for the world market. This activity is normally the responsibility of headquarters, which approves the design, overseas the test, and endorses the introduction of a new product.

To carry on with the various tasks previously described, multinationals require vast amounts of funding, and the support of an efficient and well organized market to provide this financing.

The goal of this chapter is to describe and analyze the various financial instruments used to finance the globalization of a firm. The meet this objective, the chapter:

- Describes the factors shaping the globalization of industries and the process used by firms to globalize

- Analyzes the conditions helping or constraining the process of globalization and the rules applied by the firms to globalize

- Examines the channels used by firms to finance globalization programs

FACTORS SHAPING THE GLOBALIZATION OF INDUSTRIES

Globalization is characterized by the easier access on the part of multinationals to factors of production and markets and by the large degree of integration between parents and subsidiaries in the transfer of technology.

Regarding market access, the world has experienced since 1991 a process of liberalization that has eliminated duties and exchange controls on imports of goods and services. For example, between 1994 and 1997 duties in the emerging nations fell from 34% to 14%. Also, between 1970 and 2000 the number of countries lowering trade barriers increased from 35 to 137. Similarly, under the Uruguay Round the tariffs imposed by the advanced nations on imports of manufactured goods were reduced to less than 4%.

The process of globalization has also contributed to facilitate foreign direct investment (FDI). Over the last ten years there have been, at least, 570 modifications to foreign exchange regulations and more than 1,330 bilateral investment treaties involving 162 countries. The most hospitable environment of the 1980s and 1990s toward FDI contributed to accelerate the participation of multinational corporations in the generation of FDI. For example, during the 1980-97 period FDI increased at an average rate of 13% a year compared with rates of 7% both for world exports of goods and for world GDP.[2]

The factors identified as playing a role in the increase in multinational led-FDI are the business strategies of multinational formulated on market, resource/asset, and efficiency seeking FDI.

Figure 8.1
Variables Shaping Market-Seeking FDI

Policy Frame For FDI	Economic Variables
• Economic, social and political stability • Rules regarding entry and operations • Standard treatment of affiliates • Policies on functioning and structure of markets, specially policies ruling mergers and acquisitions	• Market size and per capita income • Market growth • Access to regional and global markets • Region or country specific consumer preferences • Structure of local or regional markets

Multinational corporations identify Market Seeking FDI opportunities using information on political, social and legal, macro, and microeconomic variables focusing on a region's demand conditions. See Figure 8.1.

Multinationals use these core variables to determine the degree of a region's hospitality toward FDI, and how much a hospitable environment can help a firm to create value through FDI. To attain these goals multinationals have to run, simultaneously, normative and positive testing of FDI on regions targeted for investment. The first test is normally based on the study of the socio-political environment of the country, whereas the second check is determined by NPV associated to FDI.

Resource/asset seeking FDI is also determined by a core of socio-political and economic variables, except, that in this case, these variables are more directed to reflect the targeted region's abundance of natural resources, the availability of infrastructure to conduct international trade, and the trade and tax policies of the region. See Figure 8.2.

Efficiency seeking FDI is a relatively rare of FDI mostly conducted by multinational corporations of emerging countries seeking to have access to the latest in technology, more efficient sources of corporate funding, and lower cost of asset and resources, to implement leap frog strategies. See Figure 8.3.

In this case, testing of FDI is based on how much the acquisition of foreign assets will contribute to the NPV of cash flows related to the enhancement of the technological, managerial, or financial performance of the corporation.

Figure 8.2
Variables Shaping Resource/Asset-Seeking FDI

Policy Frame For FDI   Economic Variables

• International agreements on FDI • Privatization programs and policies • Trade policy (tariff and non tariff trade barriers) • Tax policies • Labor laws	• Availability of raw materials • Cost of skilled and unskilled labor • Availability of physical infrastructure (ports, roads and telecommunications) • Existence of technological innovative and other created assets in local firms and clusters (brand names)

Figure 8.3
Variables Determining Efficiency-Seeking FDI

Policy Frame For FDI   Economic Variables

• Investment promotion policies including image-building and investment generating activities • Investment incentives • Cost related to dealing with corruption and administrative efficiency managing FDI • Social amenities, quality of life, and after-investment services	• Cost of assets and resources adjusted for productivity of labor • Cost of transportation and communication to, from, and within the host country • Host country's membership to a regional treaty that can be conducive to establishing regional corporate networks

Transfer of Technology

While the deregulation of international trade and foreign direct investment has greatly enhanced the process of globalization, the speed in the transmission of the mechanism of globalization has been, at a large extent, due to developments in the industries associated to digital business, such as the software and electronic industries.

The new technology in this area of industrial activity provided multinationals with cheaper computer costs, better software, and faster communications. For example, in the 1960-2000 period, the cost of a unit of computer power declined 99%. In the 1930-2000 period, average revenue per mile in air transport fell from $0.68 to $0.11. In a similar fashion, the cost of a three-minute telephone call between New York and London declined from $2.44 to $0.75.[3]

Another key contribution of the electronics and software industries was the development of the internet that it is being used by every multinational to cut the cost of managing supplier relationships, streamline logistics and inventories, plan production, and reach new and existing customers more effectively.[4]

The lower cost of communicating through the integration of various technologies has also helped the process of globalization by allowing multinationals to sell more physical goods in more markets, and to increase and improve the design, production, and sale of digital goods and services.

THE PROCESS OF GLOBALIZATION

The process of globalization can start with the assessment of the demand for a product in overseas markets. If the initial market research indicates that the product under consideration is competitive, the next step is to explore alternatives of how to operate in the foreign market.

The next step is to identify the most efficient entry strategy. Effectiveness in the digital economy is ruled by how much a new project can cut costs, improve the international coordination of a firm, and contribute to diversify the presence of a multinational in the world market. For any one of these aspects to play a role, they have to be quantified in dollar terms to determine which one of the proposed entry strategies contributes with the highest net present value. The NPV assessment has to consider social constraints in the target regions as well as organizational limitations. If any one of these aspects do not pose a serious threat to the implementation of an entry strategy, the last step is to implement and monitor the internationalization project. It is important to note, that that the fundamental rule in every globalization project is to accept and implement the internationalization of a product when the project has the potential to render a positive NPV. See Figure 8.4.

Researching and Selecting the Target Market

Searching the global market starts with the gathering and organizing of information. This process provides multinationals with a picture of the political, economic, and cultural factors of a foreign market. This knowledge helps multinationals to confirm the existence of market opportunities and understand the characteristics of the new market. In addition, marketing research allows the firm to know what is important to customers and what is likely to influence their buying decisions. Research also reveals the dynamics of the target market, the trends that characterize it, and the forces driving those trends. Finally, research assists firms in determining now to operate in the market.[5]

Figure 8.4
The Process of Globalization

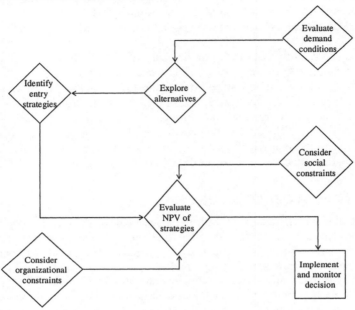

An effective research effort should not focus on a single market but rather o the comparison of various countries or regions of the world. This contrast should use information related to the type of marketing existing in each entity, the economic and political highlights of each nation or region, business information on all the target markets, the viability of finding a reliable local partner, and a detailed analysis of how to support a market entry strategy.

Entry Strategies

Based on the information provided by the market research on the target market, multinationals are able to rank the regions under scrutiny according to the most profitable way to enter and serve the market. The traditional means of market entry are grouped in five broad categories:

- Direct and indirect exporting
- Licensing and franchising
- Service contracts
- Partnering alliances
- Investing in a wholly owned subsidiary (WOS)

These entry strategies are ordered in terms of the amount of initial investment required in the implementation of each one of the market entry strategies. The least expensive entry strategy, measured in terms of initial investment is indirect exporting. In contrast the most expensive is building or acquiring a WOS. Multinationals choose from a number of international projects belonging to the same risk category, the entry strategy showing the highest NPV. To find this information, the multinationals consider:

- The amount of initial investment
- The financial capacity of the firm to meet the funding requirements of the chosen strategy
- Prices, operating and international transportation cost in the home and target markets
- Tariff and nontariff trade barriers in the target market
- The time to maturity of the project
- Business etiquette in the target market and in the industry sector to which the target market belongs

To relate market entry to initial investment, the firm has to pay attention to the size of the target market and its anticipated growth, the level of per capita income in the region measured in terms of its international purchasing power.

To estimate the market size multinationals use the number of units sold of a product in a specific market. For example, the auto industry uses the annual change in vehicle registration as a measure of market size. To measure market growth they the percentage change in the number of vehicles registered.

The level of income of a region or a country is measured by gross domestic product in terms of purchasing power parity (GDP PPP). It is the international purchasing power of the amount of goods and services produced by a country over a period, such as a quarter or a year. To illustrate the application of this concept, consider the case of Luxemburg. In the year 2000, the GDP PPP of this tiny, but rich European nation was estimated at $14.7 billion. This means that the goods and services produced by Luxemburg in the year 2000 could purchase the equivalent to $14.7 billions of goods and services in the United States.[6]

To estimate income growth, multinationals use GDP PPP growth. This is the percentage change of GDP PPP over a given period. For example, in Luxemburg, it is known that GDP PPP increased by 4.2% in the year 2000. This means that the goods and services produced by Luxemburg in the year 2000 could purchase 4.2% more goods and services in the United States in 2000 that they could in the previous year.

To provide a guide of how multinationals apply market size, market growth, and income growth to determine a best entry strategy and the initial investment required to implement this strategy, consider the case of General Motors (GM) in 1999. Prior to 1999 this company, which used to focus its strategy on serving the U.S. market, suffered from low profitability compared with other U.S. and foreign competitors. To find a remedy for this situation GM decided to internationalize. To find new markets, the company developed a model labeled the GM World Model. See Figure 8.5.[7]

Under the direction of GM Trade Director, Dr. Frances Hammond, GM gathered information on 60 countries and organized in four quadrants. Quadrant I, included countries with a market size and market growth rates higher than average such as China and Mexico. Quadrant II featured countries with larger than average size markets which were growing at rates lower than average such as the United States and Germany. Quadrangle III shows countries smaller than average markets growing at rates higher than average such as Egypt and Colombia. Finally, Quadrant IV shows countries with market size and market growth rates below average, such as Switzerland and Belgium.

The most promising markets are the countries included in Quadrant I. In contrast, by comparison, the least promising targets are the countries such as Switzerland and Belgium, located in Quadrant IV.

In addition to providing a way to prioritize target markets, the GM model also permitted the company to identify suitable entry strategies. For example, the results indicate that the most appropriate entry strategy for target market located in Quadrants I and II is some form of FDI. With respect to Quadrant III the best entry strategy is to export vehicles to those countries since the markets of this quadrant appear to be too small to provide appropriate economies of scale to render a positive NPV on FDI. In other words, the model indicates that *FDI is a viable strategy to internationalize the operations of a multinational if the markets are large, regardless of their rate of growth. In contrast, exporting is best, only when the markets are small and fast growing.*

The initial assessment is complemented with information on income per capita and income per capita growth. For example, China is a country with a very low income but is growing at a very fast pace. In contrast Mexico has a higher income and is growing fast. Considering this information, both China and Mexico are promising markets, however, in the foreseeable horizon, Mexico, in principle, should be considered best because is showing a high and fast-growing level of income per capita. However, a multinational's ultimate decision, of which country to choose will rest on the contribution of each project to value creation.

In general, *countries with high and fast-growing levels of income per capita are promising markets whereas countries having low and slow-growing levels of income per capita are not.*

Other variables contributing to estimate the quantity demanded of a product in foreign markets, and he NPV of an entry strategy related are listed in Figure 8.6.

Figure 8.5
GM World Vehicle Model, 1991-2002

Annual % change in vehicle registration

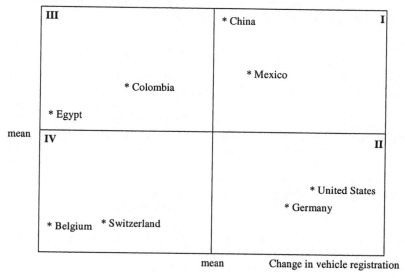

Figure 8.6
Other Variables Helping to Estimate Foreign Demand

Product's Price

Anticipations about the exchange rate

Tariff and non tariff trade barriers

Prices of substitutes and complement

Advertising expenditures

Competitor's advertising expenditure

Population size

Population trends

Consumers taste and preferences

Rules Applied to Globalize

There are not established rules of how to internationalize the activities of a firm. Globalization does not have to being with an export entry strategy and end with an investment in a WOS. In many instances, he process starts with FDI and after some adjustments may conclude with exports. For example, in the 1960a, Chrysler initiated operations in Spain with an assembly plant in Villaverde, near

Madrid. In the 1970s, due to the poor performance of the Spanish subsidiary and the overall financial conditions of the parent company, Chrysler shut down the Villaverde plant and left the Spanish market. In the late 1980s, the company returned to Spain. This time Chrysler chose to export from the United States to Spain as the preferred entry strategy.

THE THEORY AND PRACTICE OF INTERNATIONAL TRADE

In principle, as a rule of thumb, exporting is a financially viable entry strategy when the price differential between local and foreign markets is higher than the transportation cost required to ship products from home to the target market and when the exporting firms have excess capacity at home to supply a foreign market. Exporting is based on the principle of comparative and competitive advantages. The first advantage allows companies to manufacture final standardized good with the highest quality at the lowest possible cost. Comparative advantages can be structural or responsive.

Structural advantages are built into the nature of a business activity. For example, the geographic location of South Carolina and the abundance of a well-trained labor force existing in the state provide multinationals with manufacturing facilities in the region the ability to manufacture high quality output at relatively low labor cost.

Responsive advantages refer to the comparative advantage built by a multinational over time as a result of the sequence of appropriate managerial decisions. It is known that South Carolina, in an effort to attract FDI offered the German company BMW an excellent tax incentive package directed to promote training and the promise to build appropriate infrastructure to improve the state's international transportation system. The negotiations conducted by the German managers to obtain these concessions created comparative advantages that helped BMW and other companies operating in the State to lower the cost and improve the quality of producing cars in South Carolina. To illustrate how comparative advantages work considers the bilateral trade between the United States and Germany in automobile gasoline pumps and computer chips presented in Table 8.1.

The cost of producing gasoline pumps in Germany is €170. However, at the exchange rate of €1.2/$1 the dollar price of a German gasoline pump is only $141.7 compared to $144 in the United States. Regarding memory chips, the dollar price of this item produced in Germany is $113.3 but in the United States is $360. This information indicates that Germany has *absolute advantage* in the production of both gasoline pumps and computer memory chips because these items can be produced in this country at a lower dollar cost than in the United States. However, in relative terms, Germany is relatively better at producing chips because Germany can produce gas pumps only at 98% ($141.7/$144) of the cost of producing them in the United States, while in memory chips the German cost is only 31% against the cost of producing chips in the United States ($113.3/$160). Considering the cost information in relative terms, it can be concluded that Germany has *comparative advantages* producing chips and the United States producing gasoline pumps. If each country specializes and trades along comparative advantages, both countries are anticipated to be better off.

To show this point, consider that initially, each country is producing 1 gasoline pump and 1 memory chip. If the two countries specialize and trade, the United States has to shut down the memory chip plants. This closure will liberate resources that will allow the United States to produce 6.25 additional gasoline pumps with the resources liberated by the closure of the chip plant because in the United States the relative cost of 2.5 gasoline pumps is only 0.4 chips (2.5/0.4 = 6.25):

0.4 chips = 2.5 pumps
0.4 chips = 2.5 pumps
<u>0.2 chips = 1.25 pumps</u>
1.0 chips = 6.25 pumps

Similarly to the United States, if Germany specializes in the production and trading of memory chips, it will have also to shut down the plants producing gasoline pumps. This action will liberate resources in Germany to produce approximately 1.5 additional computer memory chips (more exactly, 1.25/0.8 = 1.56).

Once the countries specialize, the next issue to resolve is the term of trading gasoline pumps per chips. If the United offers to trade 3.25 gasoline pumps per one German chip, trade will take place because at this rate, the United States and Germany will benefit from their international trade.

Table 8.1
International Trade and Comparative Advantages

	Absolute cost in the United States	Absolute cost in Germany
Gasoline pumps	$144	€170 = $141.7
Memory chips	$360	€136 = $ 113.3
Exchange rate		€1.2 = $1
	Relative cost United States	Relative cost Germany
Gasoline pumps	$144/$360 = 0.4 chips	€170/€136 = 1.25 chips
Memory chips	$360/$144 = 2.5 pumps	€136/€170 = 0.8 pumps
	Gains from trade United States	Gains from trade Germany
Initial production	1.0 gas pump + 1.0 chips	1.0 gas pump + 1.0 chips
After specialization:		
Gasoline pumps produced	(1.0 + 6.25 = 7.25) gas pumps	0
Memory chips produced	0	(1.0 + 1.5 = 2.5) chips
Exports	3.25 gas pumps	1.0 chips
Imports	1.0 chips	3.25 gas pumps
Goods available in local market after trade	3.0 gas pump + 1.0 chips	3.25 gas pumps + 1.5 chips

If the United States does not specialize and trade, it will have only 1 gasoline pump and 1 chip. However, if it agrees to trade at the rate of 3.25 gasoline pumps per 1 chip, at the end of the end of this transaction, the United States will have available for local trading and consumption 3 gasoline pumps (6.25 gasoline pumps produced – 3.25 gasoline pumps traded) and 1 chip (obtained in exchange for the 3.25 gasoline pumps exported to Germany).

Comparing the pre and post international trade situations it is obvious that specializing and trading along comparative advantages has benefited the United States. Germany is also better off with this arrangement because in the post trade situation has more goods available for local trading and consumption (3.25 gasoline pumps + 1 memory chip) that it would have had if it had not specialized.

The reality of international trade is a lot more complex than the highly simplified model used previously to explain comparative advantages. Nonetheless, real world complications do not detract the importance of the concept of comparative advantages or its predictive power. However, there is detrimental aspect of specializing along comparative advantages. Michael Porter has argued that policies relying on comparative advantages hamper a country's growth and development.[8] This author further contends that a country's progress will accelerate if a nation moves from comparative to competitive advantages. It is important to underline, that under the notion of competitive advantages corporations, and not nations, are the focus of international trade and competition.

Competitive Advantages

In Porter's view four major forces define the notion of competitive advantages. These factors are firm structure and rivalry, demand and factor conditions, and the role played by related and supporting industries. See Figure 8.7. The interplay of these forces shapes the firm's strategy that has to be firmly grounded on adding value. If this is not the case, the strategy should not be implemented.

Firm structure and rivalry refers to the conditions governing the creation, organization and management of a multinational corporation. It encompasses management ideology, company goals, and employee motivations. It also includes local market rivalry that sometimes can be an excellent substitute for international rivalry when the firms are not exposed to the intense pressure of competing in the global market.

Demand conditions refer to the nature of demand for the industry's products or services. However, unlike other notions of demand conditions, the one specified by Porter in his model is related to twisted demand conditions in the home country, often created by the lack of comparative advantages that help local firms to develop know-how, technologies, and products that are unique in the world market. These unique skills, in turn, provide local firms with an incentive to innovate and create a competitive edge whose sustainability will depend on the ability of other world competitors to match it. An example of a local twisted demand forcing innovation is the case of Japan. In this country the scarcity of land forced the Japanese government, households, and business to build narrow streets, and small homes and offices. Narrows streets and small buildings in turn, created the need for small cars and tiny electronic devices in Japan. The need to satisfy this demand encouraged local companies to design products appropriate to narrow streets and small homes and offices. The implementation of the innovation led to the creation of new technologies and human skills that became later, the source of competitive advantage for Japanese companies in the global market.

Competitive advantages let firms to create a virtuous circle that starts with product differentiation and premium prices. Manufacturing with large economies of scale combined with premium prices guarantee in the short run high profit margins that allow companies to invest in expensive marketing programs that can permit them to corporations gain first, and sustain later, some market share. If the implementation of the virtuous circle is successful, it will attract competition that eventually will derail the competitive advantages of a successful firm. To renew the sustainability of the competitive edge multinationals have to sustain costly research programs to find new rounds of differentiated products to restart the virtuous circle.

Factor conditions refer to the resources or factor endowment faced by the firm in the local market. These factors include the availability of trained workforce, their skills and cost, and how they are deployed.

Related and supporting industries refer to the technological and cost edge provided by local suppliers to local corporations that help them to gain and sustain a competitive advantage. For example, in the United States the software industry provides an abundance of high quality software that helps the U.S. banking industry to be more cost effective and to offer new and more sophisticated banking services and products. By the same token, local banking provides the U.S. software industry with a very large demand and the opportunity to design software on large scale. This sequencing of firms firm's interconnections and activities is known as value chain.

Value chains are built on the notion that the firms of closely related industries are organized as a geographically proximate group of interconnected companies and associated institutions in a particular field, linked by commonalities and complementarities.[9] The value chain also depicts the firm as a collection of value-creating activities such as export and import logistics, software's production operations, trade financing, marketing and exporting, and services. See Figure 8.8.

Government and chance are two external influences that in the view of Porter stochastically sway the competitiveness of firms. Porter does not consider the role of the government vital in the process of creating and sustaining competitive advantages. He reduces the role of this entity to providing the ground to enhance security, education, and manpower skills.

Figure 8.7
Model of Competitive Advantages

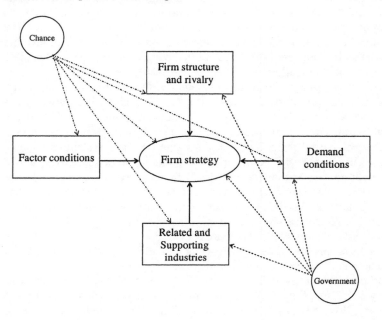

Figure 8.8
E-Commerce Value Chain

Firm structure: E-commerce directed to local and international trade				
Human resources: Software developers for international trade & finance				
Procurement: sourcing final goods from local and foreign suppliers				
Procurement: sourcing final goods from local and foreign suppliers				
Import and export logistics	Software's production operation	Trade financing	Marketing And exporting	Software and financing services

TRADE FINANCE

Imagine that an e-commerce company with a great product which has a well-designed export strategy and is ready to ship its output to world markets receives a very large order needed within a very short period. At first company executives are elated. However, they quickly realize that they need more production capacity and financing to fill the order. Similarly they realize they also become conscious that the buyer is requesting a relatively long 180-day payment plan. This request brings to the forefront the issues of funding and risk. Where will the financing come from? What if the buyer defaults or goes out of business before paying?

For a new or small e-commerce firm engaged in international trade, the financing of exports is very important. This aspect can be the difference between success or failure. To avoid failing, exporting firms need to have a well defined financial program, which includes a detailed cash budget plan to cover the anticipated export activities within forthcoming three years of activity.

The financial plan should also include a long-term capital budget program detailing investment expenditures and anticipated future export cash flows. The cash budget helps the exporter to estimate the timing and amount of cash expenditures and provides an overview of the funding required to completing different export projects. It will also provide an indication of the time required for the business to generate positive cash flows.

If cash flow analysis is very important in a domestic business transaction, it is even more crucial in an international trade transaction because in this setting the payment of account receivables take longer to settle. Therefore, to avoid lacking liquidity to meet international payments, exporting companies need to ensure an abundance of cash flow or the availability of reliable lines of credit. Cash flow planning helps exporting companies to avoid short-term cash shortages due to the following problems:

- Unexpected changes in the exchange rate
- Delay in the transmission of an international payment
- Inability to collect payments due to unexpected political events
- Slow collection of international payments due to bureaucratic red tape prompted by exchange controls

Collection of international payments can be executed in at least four ways: cash in advance, LC, documentary credit and collection and open accounts.

Cash in advance is the most secured option to receive export proceeds since it eliminates all risk of nonpayment and enhances the working capital of the exporting firm. Unfortunately, it is an option that very few importers are willing to incur, because it places all the risk of the transaction on them.

A *Letter of credit* (LC) is the most popular form of collecting international payments because they provide some measure of financial security to both exporters and importers. This instrument relies on services normally provided by commercial banks, which receive and confirm shipping documents and guarantee payments once the conditions of an international trade transaction are met. Both importer and exporters should carefully review LC specifications, especially small fine printing stipulations that may include conditions shifting the cost of financing a transaction from the exporter to the importer or the other way around.

A LC contains a payment undertaking given by a bank (issuing bank) on behalf of a buyer (importer) to pay a seller (the exporter) a given amount of money on presentation of specified documents representing the supply of goods (exports) within specific time limits. These documents have to presented, to allow for collection, at a specified place and have to meet the terms and conditions set out in the LC.[10]

The first action to start processing a LC is for the exporter and importer to agree on the terms of the LC, including means of transportation, period of the credit offered, latest date of shipment, and Incoterm to be used.

In a subsequent activity the importer applies, with a commercial bank (issuing bank), for a LC. The bank evaluates the importer's credit standing and issues the LC if the credit rating is suitable.

The issuing bank sends notice of LC approval to the advising bank. This bank confirms the authenticity of the LC and informs the exporter. At this point the exporter should carefully review the LC to insure that it meets the conditions of the initial agreement and that all its terms can be satisfied. If this is the case the exporter ships the goods and organizes all the documents according to the specifications of the LC.

The LC documentation is presented to the advising bank, which reviews it. If the documents comply with all the specifications the advising bank pays the exporter and forwards the documents to the issuing bank. If the documents are correct, the issuing bank reimburses the seller immediately. The issuing bank debits the reimbursement in the importer's bank account and releases the documents that will allow the importer to claim the goods from the carrier.

LC can be categorized as revolving, transferable, and confirmed.

A *revolving LC* is designed to satisfy exporters and importers when they trade regularly and for sustained periods. This instrument allows the payment of a sequence of transactions with only one LC. For example this letter could mandate the payment of exports executed every other month during a year period to the same exporting company. To introduce reliability for both parties a revolving LC usually states a maximum amount of payment on each delivery.

A *Transferable LC* allows the payment to be directed, partially or totally, to a commercial bank granting a start up loan to the exporter. This LC allows the financial institution funding the start up transaction to recover the interest plus the principal when all the conditions of the international trade transaction are met. This type of LC is well suited to the needs of small trading companies lacking the cash required to finance a large export shipment.

A *confirmed LC* refers to financial documents guaranteeing that the Advising bank will make a payment to the exporter meeting all the conditions stated in the LC. These letters are designed to protect an exporter against the risk of failing to recover revenues from an export transaction meeting all the importer's demands. An even more beneficial LC to the interest of an exporter is one that is confirmed and irrevocable.

Documentary credits are financial documents entitling the exporter to receive payment on an export transaction and are also known as drafts. They are issued by commercial banks and can adopt two forms: sight and term drafts. A sight draft allows the exporter to collect a payment upon the presentation of the document to the issuing bank. A term draft let the importer to settle the transaction over a pre-specified period of 30, 60, or 90 days. Other longer terms are also available.

In a *collection,* the exporter ships goods and forwards the shipment documents to a collection bank or agency, which secures the payment of the shipment to the exporter in exchange for the documents. In a collection arrangement, the exporter is exposed to the risk associated with the transaction because the financial institutions in charge of collecting for the exporter do not commit to paying in advance upon presentation of the shipment documentation. The conditions implicit in a collection compel the exporter to financing the shipment until the importer receives the goods if the collection (sight draft). In other circumstances, the exporter is paid later at a pre specified date if the collection is stated in terms of a term draft.

Open accounts is a financial arrangement between two trading parties where the exporter is required to ship the goods and transfer the title of the shipment to the importer in anticipation of payment for the consignment. In this case, the exporter is fully exposed to the credit risk involved in the transaction. This risk is aggravated if the payments specified in the document are postponed.

SUMMARY

This chapter reviewed and analyzed the instruments used by multinational corporations to globalize and to finance the internationalization of their business activities.

The process of globalization starts with an evaluation of the demand conditions existing in various target markets that may involve a single country or a region. If the market research indicates that a business opportunity exists in one or several of the target markets, the next step is to identify and rank entry strategies according to NPV. To determine and rank the NPV of each entry strategy multinationals gather information on key variables such as market size, growth potential, an others. They use this information to determine the entry strategy, the initial investment required to implement the strategy, the cash flows, and the NPV of each alternative.

Entry strategies are grouped into five broad categories: direct and indirect exporting, licensing and franchising, servicing contracts, partnering alliances, and investing in WOS.

Case: Wendy's in Saudi Arabia

Brion G. Grube, Senior Vice President of Wendy's International while waiting for the flight that will take him from New York to Riyadh, the Capital of Saudi Arabia, began to ponder the prospects of a further expansion in this country, and the Middle East in general, after the tragic events of September 11, 2001 in the United States, and the unexpected passing away of founder Dave Thomas on January 8, 2002.

Prior to these events, Wendy's was looking forward to a more aggressive expansion program in the Middle East. However, under the new political landscape of the region, the Board had asked him to present a new long-term business plan, stating the full market potential for Saudi Arabia under the new political scenario, and the best way to implement the expansion program. Wendy's had already 13 restaurants operating in the Gulf country.

THE MARKET POTENTIAL OF SAUDI ARABIA

To estimate the extent of Wendy's expansion in Saudi Arabia, Mr. Grube and his research team consider the population of the largest cities in Saudi Arabia because in overseas markets Wendy's restaurants are profitable only in large urban centers having relatively high levels of income.[11] The factors required to have an initial estimate of a region's potential are summarized below:

- The ratio of population of largest cities in Saudi Arabia to the number of customers needed to support an average Wendy's restaurant in the United States (TPC_{saudi}/CNR_{us})

- The ratio of hamburger consumption per capita in Saudi Arabia to hamburger consumption per capita in the United States ($HCPC_{saudi}/HCPC_{us}$)

- The ratio of income per capita in Saudi Arabia to the income per capita in the United States (IPC_{saudi}/IPC_{us})

- Te ratio of the proportion of income spent on hamburgers in Saudi Arabia to the proportion of income spent on hamburgers in the United States (PSH_{saudi}/PSH_{us})

All the ratios previously described are summarized in the following equation:

Market potential = $[(TPC_{saudi}/CNR_{us}) \times (HCPC_{saudi}/HCPC_{us}) \times (IPC_{saudi}/IPC_{us}) \times PSH_{saudi}/PSH_{us})]$

Capital Requirements

The expansion plan to be prepared by Gruber's team depends to a large extent on the number of outlets required to serve Saudi Arabia, as well as on the mix between company-owned restaurant and franchises. Another factor playing a role is the ratio of independent restaurants to mall-type stores.

The cost of a building and land for an independent unit is $2 million. The average of a mall-type store ranges from $500,000 to $1 million. Mall-type restaurants in Saudi Arabia are not unusual since half of the existing restaurants are located within malls in this country.

Restaurants are built according to company's specifications concerning exterior style and interior décor. The majority are free-standing, one-story brick buildings, substantially uniform in design and appearance, constructed on sites of approximately 40,000 square feet, with parking for approximately 45 cars.

Within each restaurant there is a preparation area, a dining room capacity for 90 customers, and double pick up windows for drive-through service.

Depreciation

Depreciation is straight line for buildings, kitchen equipment, and restaurant furniture. For the edifice, depreciation is estimated using an average life span of 40 years and for the kitchen equipment and furniture items depreciation is estimated considering that they last 7 years.

THE COMPANY

With no real intention to be a national chain, Wendy's began to operate in 1969 as a single unit in downtown Columbus, Ohio. A second unit quickly followed on the opposite side of the city. The next step in the development of the company was the opening of the first franchise in Indianapolis, Indiana, in 1972, which was followed by many more Wendy's restaurants within and outside the United States.

By the end of 1997, Wendy's had 4,993 outlets, from which 481 were located outside the United States and Canada. By January of the year 2000, the company had grown to 7,652 restaurants. Out of this total, 578 were located in markets outside the U.S. and Canada.[12]

Market Intensity and Brand Recognition

Wendy's market intensity in the US is estimated at 61,055 people per unit. Comparatively, McDonald's has one restaurant for every 22,000 persons. Another interesting comparison between the two companies is that McDonald's has the third most recognized brand name in the world, whereas Wendy's is barely known outside the US. Another intriguing aspect of the hamburger war is advertising. Wendy's has the second highest advertising awareness among the US fast food service restaurants in spite of the fact that McDonald's, which is in the number one position, outspends Wendy's by a proportion of five to one.

Financial Indicators

Wendy's total assets amounted in 1995 to 1.5 billion. The next year they increased 32%. However, after 1996, the path of growth has been unstable.

With respect to equity, there are 200 millions shares outstanding. The largest stockholders are executive officers holding 19.4% of Wendy's stock, followed by Canadian investor Ronald V. Joyce with 13.7% and, the company's founder, David Thomas, with 4.3%.

Regarding value creation, Wendy's performance has been rather lackluster. If an investor had purchased $100 of Wendy's shares in 1995, by the year 2000, the value of this investment would have grown to $131.16. That is, a rate of growth of 31% over a five year period, which is equivalent to a 6% growth per year. By contrast, if the same investor had placed $100 in stock of companies similar to Wendy's (Peer Group) the investor would have gained a return totaling between $54 to $66, which is almost twice as much as the return provided by Wendy's. To uphold the price of its shares given the previously discussed stock trends, Wendy's began in 1998 a share repurchase program. By the end of the year 2000, it had acquired 21.9 million shares at an average price of $22.42. These transactions amounted to $491 million. Part of this package was the stock purchase exercised in the year 2000, which amounted to 5.4 million shares at an average price of $17.22.[13]

The company manages its debt portfolio in response to changes in interest rates and foreign exchange rates by periodically retiring, redeeming, and repurchasing debt. These policies have helped the company to maintain a very strong balance sheet with a debt-to-equity ratio of 22% and a debt rating of BBB and Baa-1. Wendy's ratings have been the same since 1995. Wendy's financial position, however, is not as strong as the position held by McDonald's which has Moody's ratings at Aa2 and AA+. Wendy's most recent interest rates on debt averaged 6.08% in the year 2001. Previously, it had had experience rates of 7.1%.

Expansion Strategy

The McDonald's Company is on course to be turned into a global brand rivaling Coca Cola. By the year 2000, the company had hit two key benchmarks: first, the opening of a restaurant in February of 1999 in Tbilisi, Georgia. This event marked the 115th country to play host to the Golden Arches. The second major achievement was the inauguration in August 1999, of the company's 25,000th restaurant in Chicago. Since then McDonald's has added more outlets and countries. It is estimated that at the beginning of the 2000, McDonald's had 29,000 restaurants in 120 countries.

McDonald's success in world markets has been attributed to its tradition of adapting to the conditions of local demand. For instance, it serves a non-beef hamburger in India and Saudi Arabia, while offering a teriyaki burger in Japan, and falafel in Egypt. In Switzerland, it cancelled its breakfast service to avoid conflicting with "cultural nuances."[14] Another important aspect of McDonald's strategy in world markets is its program to develop local suppliers. For instance, in Brazil invested a significant amount of resources into helping farmers master the cultivation of potatoes.[15]

McDonald's however, has hit some walls. It has been targeted by environmentalists in Europe where it has been battered by the upsurge of mad-cow disease, and his growth has slowed down considerably in the United States.

Unlike McDonald's the promotional marketing abroad for Wendy's has been rather limited due to lack of economies of scale in advertising. The minimum scale required to launch a national advertising program is 25 stores per country. So far, in the global market only Canada (324), Japan (100), Indonesia (27), Philippines (49), Venezuela (47), and Puerto Rico (35) are meeting the Wendy's standard required to launch national advertising campaigns.[16] While McDonald's, expanded one store at a time, Wendy's preferred to unfold in blocks. In 1995, it entered into a strategic alliance with Tim Horton, a Canadian fast food retailer, which gave Wendy's access to more than 1,323 restaurants in the North American Country.[17] This number had grown to 1,980 restaurants at the end of the year 2000. Recently, however, the franchise industry reached maturity. To respond to this new market reality, Wendy's decided to grant new franchises both in the United States and foreign countries on unit-by-unit basis.[18]

Wendy's Franchising System

At the end of the year 2000, Wendy's operated 5,792 restaurants in 50 states, the District of Columbia and 26 other countries and territories. The Restaurant Franchise Document details the conditions that rule a franchise. Under the conditions of this document, the Company grants the franchisee the right to construct and own, or lease a restaurant upon a site it approves. After submitting an approved application and financial information, an individual becomes an accepted applicant upon the execution of a Preliminary Letter of Agreement. This document does not guarantee acceptance as a franchise owner. It only entitles the applicant to commence a training program intended to allow both parties the opportunity to assess the prospects for a long-term relationship.

Upon the execution of the Preliminary Letter of Agreement, which gives the applicant only the right to be considered, the prospective candidate for a Wendy's franchise is required to pay a nonrefundable fee of $5,000. If the application is accepted, the franchisee pays a technical assistance fee of $30,000. Once this is met, the franchisee can purchase the franchise at a price of $350,000. The acquisition of the franchise gives the franchisee the right to have a site to build a restaurant, or a building to be leased from Wendy's. In this case the franchiser is entitled to receive rent and royalties, which are, 12.5% and 4% of gross sales, respectively.

Most foreign operations fall into the first classification. That is, land and building are owned by the franchisee. Wendy's has the capabilities to locate and secure real estate for a new restaurant development. Wendy's obtain all licenses and permits necessary to construct and operate the restaurant with the franchisee having the option of building the restaurant or having Wendy's to construct it. In the second instance, the franchisee pays Wendy's a fee for its services and reimburses Wendy's for all out-of-pocket expenses Wendy's incurs in locating, securing, and /or constructing the new outlet. All the expenses associated to the real estate development of a new restaurant are estimated at $2 million.

In addition to paying all the fees and expenses previously discussed, the franchisee has to supply kitchen equipment and restaurant furniture, which cost $400,000. Every franchise is also required to spend 4% of its gross receipts in advertising and promotion. This can be increased at Wendy's request to 5%. Half of the advertising fee is allocated to local and regional advertising and the other half goes to Wendy's Advertising Program. The franchise agreement is for an initial term of 10 years or the term of the lease, whichever is shorter.

THE PROFILE OF SAUDI ARABIA

Saudi Arabia is located in the Middle East, bordering the Arabian Gulf and the Red Sea, north of Yemen. It has a territory of 1.96 million of square kilometers, which is equivalent to one fifth of the United States. It is integrated by 13 provinces: Bahah, Hudud Shamaliyah, Jawf, Madinah, Qasim, Riyad, Ash Sharqiyah, Asir, Hail, Jizan, Makkah, Najran, and Tabuk. The population of these provinces is heavily concentrated in few major cities, due to the harsh climate of Saudi Arabia, often characterized by dry desert featuring frequent sand and dust storms.[19]

The currency of the country is the Saudi riyal (SR) which has been pegged to the dollar since 1982, at a rate of SR3.75 per one US dollar.[20]

Saudi Arabia is an oil-based economy with strong government controls over major economic activities. It has the largest reserves of petroleum in the world—260 billion barrels of proven reserves which are equivalent to 26% of world's proven reserves—ranks as the largest exporter of petroleum, and plays a leading role in the Organization of Petroleum Exporting Countries (OPEC).[21] For example, Saudi Arabia was a key player in the successful efforts of OPEC and other oil producing countries to raise the price of oil in 1999-2000 to its highest level—$26.81 a barrel in 1999, compared with $17.45 in 1999—since the Gulf war by reducing production.[22]

The petroleum sector employs 1.5% of the Saudi Arabian labor force but accounts for roughly 75% of government revenues, 40% of gross domestic product (GDP), and 90% of export earnings. About 35% of GDP comes from the Saudi private sector.[23] Currency can be transferred in and out of Saudi Arabia with no restriction. Credit is widely available to both Saudi and foreign entities from the commercial banks and is allocated on market terms. The nominal cost of borrowing, for 5 years, is 7.5%. However effective interest rate is 13.3%, as a result of how banks charge interest. [24] There are no restrictions on converting or transferring funds associated with an investment—including remittances of investment capital, earnings, loan repayments, and lease payments—into a freely convertible currency and at a legal market clearing rate. There have been no recent changes, nor are there plans to change remittance policies.[25]

There are no delays in effect for remitting investment returns such as dividends, return of capital, interest and principal on private foreign debt, lease payments, royalties and management fees through normal legal channels. There is no need for a legal parallel market for investor remittances. There is no limitation on the inflow or outflow of funds for remittances of profits, debt service, capital, capital gains, returns on intellectual property, imported inputs, etc. There is, however, a tax—up to 45%—on corporate profits and capital gains on the income of a foreign partner in a joint venture.[26]

Gross Domestic Product and the Saudi Arabian Markets

The gross domestic product of Saudi Arabia amounted to $232 billion in the year 2001. On a per capita basis, it was equivalent to $10,200. This is an important index for the fast food industry, since it is well known that the consumption of beef and hamburgers consumption, up to a point, are positively correlated with income. For example, empirical estimates indicate that the income elasticity of beef and chicken hamburgers is 1.05 and 0.28 respectively. [27] It has been also estimated that the consumption of hamburgers per capita in Saudi Arabia is equal to 0.37 of the consumption per capita in the United States. This last variable, in turn, is equal to Wendy's average restaurant sales divided by market intensity.

The average price of a hamburger meal in Saudi Arabia is 12 Saudi riyals ($3.20). In the US, Germany, Japan, and Switzerland are $2.56, $2.69, $2.08, and $3.87 respectively.[28]

Population

The population of Saudi Arabia at the end of 1991 was estimated at 22.7 million. From this total, 5.3 million were foreign nationals, mostly guest workers. The Saudi population is 100% Muslim and grows, as previously indicated, at a rate of 3.5% per year.[29]

According to the Saudi Arabian Monetary Agency explains the high rate of population growth by the high rate of fertility which is equal to seven infants per mother.[30] According to SAMA, the other contributing factor to population growth is the improvement in living, and health conditions in the Kingdom, which have raised the life expectancy to 70 years for men and 74 years for women. Considering all these factors, SAMA forecast that the Saudi population in the Kingdom will rise to 30 million at the end of the year 2020.[31]

Currently, Saudi household average 9 members, and each person averages an income per capita of $10,200 per year.[32] Most of the Saudi population is urban and is located in the cities of Riyadh (the capital), Jeddah, Makkah, Madinah, and Dammam.[33]

The Labor Market in Saudi Arabia

In this overwhelming Muslin country, the number of people employed amounted to 7.2 million in 1999. From this total, the Saudi population accounted for 44.2% (3.2 million workers) and the non-Saudi 55.8% (4.0 million). Unemployment among Saudis was estimated, for the same year, roughly, at 25.1%.

This relatively high level of unemployment is usually explained by the cost disparity between local and foreign labor. The hourly wage rate for a Saudi national is estimated at $3.98 per hour. By contrast, foreign labor, while often unskilled, costs only $0.66 an hour. Another factor playing a factor in local unemployment is the unwillingness of young Saudis to accept menial or laborer's jobs.

The normal workload for white collar jobs is 8 to 9 hours per day. For unskilled workers it consists of two shifts. The first starts at 8:00 AM until 13:00, which is followed by a 3-hour break. The second shift starts at 4:00 PM and often runs until 8:00 PM. However, for restaurant and retailing business activities the night shift can be extended until 10:30 PM or later. In average, the workload for an employee in the restaurant industry is estimated, roughly, at 50 hours per week.[34]

Labor Regulations

Under the 1969 Labor and Workman regulations, 75% of a firm's work force and 51% of its payroll must be Saudi, unless an exemption has been obtained from the Ministry of Labor and Social Affairs.[35] The Saudi Government recently implemented a regulation requiring each company employing over 20 workers to include a minimum of 5% Saudi nationals. Companies not complying with the 5% rule—which will increase in annual increments of 5%—will not be given visas for expatriate workers. However, these laws have not had the expected impact on local labor employment since Saudis represent only about a third of the estimated 7 million workers in Saudi Arabia. Since few firms have been able to meet local labor requirements, then, foreign firms are under constant pressure to employ more nationals.

Recruitment of expatriate labor is regulated jointly by the Ministry of Interior and the Ministry of Labor and Social Affairs, which encourage the recruitment of Muslim workers, either from Muslim nations or from countries such as India and Sri Lanka with sizable Muslim populations. The largest groups of foreign workers now come from Pakistan, the Philippines, and India. Since September 1994, the Ministry of Labor and Social Affairs requires a certification that there are no qualified Saudis for a particular job before it can be filled by an expatriate worker. In addition, the Ministry of Interior must approve all transfers of expatriate workers from one firm to another. In spite of these limitations, firms wishing to import foreign labor can normally obtain bloc visas to hire workers recruited abroad. Saudi labor law forbids union activity, strikes, and collective bargaining.

However, there is no forced or compulsory labor; any required overtime, over and above the usual five and one-half to six-day week, is compensated normally at time-and-a-half rates. The minimum age for employment is 14. According to U.S. Embassy analysts, the Saudi Government does not adhere to the International Labor Organization Convention, which is a well-respected organization ruling on workers' rights.[36]

FOREIGN DIRECT INVESTMENT

The Saudi Government generally encourages foreign direct investment (FDI) particularly joint ventures with Saudi partners. Though Saudi Arabia technically allows wholly foreign-owned firms to operate, such corporate are rare. With the desire to stimulating greater foreign investment to strengthen the non-oil private sector, Saudi Arabia is revising its 30-year-old investment code and tax code.

However, some U.S. analysts working for multinational corporations in Saudi Arabia believe that there is a great deal of disincentives for FDI. Some deterrent mentioned include a high tax rate on a foreign partner's corporate profits, a policy of forced hiring of Saudis, the practical requirement for a foreign investor to have a Saudi partner, a very conservative cultural environment, and the extreme desert climate of the country. The Saudi government encourages foreign direct investment, particularly, joint ventures with Saudi partners.[37] The current foreign capital investment code specifies three conditions for foreign investments: The undertaking must be a "development project." The investment must generate technology transfer. A Saudi partner should own a minimum of 25% equity—although this last stipulation can be waived.

To initiate a new industrial project, the Saudi government normally requires 25% capitalization, although it may be higher for some industries. Additionally, 10% of profits must be set aside each year in a statutory reserve until it equals 50% of the venture's authorized capital.[38]

The Ministry of Industry and Electricity licenses FDI except for mineral concessions. For ventures with Government participation, the process of obtaining an FDI license is only a formality. To get a license for a purely private venture may require a considerable amount of time and effort. New joint venture must apply for a commercial registration number from the Ministry of Commerce.

The Foreign Capital Investment Committee of this ministry evaluates projects using a variety of factors. Foremost is the project's compatibility with Saudi Arabia's basic economic goals:

- Economic diversification

- Access to modern technology

- Development of a trained Saudi labor force to reduce dependence on foreign labor

In the view of U.S. Embassy analyst reporting on Saudi Arabia's investment climate, there is a hierarchy of privileges and preferences in Saudi Arabia that favors Saudi companies and joint ventures with Saudi participation.[39] For instance, they indicate that only firms with at least 25% Saudi ownership are eligible for tax holidays and interest-free loans from Government credit institutions such as the Saudi Industrial Development Fund.

They also report that only foreign-owned corporations and the foreign-owned portion of joint ventures are subject to the corporate income tax, which can range up to 45% of net profits. Only Saudi companies or citizens, or those from the other Gulf Cooperation Council (GCC) countries—Kuwait, Bahrain, Qatar, United Arab Emirates and Oman—may own land or engage in internal trading and distribution activities. Similarly, only joint ventures with at least 51% GCC ownership interest are permitted to export duty-free to other GCC countries. In the view of the U.S. analysts, the privileges granted to Saudi firms, taken together, represent a formidable array of preferences, which can severely disadvantage a foreign investor attempting to operate a wholly owned company in Saudi Arabia.

To get around this regulation, in the recent past, some Saudis, in violation of legal regulations, lent their names to foreign-owned and operated business. This scheme labeled "cover up" was curtailed by Royal Decree m/49 of May 21, 1989. Under this regulation Saudi nationals and foreigners engaging in "cover-up" are subject to severe penalties, including imprisonment, stiff fines, and deportation for the foreigner.[40]

Another aspect identified as detrimental to FDI in Saudi Arabia is the access to visas. According to U.S. analysts, one of the leading obstacles for foreign investors is a restrictive Saudi visa requirement.[41] Investors or potential investors wishing to visit Saudi Arabia must have a Saudi sponsor to obtain the necessary business visa.

On rare occasions the Saudi Embassy or Consulates grant, at their discretion, sponsor-less business visas to employees of prominent American firms. Business visas are valid for only one entry for up to two months. Recently, to overcome this problem, the Saudi Ministry of Foreign Affairs has pledged to provide business executives from recognized Multinational Corporations multiple-entry visa.

Protection of Property Rights

The Saudi legal system protects and facilitates acquisition and disposition of private property in accordance with Islamic laws governing private property. These laws, however, forbid non-Saudis from acquiring real estate in Saudi Arabia. Nonetheless, this regulation has never led to a case of expropriation or nationalization of foreign-owned assets in the Kingdom.[42] The term of protection is 15 years. The patent holder may apply for a 5-year extension. Saudi Arabia has a Copyright Law. However, this law does not extend protection to works that were first displayed outside of Saudi Arabia unless the author is a Saudi citizen.

Bribery

Saudi Arabia has laws aimed at limiting the abuse of foreign direct investors. For example, the Agency Law limits a Saudi agent's commission to 5% of the value of a contract. Ministers and other senior Government officials appointed by royal decree are forbidden from engaging in business activities with their Ministry or Government organization while being employed by the government.[43] In spite of existing anti-corruption laws, U.S. Embassy analysts advising American corporations wishing to invest in Saudi Arabia believe that bribery is an obstacle to FDI in Saudi Arabia. To support this contention, Embassy reports mention the request of "commission payments" as a form of disguised bribery.[44]

Dispute Settlement

Dispute settlements in Saudi Arabia are time-consuming and uncertain. Even after a decision is reached in a dispute, effective enforcement of the judgment can still take years.

In the view of multinational corporations, Saudi litigants have an advantage over foreign parties in almost any investment dispute, because of their first-hand knowledge of Saudi law and culture and the relatively amorphous dispute settlement processes. To overcome this disadvantage, foreign partners involved in a dispute find it advisable to hire local attorneys with knowledge of Saudi legal practices. The U.S. Embassy has reported cases where disputes between local and foreign investors have caused serious problems to foreign investors. They point to instances where Saudi partners have blocked foreigners' access to exit visas, forcing them to remain in Saudi Arabia against their will.

The Saudi Arabian legal system is derived from the legal rules of Islam, known as the Shari'a. The Ministry of Justice oversees the Shari'a-based judicial system, but most ministries interpret the rules on matters under their jurisdiction. Of principal interest to investors who have disputes with private individuals are the Committees for Labor Disputes—under the Ministry of Labor—and the Committee for Tax Matters—under the Negotiable Instruments Committee, also called the Commercial Paper Committee.[45] The Ministry of Finance has jurisdiction over disputes involving letters of credit and checks, while the Banking Disputes Committee of the Saudi Arabian Monetary Agency (SAMA) adjudicates disputes between bankers and their clients. Judgments of a foreign court are not yet accepted and enforced by the local courts. Monetary judgments are based on the terms of the contract; i.e., if the contract is in dollars, the judgment would be in dollars; if unspecified, the judgment is denominated in Saudi riyals.

OPIC and Other Investment Insurance Programs

The Overseas Private Investment Corporation (OPIC) is a U.S. institution created to provide insurance protection to U.S. investors. This organization has ceased to provide U.S. exporters with insurance protection on cargos to Saudi Arabia. In 1995, OPIC removed Saudi Arabia from its list of countries approved for OPIC coverage due to the failure of Saudi Arabia to take steps to comply with internationally recognized labor standards.[46]

THE FRANCHISING INDUSTRY IN SAUDI ARABIA

Prior to 1990, the franchising industry did not exist in Saudi Arabia. However, it took off with the globalization of industries during the last decade of the 20th Century. Local factors, however, also contributed at a very large extent to the tremendous expansion of this industry in the Gulf country. Among them, the existing high concentration of income, the high local rates of private savings prompted by government subsidies on housing and food, the fascination of the Saudi consumer with American fashions, and the bond and composition of Saudi households.

All these factors contributed to a phenomenal growth of the franchising industry in Saudi Arabia, which grew from ground bottom in 1990 to $214 million sales by the end of 1997 and $249 million in 1999. Food franchise industry, with McDonald's leading the pack, represented 40% of total sales.

However, the success enjoyed by the industry, was also the cause of its decline. As more and more companies entered into the franchise market, several unpleasant trends began to unfold. To begin with, quality of the products sold by the franchises faded. The franchise products did not seem to match the quality featured by the items sold by the parent company in the home market. Naturally, dwindling quality led to a decline in sales and profit margins.

A study conducted on the franchise industry in 1997, concluded that the industry was facing lack of quality (38%), limited financial resources and know-how (26%), poor labor training (20%), and a small demand for franchise products (16%).[47]

Another factor affecting the performance of the industry is international politics. U.S. based corporation doing business in the Middle East, have tried very hard to present themselves as neutral in regional conflicts. However, this has been easier said than done since local groups with diverse background and nationalities, at times, have issued calls to boycott American products.

Case Table 8.1
Wendy's Stock Performance

Year	2000	1999	1998	1997	1996	1995
Wendy's	$131.6	$102.40	$106.31	$115.96	$ 97.7	$100.00
Peer group	$165.9	$172.33	$177.61	$115.49	$103.93	$100.00

Case Table 8.2
Wendy's U.S. Net Sales per Restaurant

Year	2000	1999	1998	1997	1996	1995
Company (000)	1,314	1,284	1,174	1,111	1,049	1,014
Growth	0.02	0.09	0.06	0.06	0.03	
Franchise (000)	1,130	1,102	1,031	1,017	978	974
Growth	0.03	0.07	0.01	0.04	0.00	

Source: Wendy's International, Annual Report, 2001.

Case Table 8.3
Wendy's Cost of Sales and Distribution (% of sales)

ITEM	2000	1996	1995
Cost of sales	63.0	60.1	58.7
Distribution of cost of sales			
Food cost	29.0	30.0	29.1
Labor cost	30.0	26.0	25.6
Other	4.0	4.1	4.0
Total	63.0	60.1	58.7

Source: Wendy's International, Corporate Profile, March 2002, p. 20.

Case Table 8.4
Operating Profit Margin (% of sales)

ITEM	2000	1995
Retail Sales	100.0	100.0
From which:		
Cost of sales	63.0%	58.7
Operating cost	26.6%	26.2
Operating Margin	10.4%	15.1
Income tax	38.8%	33.3

Source: Wendy's International, Corporate Profile, March 2002, p. 22.

Case Table 8.5
Wendy's Debt to Equity Ratio

Year	2000	1999	1998	1997	1996	1995
Long term debt	248	249	246	250	242	337
Equity	1,126	1,065	1,068	1,184	1,057	8,19
Debt/equity ratio	0.22	0.23	0.23	0.21	0.23	0.41

Source: Wendy's International, Corporate Profile, March, 2002, p. 22.

Case Table 8.6
United States and Saudi Arabia, Statistics

Key Statistics (2001)	US	Saudi Arabia
Area (square kilometers)	9,372,610.00	1,960,582.00
Population (million, 2000)	266.40	22.70
Population growth (%)	0.91	3.50
Labor force (million)	132.20	7.00
GDP ($, billion)	7,240.00	232.00
GDP growth (%)	2.10	4.00
GDP per capita ($)	27,500.00	10,200.00
Inflation (%)	2.50	0.50
Unemployment rate (%)	3.60	25.90
Hourly wages ($)	13.22	3.98

Source: Central Intelligence Agency, *The World Fact Book*, 1998, and 2000, http://www.odci.gov/cia/publications/factbook/index.html. (Accessed March 5, 2002).

Case Table 8.7
Population, Major Cities of Saudi Arabia, 2001

Rank	City	Population (000)	Region	Proportion
1	Riyadh	3,627	Riyadh	0.16
2	Jeddah	2,674	Makkah	0.12
3	Makkah	1,154	Makkah	0.05
4	Madinah	818	Madinah	0.04
5	Dammam	675	Sharquiyah	0.03
6	At-Taif	634	Makkah	0.03
7	Tabuk	382	Tabuk	0.02
8	Buraydah	325	Qasim	0.01
9	Mubarraz	286	Sharquiyah	0.01
10	Hufuf	286	Sharquiyah	0.01
	Saudi Arabia	22,700		1.00

Source: http://www.gazetteer.de/fr/fr_sa.htm. (Accessed February 1, 2002).

Case Table 8.8
Wendy's Consolidated Income Statement

$ (million)	2000	1996	1995
Retail sales	1,807.00	1,170.0	1092.00
Franchise revenues	429.00	238.0	194.00
Total revenues	2,236.00	1,408.0	1,286.00
Cost of sales	1,140.00	729.0	662.00
Operating cost	382.00	284.0	260.00
Other cost	86.00	39.0	42.00
General and Administrative	208.00	96.7	96.10
Amortization of property	108.00	66.1	59.30
Special charges	18.00	0.0	27.00
Interest net	15.00	5.1	8.10
Total cost	1,957.00	1,220.0	1,155.00
Income before taxes	279.00	188.0	132.00
Income taxes	102.00	72.4	40.12
Net income	177.00	116.0	91.00
Earnings per share	1.48	0.9	0.76

Source: Wendy's International, Corporate Profile, Annual Report, 2001.

Case Table 8.9
Wendy's Restaurants in the World Market

Country	1996 Company	1996 Franchise	2000 Company	2000 Franchise	Change
Argentina	11		0		−11
Canada	105	98	114	210	
El Salvador		5		7	2
Greece		8		9	1
Guatemala		3		7	4
Honduras		5		16	11
Hong Kong		7		0	−7
Indonesia		18		27	11
Japan		54		100	46
Mexico		8		9	1
Philippines		31		35	4
Puerto Rico		19		35	16
Saudi Arabia		14		13	−1
South Korea		6		0	−6
Switzerland		3		0	−3
Taiwan		12		0	−12
Britain	6	1		3	−4
Total	122	292	114	471	52

Source: Securities and Exchange Commission, Form 10-K, 1997 and 2000, http://www.wendys-invest.com/library/annual/00/wen00ann.pdf. (Accessed March 4, 2002).

Case Table 8.10
Wendy's Total Restaurants, 1994-2000

	2000	1996	1995	1994
Open at the end of the year	5,792	4,993	4,667	4,411

CASE PROBLEMS

Please help Mr. Grube to prepare a report to the Board indicating whether Wendy's should contract, expand, or remain as it is. The key consideration shaping the recommendation is value creation. The Board will be willing to approve an expansion, if there is value creation in this strategy.

To quantify value creation, you have to estimate first, the number of additional restaurants that the economy of Saudi Arabia can support. To do so, you have to use the formula included in the case.

Once you have estimated the number of new restaurants, you need to determine how to distribute the restaurants in the major cities of Saudi Arabia. For instance, you have to indicate how many restaurants for Riyadh, the capital of this country.

In a second stage, you have to justify the expansion with an analysis of value creation. That is, you have to estimate the net present value of adding new restaurants in Saudi Arabia. To perform this task, you need, to find out the Saudi riyal (SR) value of the cash flow from the perspective of Wendy's. To estimate the cash flow it is necessary to find out the profit per restaurant plus depreciation.

The estimation of profits is very straightforward. It is equal to gross sales less operating expenses, less depreciation, minus taxes. You should ignore interest expenses and treat the project as if there were no interest payments.

It is also necessary to determine the life of the project or time to maturity. To do so, you can use as parameter the life expectancy of the building or the kitchen equipment.

Additionally, it is necessary to estimate discount rate. If the project is funded with Saudi funds, you need to use a local interest rate. If Wendy's finances the project, you need to calculate the company's discount rate. You can find information in the case to estimate Wendy's discount rate applying the concept of WACC.

In your analysis of value creation, you have to consider the social, political, and cultural constraints imposed by the country on the expansion project, as well as the organizational constraints.

NOTES

1. Lli, Carlos, "Ford Strategy for the New Millenium," mimeo prepared under the Direction of Dr. Francisco Carrada-Bravo, Thunderbird, The American Graduate School of International Management, Glendale, Arizona, May 1999, p. 20.

2. Mallampally, P., and Sauvant, K. "Foreign Direct Investment in Developing Countries." *Finance Development*, March 1999, vol. 36, number 1, pp. 1-7.

3. Wolf, Martin, "Prospective: The Heart of the New World Economy." *The Financial Times*, October 1, 1977, p. 20.

4. Margherio, Lynn, *The Emerging Digital Economy*, Washington, D.C: U.S. Department of Commerce, http//www.ecommerce.gov, p. 2. (Accessed March 18, 2001).

5. A Team Canada Inc, *A Step-by-Step Guide to Exporting*. Toronto, Canada, p. 16. http//www.exportsource.gc.ca. (Accessed March 23, 2001).

6. Central Intelligence Agency, *The World Fact Book 2000*.

7. Hammond, Frances, "GM Trade Model," mimeo, presentation prepared for the course International Trade Strategies, Thunderbird, The American Graduate School of International Management, Glendale, Arizona, March 1999, p. 2.

8. Porter, Michael, *The competitive advantage of nations*. New York, NY: The Free Press, 1990.

9. The concept of the value chain was developed by Michael Porter. See Chapter 2 of *Competitive Advantage,* New York, NY: Free Press, 1985.

10. Mantissa e-learning, "Quick Guide to Letters of Credit." http://www.mantissa.co.uk/Top2_1.htm. (Accessed April 8, 2002).

11. Rocío Alcazar developed this formula under the direction of Professor Francisco Carrada-Bravo. The formula was developed originally for America's Favorite Chicken Company.

12. Securities and Exchange Commission, Wendy's International, Inc., Form 10-K, December 31, 2001

13. Wendy's International Inc. Investor Relations, "Stock Performance." www.wendy's i-invest.com/main/stkprf.htm. (Accessed January 31, 2002).

14. Gray, Steve, and Burns, Melanie, McDonald's Corporation, personal interview, Fall 1996.

15. Wilman, John, "Perspective: Managing Global Brands," in *the Global Company, the Financial Times*, London, United Kingdom, October 22, 1997.

16. Gray, Steve, and Burns, Melanie, McDonald's Corporation, personal interview, Fall 1996.

17. Tim Horton is a Canadian baked goods and coffee retailing company.

18. Securities Exchange Commission, Wendy's International, Inc., Form 10-K, December 31, 2001, p. 6.

19. Central Intelligence Agency, *the World Fact Book*. Washington, D.C.: 1998 and 2000, www.odci.gov/cia/publications/factbook/index.html. (Accessed April 8, 2002).

20. Central Intelligence Agency, the World Fact Book. Washington, D.C., 2000, www.odci.gov/cia/publications/factbook/index.html. (Accessed January 7, 2002).

21. I owe this information to Professor Musa Essayyad, College of Industrial Management (CIM), King Fahd University of Petroleum & Minerals, Saudi Arabia, March 2, 2002.

22. Central Intelligence Agency, the World Fact Book, 2000. www.odci.gov/cia/publications/factbook/index.html. (Accessed March 5, 2001).

23 Ministry of Finance and National Economy, Saudi Arabian Monetary Authority. Riyadh, Saudi Arabia, *Thirty Seventh Annual Report*, 2001, p. 265.

24. I owe this observation to Finance Professor Ali Al-Elg, College of Industrial Management, King Fahd University of Petroleum and Minerals, March 2, 2002.

25. Ministry of Finance and National Economy, Saudi Arabian Monetary Agency. Riyadh Saudi Arabia, *Thirty Seventh Annual Report*, p. 265.

26. "Saudi Arabia, Investment Climate Statement," p. 7.

27. Suits, B. Daniel, "Agriculture," in *Structure of the American Industry*, 7th ed. (W. Adams, editor). New York, NY: McMillan, 1986.

28. The Economist, "Big Mac Currencies," April 11, 1998, p. 58.

29. Saudi Arabian Monetary Authority, *Thirty-Seventh Annual Report*, 2001, p. 265.

30. In the rest of the world and in Muslim countries, this rate is only of 2.7 and 3.5 infants per mother.

31. Central Intelligence Agency, *The World Fact Book*. Washington, D.C., 2000, http://www.odci.gov/cia/publications/factbook/index.html. (Accessed February 1, 2002).

32. Central Intelligence Agency, *the World Fact Book*. Washington, D.C., 2000, http://www.odci.gov/cia/publications/factbook/index.html. (Accessed February 5, 2002).

33. www.gazetteer.de/fr/fr_sa.htm. (Accessed February 1, 2002).

34. Interview with the Mr. Sulaiman Hassan, manager of the restaurant Mishwar, Dhahran, Saudi Arabia, February 2, 2002.

35. "Saudi Arabia, Investment Climate Statement," p. 6.

36. "Saudi Arabia, Investment Climate Statement," p. 7.

37. United States Embassy, "Saudi Arabia Investment Climate Statement," Riyadh, Saudi Arabia, November 1997, p. 2. http://www.awo.net/business/invest/sau1.asp. (Accessed February 6, 2002).

38. "Saudi Arabia, Investment Climate Statement, "p. 3.

39. "Saudi Arabia, Investment Climate Statement," p. 3.

40. "Saudi Arabia, Investment Climate Statement," p. 4.

41. "Saudi Arabia, Investment Climate Statement," p. 4.

42. "Saudi Arabia, Investment Climate Statement," p. 5.

43. "Saudi Arabia, Investment Climate Statement," p. 6.

44. "Saudi Arabia, Investment Climate Statement," p. 7.

45. "Saudi Arabia, Investment Climate Statement," p. 9.

46. "Saudi Arabia, Investment Climate Statement," p. 10.

47. www.exporthotline.com, "Saudi Arabia, Industry Report—Franchising." (Accessed April 8, 2002).

SUGGESTED ADDITIONAL READINGS

Business Advisors. "Trade Finance." http//www.business.gov/busadv/maincat. cfm?catid=98. (Accessed April 8, 2002).

Eiteman, D., et al. *Multinational Business Finance.* 9th ed. Reading MA: Addison Wesley Longman, 2001.

Luca, C., Trading in the Global Currency Markets. 2nd ed. New York, NY: *2000. NYIF* http://www.liffe.com/. (Accessed November 12, 2001).

National Bureau of Economic Research (NBER). "NBER Papers on International Trade and Investment." http://papers.nber.org/papersbyprog/ITI.html. (Accessed November 24, 2001).

Organization for Economic Cooperation and Development. "Trade and Competition Policies: Options for a Greater Coherence," May-July 2001. http://www.oecdwash. org/PUBS/BOOKS/RP013/rp013ti.htm. (Accessed November 12, 2001).

Shapiro, A. *Multinational Financial Management.* 6th ed. New York, NY: John Wiley, 1999. See Chapter 12.

Shapiro, A. *Foundations of Multinational Financial Management.* 4th ed. New York, NY: John Wiley, 2001. http://www.hg.org/trade.html. (Accessed April 10, 2002).

9

Exchange Rate Risk Management

Multinationals accept and make payments in currencies different from their own, as such; they are confronted with the problem of consolidating the financial results o their subsidiaries in terms of the home currency. Furthermore, they need to be assessing continuously the financial performance of each facility overseas. In addition, they need to estimate how much each one of them is worth in terms of the currency of the parent company.

Whether a multinational is clearing international payments, consolidating financial statements, evaluating the performance of overseas facilities, or defining the worth of a subsidiary, there is a common thread in all these activities. These tasks take time, and through the passing of time, they are exposed to the financial hazards created by changes in the exchange rate. This last aspect is known in the global finance literature as *exchange rate risk*.

Multinationals traditionally, have considered the management of exchange rate risk a key activity that is normally the responsibility of a Treasury Department. There are several reasons justifying the importance of this activity. Changes in the exchange rate may:

- Increase the cost of raw material imports
- Raise the price of exports
- Cut export revenues
- Lower the local currency value of accounts receivable
- Increase the local currency value of accounts payable
- Decrease the value of a subsidiary, measured in terms of the parent's currency, some times, with a great deal of severity

The goal of this chapter is to provide the reader with all the technical tools required to understanding and managing exchange rate risk. To meet this goal, this chapter:

- Explains the difference between exchange rate, or currency risk, and exchange rate risk exposure
- Describes the profile of the different variants of exchange rate risk
- Provides the financial tools required to managing this risk using spot and forward contracts

Currency Risk and Exchange Rate Risk Exposure

Prior to explaining how exchange rates affect the performance of a multinational corporation, the reader has to be aware of the differences that distinguish currency risk from exchange rate risk exposure.

Currency risk exists when the movements of a monetary unit in the foreign exchange market deviate from expectations. In other words, it happens when a currency variation, such as depreciation, is not anticipated.

Exchange rate risk exposure happens when multinational corporations hold assets and liabilities stated in terms of foreign exchange because the home currency value of these items can be affected by changes in the exchange rate.

The degree of exchange rate risk exposure depends on how much of the assets and liabilities are exposed. For example, a U.S. resident holding assets and liabilities in dollars is not exposed to exchange rate risk. A U.S. corporation holding a bank account deposit worth £10 million has a £10 million exposure. If the pounds are converted into dollars, the currency exposure is eliminated.

Alternative Measures of Exchange Rate Risk Exposure

Exchange rate risk effects on corporate performance are usually classified under the terms of *translation*, *transaction*, and *operating exposure*. Transaction and operating exposures combine to create *economic exposure.*

Translation Exposure

This is also known as *accounting exposure,* and refers to changes in the value of the income statement and balance sheet items when they are re expressed at consolidation from local currency terms to the monetary unit of the parent company. The degree of accounting or translation exposure depends on the conditions and composition of the financial statements. To measure the extent of a firm's exposure to exchange rate risk, the financial statement items can be classified either as exposed or nonexposed. To judge the degree of translation exposure is not an easy task, because it depends on the nature of the items and the method used to measure the exposure.

The most commonly applied methods to measure translation exposure are the *current*, *current/noncurrent*, and *monetary/nonmonetary* methods.

Under the *current method*, there is the presumption that the assets and liabilities are always exposed to currency risk. Consequently, under this method all the assets and liabilities of a subsidiary are translated at the current exchange rate.

Under the *current method*, a depreciation of the local currency raises the value of a company if the assets held in foreign exchange exceed its liabilities in the same currency. By contrast, a revaluation of the home currency has the opposite effect.

For instance, if a Mexican company has $100 million in assets and $50 million in liabilities and the spot rate is $0.109/MxP$1, then it has a net exposure of $50 million. An appreciation of the dollar (a depreciation of the peso, which in this case is the home currency) to $0.098 per one peso raises the net worth of the Mexican entity because the increase in the peso value of the $100 million asset exceeds the increase in the peso value of the $50 million liability, as it shown below.

Net exposure × (MxP$/S1)		million
($100 – $50) × (MxP$1/ $0.109)	= ($50/$0.109) × MxP$1	= MxP$458.7
($100 – $50) × (MxP$1/ $0.098)	= ($50/$0.098) × MxP$1	= MxP$510.2

At one time, the *current/noncurrent method* was used by most of the U.S. corporations. The key consideration under this accounting system is maturity. Under this method, the current assets and liabilities of a foreign subsidiary are translated into home currency at the *current exchange rate*. All noncurrent assets or liabilities are translated at the historical rate, that is, the rate in effect at the time the assets were acquired or the liabilities incurred.

Under this method, an appreciation of the parent's currency will give rise to a translation loss if the subsidiary is having a positive local working capital. A depreciation of the parent's currency will have the opposite effect.

The income statement is translated at the average exchange rate of the period except for the case of revenue and expense items related to noncurrent assets or liabilities. One of the items classified as noncurrent is depreciation, which is translated at the historical rate, which is the rate prevailing when the capital equipment was purchased.

Under the *monetary/nonmonetary method*, the assets are first classified according to their liquidity. Monetary or liquid assets include cash, accounts receivable, and securities. Monetary liabilities include accounts payable and long-term debt items. In contrast, nonmonetary assets include "physical items" such as inventory and fixed assets. Once the items are classified into monetary and nonmonetary, they are translated.

Monetary assets are consolidated into the financial statement of the parent company at the current (spot) rate. Nonmonetary items are translated at historical rates.

Income statement items are translated using the average exchange rate. Depreciation and the cost of goods sold are translated at their historical rate.

Transaction Exposure

Transaction exposure refers to the effect of exchange rate variations on the value of accounts payable and/or receivable. Consider the case of a U.S. firm holding a yen payable and a German company having a dollar receivable. Under the proposed scenario, the two firms are exposed to unexpected variations of the dollar in the foreign exchange market. Dollar depreciation against the yen worsens the financial situation of the U.S. firm by raising the dollar cost of the yen payable in proportion to the devaluation. For example, if the U.S. firm has an account payable worth ¥100 million when the exchange rate is $1/¥100 then the dollar cost of the payable is $1 million.

If the dollar depreciates to $1.2/¥100, then the cost of the payable in dollar terms raises to $1.2 million.

¥100 × ($1/¥100)	= (¥100/¥100) × $1	= $1 million
¥100 × ($1.2/¥100)	= (¥100/¥100) × $1.2	= $1.2 million

A dollar depreciation against the euro also affects the finances of the German company since the devaluation lowers the euro value of its receivable. Again, let us suppose that the German corporation is holding a $10 million account receivable when the exchange rate is $0.9/€1. Then the euro value of the dollar receivable is € 11.11 million. If the dollar depreciates to $0.92/€1, the euro value of the dollar receivable declines to €10.87 million.

$10 × (€1/$0.9)	= $10/$0.9) × €1	€11.11 million
$10 × (€1/$0.92)	= $10/$0.92) × €1	€10.87 million

Operating Exposure

Multinationals are always interested in assessing the operating income of their subsidiaries, in terms of the parent's currency. Operating income is equal to revenues minus the cost of goods. Both items change with exchange rate variations. Therefore, *operating exposure* refers to the effect of variations in the exchange rate on the value of a subsidiary's operating income, measured in terms of the parent's currency.

The measurement of this risk requires a long-term perspective, viewing the subsidiaries as a dynamic entity with primary business activities exposed all the time, to changes in the exchange rate. Operating exposure occurs when a multinational invests in servicing a local market subject to intense foreign competition, or when the company purchases a plant overseas that requires to import foreign parts (or other inputs) to manufacture locally. Under these two scenarios, a variation in the exchange rate for example a depreciation of the home-currency, increases the local and international competitiveness of the subsidiary's output but raises the cost of sourcing goods and inputs from overseas. The overall impact of the change in the exchange on operating income will depend on the degree of foreign competition in the local market, and the proportion of foreign inputs into the cost of manufacturing locally.

ECONOMIC RISK

To estimate the market value of a subsidiary, multinationals pay special attention to the present value of anticipated future cash flows and exchange rate forecasting. Very often, however, exchange rate expectations are not fulfilled. As a result, the actual cash flows and market value of the firm are different from the ones originally anticipated. The sensitivity of a firm's cash flows and market value to variations in the exchange rate is known as *economic exposure.*

To estimate the market value of a subsidiary, international managers and investors usually factor into their calculations anticipated changes in the exchange rate because the value of the relevant financial statement items required calculating the value of the subsidiary vary in accordance with the path of the exchange rate. Naturally, unexpected variations in the exchange rate are not included in a manager's calculations. In consequence, exchange rate divergence from the expected path may lead to future cash flows different from the ones initially anticipated. This variation in the value of a firm resulting from changes in the exchange rate is defined as *economic risk.*

Economic risk may be assessed in the short term, medium term, and long run. *Short-term economic exposure* is the effect of unanticipated exchange rate changes on the one-year cash flows. *Medium-term economic exposure* refers to the consequences of the exchange rate change on the cash flows of the firm during the next two to five years following the unanticipated change. These relative long-term effects are explained by the inability of the firm to adjust its cost and price structure to a new competitive environment. *Long-term economic exposure* pertains to the exchange rate effects on the cash flows of the firm beyond five years.

Managing Transaction Exposure

When a firm is in possession of a financial instrument that requires settlement in foreign exchange, it is automatically exposed to transaction risk. To manage this risk, the firm may resort to hedging either in the spot market— also known as the money market—or in the forward market. Other hedging methods are available with futures, options, and swap contracts, but they are beyond the purpose of this chapter.

Managing Transaction Exposure with Spot and Forward Contracts

To provide a flavor for transaction risk, consider the case of MCI, a U.S. telecommunications company, which is known to hold accounts payable and receivable, stated in terms of Mexican pesos, British pounds and many other currencies. In the event of a dollar depreciation across currencies —against the Mexican peso, and the pound—the dollar value of the payables held by MCI increases in proportion to the dollar devaluation. In the case of the receivables, the opposite occurs. Their dollar value increases with the dollar depreciation.

The net result of dollar devaluation on the value of assets and liabilities held by MCI, in terms of foreign exchange, will depend on the balance between payables and receivables, the currency in which these items are stated, and the degree of the devaluation. To minimize the transaction risk associated with variations in the exchange rate, multinationals hedge their foreign currency accounts payable or receivable.

Hedging a Receivable with a Spot Contract or Money Market Hedge

To describe how a firm can hedge a receivable with spot contracts, consider the case of a U.S. exporter who is scheduled to receive a Swf10 million payment for exports to Switzerland in 90 days. If the exporter fears a Swiss franc devaluation against the dollar, this person can hedge the risk of the Swiss franc devaluation by implementing a spot hedge, also known as a *money market hedge*. The first action in implementing this hedge is either to borrow—in Swiss francs—the equivalent of the present value of the receivable or to submit the Swiss franc receivable for discount. The second step is to trade the Swiss francs in the spot. At this point, regardless of what happens to the dollar, the trader has secured dollar revenue for the 90-day Swiss franc export. The hedging of an export transaction is described in detail in Figure 9.1, and is explained below using the information provided in Table 9.1.

Figure 9.1
Money Market Hedge of an Account Receivable

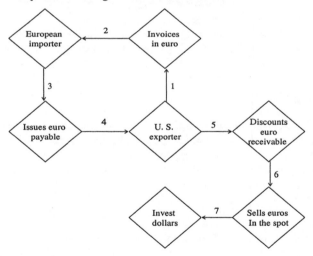

Table 9.1
Foreign Exchange and Interest Rate Quotations

Country	Exchange rate $/Swf1	Annual interest rates (%)
Switzerland		
Spot	$0.5995	
90-day forward	$0.6013	
		3.0
United States		4.2

Performing a Spot Hedge

- Borrow Swiss francs against the Swiss franc receivable. The maximum amount of Swiss francs that the firm can borrow, when using the Swiss franc receivable as collateral, is the present value of the receivable discounted at the Swiss franc interest rate of 3% (or 0.75% quarterly).

- Present value of Swiss franc receivable = Account receivable/(1 + interest rate in Switzerland/4)
  PV = Swf 10,000,000/(1 + 3%/4)
  = Swf 10,000,000/(1.0075)
  = Swf 9,925,558

- Once the loan has been granted, the U.S. exporter can convert the Swiss francs borrowed into dollars by trading francs in the spot market.

  Present value (in dollars) = Present value in Swiss francs × spot rate
  PV($) = Swf 9,925,558 × ($0.5995/Swf1)
  = Swf 9,925,558 /Swf1) × $0.5995
  = 9,925,558 × $0.5995
  = $5,950,372

Hedging a Receivable with Forward Contracts

To perform a forward hedge on the Swf10 million receivable, the exporter needs to find the best forward rate and a bank willing to pre purchase Swiss francs at that rate. If this transaction brings a higher dollar value than a money market hedge, the exporter should implement it. Otherwise, it should not.

To find out which hedging offers the higher dollar return the exporter has to compare them. To be able to contrast these alternatives, the hedger has to make sure that both of them are expressed in terms of dollars measured at present value. If the present value of the forward hedge provides a higher dollar income than the spot hedge, the U.S. trader can enter into a forward contract.

In a step-by-step fashion, the following section describes the implementation of a forward hedge on the Swf10 million.

- Sell the Swiss francs to be received at the best forward rate available. In this case, there is only one rate listed in Table 9.1, which is $0.6013/Swf1. If the francs can be sold at this rate, the dollar value of the forward transaction is $6,013,000.

  Future dollar value of forward contract = Account payable × the forward rate
  FV($) = Swf10,000,000 × ($0.6013/Swf1)
  = (Swf10,000,000/Swf1) × $0.6013
  = 10,000,000 × $0.6013
  = $6,013,000

- To compare the forward with the spot hedge, the trader has to bring the dollar value of the forward transaction to present value. This happens to be $5,950,520

Present value of forward hedge = future value of forward hedge/(1 + U.S. interest rate/4)

PV($) = $6,013,000/(1 + 4.2%/4)
= $6,013,000/(1 + (0.0105))
= $6,013,000/(1.0105)
= $5,950,520

- Since the present value of the forward transaction is slightly higher than the value of the spot hedge, perhaps the U.S. exporter should hedge the exposure buying forward contracts

- If this is the case, at maturity the exporter settles the forward contracts. It can be done by collecting the Swiss francs and delivering them to the holder of the forward contract.

Hedging Imports

To illustrate how to hedge a payable, consider the case of a U.S. company importing Swiss watches for distribution and sale in the United States. The total value of the transaction is Swf6 million over a two-year period. The delivery of the product is quarterly. Each cargo is worth Swf750,00 invoiced as a 90-day payable. Given the size of the commitment and the fact that the U.S. importer is expecting a dollar depreciation against the Swiss currency, the trader decides to hedge the Swiss franc payable. All the information required to execute an import hedge is presented in Table 9.2. An explanation of a money market hedge is presented in Figure 9.2. A detailed presentation of the hedging process is described in Table 9.3.

Hedging Imports with a Spot Contract (Money Market Hedge)

- To implement a spot hedge, the importer has to estimate the present value of each one of the eight Swiss franc payables. The discount rate is 3% (0.75% per quarter). See Table 9.2.

For example, to implement a money market hedge on the first payable the U.S. importer has to estimate the present value of the payable in terms of Swiss francs

PV = Principal $(Swf)/(1 + R_{Swf}/4)$
PV = Swf750,000/(1.0075)
PV = Swf744,417

To estimate the present value of the eighth payable is as follows

PV = Principal $(Swf)/(1 + R_{Swf}/4)^8$
PV = Swf750,000/(1.0075)^8
PV = Swf706,482

The present value of the remaining quarters are presented in Table 9.3.

Table 9.2
Hedging Imports with Spot Contracts

Information	United States	Switzerland
Spot rate	$0.5995/Swf1	
Anticipated 90-day forward rate $= E_0 \times [(1+R_{us})^t/(1+R_{Swf})^t]$	$= \$0.5995 \times [(1+0.042/4)^t/(1+(0.0075)^t]$ $= \$0.5995 \times [(1.0105)^t/(1.0075)^t]$ $= \$0.5995 \times 1.0029 = \$0.6013/Swf1$	
Interest rate	4.2%	
		3%
Transaction		
Total value of imports	SwF 6 million	
Period	2 years	
Equal quarterly payments	Swf750,000	

Table 9.3
Present Value of Swiss Franc Payables

Invoice	Value of invoice (Swf)	Discount Factor (DF) @ 0.0075/qtr	Present Value = Payment/(1.0075)^t = Payment × DF	PV (Swf)
1	750,000	$1/(1.0075)^1= 0.993$	750,000 × 0.993	744,417
2	750,000	$1/(1.0075)^2= 0.985$	750,000 × 0.985	738,875
3	750,000	$1/(1.0075)^3= 0.978$	750,000 × 0.978	733,375
4	750,000	$1/(1.0075)^4= 0.971$	750,000 × 0.971	727,916
5	750,000	$1/(1.0075)^5= 0.963$	750,000 × 0.963	722,497
6	750,000	$1/(1.0075)^6= 0.956$	750,000 × 0.956	717,119
7	750,000	$1/(1.0075)^7= 0.949$	750,000 × 0.949	711,780
8	750,000	$1/(1.0075)^8= 0.942$	750,000 × 0.942	706,482
Total	6 million			

- Once the Swiss franc present value of each account payable is known, the U.S. importer has to find out the dollar value of each payable using the spot rate given in Table 9.2 ($0.5995). For example, the present value, in dollar terms, of the first invoice is as follows:

Present value ($) = Present value (Swf) × ($/Swf1)
PV ($) = Swf744,417 × $0.5995/Swf1
PV ($) = Swf744,417/Swf1 × $0.5995
PV = $446, 278

The present value of the invoice number eight is as follows:

PV ($) = Swf766,492 × $0.5995/Swf1
PV ($) = Swf706,482/Swf1 × $0.5995
PV = $423,536

The present value for the remaining invoices is presented in Table 9.4.

Figure 9.2
Money Market Hedge of an Account Payable

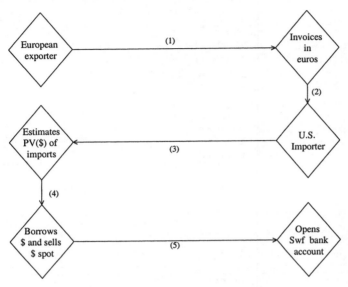

- To meet the first quarter payment in the first year the U.S. importer has to open a savings account for Swf744,417. In 90 days, this investment will increase to Swf750,000. To open this account the U. S. importer needs to trade in the spot $446,278. To cover for the eight payables, the U.S. company needs to trade $3,478,575 that purchase enough Swiss francs to open the eight savings accounts required to hedge imports. See Table 9.4.

Hedging Payables with Forward Contracts

To illustrate the forward hedge of a payable consider again the case of the American company importing Swf6 million over a two-year period. To cover the eight Swiss franc invoices the U.S. company has to find the best forward rate matching the maturity of each payable and find a financial institution willing to pre sell Swiss francs at that rate, if the present value of this transaction measured in dollars is less than the cost of hedging in the money market. If this is the case, the U.S. importer should purchase eight forward contracts to secure the dollar cost of the payables.

Forward hedging is described in Figure 9.3. A detailed numerical of the forward cover is presented in Table 9.5.

For example, the dollar present value of the first Swiss franc invoice is PV($) = Future value of invoice measured in dollars/ (1 + U.S. interest rate).

PV =[FV(Swf) × forward rate]/(1 + Rus/4)
= Swf750,000 × $0.6013/Swf1)/((1 + 0.042/4)
= (Swf750,000/Swf1 × $0.6013)/(1.0105)
= $452,307/1.0105

= $452,307 × 0.99

= $446.278

The dollar present value of the last invoice is as follows:

PV($) = Future value of invoice measured in dollars/ (1 + U.S. interest rate)

= Swf750,000 × \$0.6013/Swf1)/((1 + 0.042/4)^8

= (Swf750,000/Swf1 × \$0.6013)/(1.0105)^8

= \$452,307/1.087153

The dollar present value of the payable can be also as follows:

PV($) = $452,307 × 0.92

PV = $423,536

The present value estimates for the remaining quarters are presented in Table 9.5.

Table 9.4
Dollar Present Value of Swiss Franc Invoices

Present value ($)	Present value ($)	
Swf 744,417 × \$0.5995/Swf1	= Swf 744,417/Sfw1 × \$0.5995	$446,278
Swf738,875 × \$0.5995/Swf1	= Swf 738,875/Sfw1 × \$0.5995	$442,956
Swf 733,375 × \$0.5995/Swf1	= Swf 733,775/Sfw1 × \$0.5995	$439,658
Swf 727,916 × \$0.5995/Swf1	= Swf 727,916/Sfw1 × \$0.5995	$436,385
Swf 722,497 × \$0.5995/Swf1	= Swf 722,497/Sfw1 × \$0.5995	$433,137
Swf 717,119 × \$0.5995/Swf1	= Swf 717,119/Sfw1 × \$0.5995	$429,913
Swf 711,788 × \$0.5995/Swf1	= Swf 711,780/Sfw1 × \$0.5995	$426,712
Swf 766,492 × \$0.5995/Swf1	= Swf 706,492/Sfw1 × \$0.5995	$423,536
Total present value		$3,478,575

Table 9.5
Dollar Present Value of Swiss Franc Payables

Payable × forward rate ($/Swf)	PV = FV /(1.0105)^t = FV× discount factor	PV (Swf)
Swf750,000 × \$0.6013/Swf1 = \$450,964	450,964 × 0.99	446,278
Swf750,000 × \$0.6031/Swf1 = 452,307	452,307 × 0.979	442,956
Swf750,000 × 0.6049/Swf1 = 453,653	453,653 × 0.969	·439,658
Swf750,000 × \$0.6067/Swf1 = 455,004	455,004 × 0.959	436,385
Swf750,000 × \$0.6085/Swf1 = 456,359	456,359 × 0.949	433,137
Swf750,000 × \$0.6103/Swf 1 = 457,718	457,718 × 0.939	429,913
Swf750,000 × \$0.6121/Swf1 = 459,081	459,081× 0.929	426,712
Swf750,000 × \$0.6139/SwF1 = 460,448	460,448 × 0.920	423,536
Total PV($)		3,478,575

Figure 9.3
Forward Hedge on an Account Payable

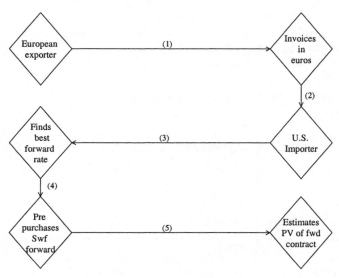

Contrasting Money Market and Forward Hedges

A comparison of the costs involved in both the spot and the forward hedge to cover the first of the eight payments suggests that the U.S. importer is indifferent between either of the methods because the costs are usually the same. Not surprisingly, this result reflects interest rate parity. Normally, due to arbitrage, interest rate parity holds pretty well in the international financial markets. As a consequence, both the money market and the forward hedge options yield similar results most of the time. If this is true, interest rate parity renders the practice of comparing spot and forward hedges somewhat meaningless.

There are, however, some compelling reasons to recommend an understanding of how to hedge in either one of these two markets. The first reason is the existence of market imperfections that may lead to short-term discrepancies between spot and forward hedges. Another reason is the fact that even if forward contracts exist, they are not always offered with the maturity required to meet the needs of the traders. In this last instance, the treasury of a multinational corporation may be forced to engage in a combined hedge —that is, to cover some portion of the transaction with a forward hedge, and the remaining with a spot hedge. To determine the most convenient hedging mix, the trader has to compare both money market and forward hedge results.

SUMMARY

Multinational corporations are always exposed to currency risk. This happens when the movements of a monetary unit in the foreign exchange market deviate from the value initially anticipated for that currency.

This risk affects the financial performance of a global business in a variety of forms that have been encapsulated into four major classifications identified as translation, transaction, and operating risk. The last two forms of exposure, in turn, create another financial hazard known as economic exposure.

Translation or accounting exposure refers to changes in the value of the income statements and balance sheet of a subsidiary when they are re-expressed at consolidation, from local currency to parent's currency terms. Transaction exposure is related to the effect of exchange rate variations on the home currency value of accounts payable and receivable stated in terms of a foreign currency. Operating income exposure is defined as the financial impact of foreign exchange rate variations on the operating income of a subsidiary, expressed in terms of the parent's currency. Economic risk refers, to the effect of changes in the exchange rate on the value of the cash flows of a subsidiary, when they are expressed in terms of the currency of the parent company.

After a detailed discussion of the different variants of exchange rate exposure, the chapter provides several examples to illustrate how multinational corporations can cover for translation risk using spot and forward contracts.

PROBLEMS

1. A Swiss firm buys parts from Japan worth ¥15 million payable in 90 days. It has yen receivables valued at ¥5 million, due in 90 days. It is the policy of the firm to hedge all residual currency positions.

Information	France	Japan
Spot rate	€1/¥84.00	
90-day forward rate	€1/¥86.25	
Interest rate	3%	0.5%

   a. What is the amount of the payable in euro if the Swiss company hedges in the money market?

   b. What is the amount of the payable in euro if the Swiss company hedges in the forward market?

   c. Which option is best?

2. A U.S. firm has a €200,000 payable due in six months. Assume that the 180-day euro interest in annual terms is 4% and the spot rate is $.0.8/€1. What is the value of the payable in dollar terms if the company implements a money market hedge?

3. Assume the following information:

Rate	Canada	United States
Spot	$0.64/CD$1	
One-year forward	$0.60/CD$1	
Interest rate	4%	5%

Additionally, assume that a U.S. exporter denominates its Canadian exports in Canadian dollars and expects to receive CD$600,000 in one year. What will be the appropriate value of these exports in dollars if the firm executes a money market hedge?

4. The U.S. subsidiary of the Mexican corporation Vitro, S.A. is filling an order from a Taiwanese company for machinery worth Tw$4,800,000. The export sale is due in 90 days and is denominated in Taiwanese dollars. The opportunity cost of funding for Vitro in the United States is 8%. The interest rate on 90-day securities in Taiwan is 10%. The spot rate is Tw$20/$1, and the 90-day forward rate is selling at a 20% discount per year. The finance staff of Vitro forecasts that the Taiwanese dollar will depreciate 10% at a steady rate over the next year. Vitro faces the following choices: hedge in the spot or forward market. Which is the best option for hedging?

Case: Grey Goose in the United States

Grey Goose is a company from the famous French region of Cognac, engaged in the production and distribution of vodka. This business activity is rather unusual in a region whose fame is tied to the production and distribution, at worldwide scale, of Cognac's *eau de vie*, otherwise "water of life."

During the 17th century, the population of Cognac was primarily Protestant in a heavily Catholic country. To protect the rights of this religious minority, the French crown issued the Edict of Nantes that guaranteed the freedom of faith, worship, and safe haven.

Louis XIV canceled the edict, and that prompted a major migration of French families to England, Ireland, and Holland.

Many French expatriates began to import wines from the Cognac region. However, lengthy export journeys through the Charente River often spoiled the wine shipments. To prevent wine deterioration, the French exporters double-distilled them and turned the wine into alcohol that later was stored in oak barrels. Upon arrival to final destination, the alcohol was supposed to be diluted back.

By chance, the French wine exporters realized that the quality and flavor of the "water of life" improved when placed in oak wood. The longer the contact of alcohol with oak wood, the better its taste. Upon this realization, exporting companies began to ship wine in corked bottles rather than oak barrels. This change in packaging led to a new economic cycle that helped to create factories producing bottles, boxes, corks, labels, and brands. These activities turned Cognac into a dynamic and fast-growing economic region.

At a later stage, the trading activities of Cognac extended to incorporate bottling of clear mineral water of exceptional quality. This activity is still thriving.

The quality of the water from Cognac is at the heart of Grey Goose strengths, since the quality of its vodka rests on the quality features of this water. This strength was further enhanced by a careful selection of ingredients and the implementation of a very labor-intensive distilling process requiring the use of copper pots.

As a result of the quality of processing and distilling, the vodka of Grey Goose received several quality awards, both in France and abroad. In 1999 the Swiss Tasting Institute granted Grey Goose the Platinum Medal, and the U.S. Beverage Tasting Institute awarded Grey Goose's vodka a rating of 96 out of 100 possible points. Because of the uniqueness and quality of Grey Goose vodka, Sidney Frank Importing Corporation, a distributor of spirits from the United States approached the French producer and negotiated the U.S. distributorship of the Grey Goose products.

Under the terms of the agreement reached by the two companies, Sidney Frank must to import a minimum of 100,000 batches of vodka each year. This amount can be increased if demand in the United States is larger than expected.

Considering the market conditions in the United States, Sidney Frank requested the delivery of 30% of the vodka imports in equal deliveries of 10,000 units in the first, second, and third quarters with the remaining 70% due for delivery at the beginning of the fourth quarter.

The vodka is normally packaged in batches of 10 bottles, and each batch is priced at $73.80.

The French company delivers the product at the beginning of each quarter. Payment and invoices of the delivery are in the form of a 90-day dollar payable. Both Grey Goose and Sidney Frank have agreed to maintain the price of the French exports to the United States in dollars.

Recently, the dollar has depreciated against the euro. The management of Grey Goose is worried about future dollar swings in the foreign exchange market. Therefore, the company is interested in hedging with spot and forward contracts in euros, the value of its first-year exports to the United States.

CASE PROBLEMS

1. Prepare a hedging sheet detailing both spot and forward hedging using French franc and euro contracts.

2. What is the best option to hedge, measuring the results in euro terms?

Case Table 9.1
Spot and Forward Rates

Exchange Rates

	Spot	30-day forward	90-day forward	180-day forward	One-year forward
Euro	$0.9256/€1	$0.9275/€1	$0.9305/€1	$0.9375/€1	$0.9429/€1

Interest Rates (annual)

	Overnight	30-day forward	90-day forward	180-day forward	One-year forward
Euro	4.37%	4.34%	4.62%	4.87%	5.125%
Dollar	5.65%	6.5%	6.75%	6.68%	7.0%

SUGGESTED ADDITIONAL READINGS

Eiteman, D., et al. *Multinational Business Finance*. 9th ed. Reading, MA: Addison Wesley. Longman, 2001. See Chapter 6.

National Bureau of Economic Research (NBER), "The NBER Project on Exchange Rate Crises in Emerging Market Countries." http://www.nber.org/crisis/. (Accessed April 14, 2002).

OFZREX. "Foreign Exchange: The Basics." http://www.ozforex.com.au/thebasics.htm. (Accessed November 12, 2001).

Peugeot–Citroen. "Notes to the Consolidated Income Statements: Foreign Exchange and Interest Rate Risk Management." http://www.psa-peugeot-citroen.com/finances/resultats00/comptes00/en_p6_36_euro.html. (Accessed November 10, 2001).

Shapiro, A. *Multinational Financial Management*. 6th ed. New York, NY: John Wiley, 1999. See Chapters 10 and 11.

Shapiro, A. *Foundations of Multinational Financial Management*. 4th ed. New York, NY: John Wiley, 2001.

10

Transaction Risk Management with Futures and Options

The futures and options markets offer standardized currency contracts written against futures clearinghouses, such as the Chicago Mercantile Exchange (CME) or the Chicago Board of Trade. These contracts include detailed specifications describing a fixed number of currency units and their term to expiration, which are used by multinationals and global financial institutions to limit exchange rate exposure or to speculate with currencies.

The purpose of this chapter is to describe the nature of the futures and options markets, and to explain how multinationals use futures and options contracts to hedge exchange rate risk or to speculate. To meet these goals, this chapter:

- Describes the nature and valuation of currency futures and options
- Shows how futures and options contracts can be used to manage the exchange rate risk involved in international trade transactions
- Explains how to take speculative positions with foreign currencies

VALUATION OF CURRENCY FUTURES AND OPTIONS

The futures and options markets are best described as continuous auction markets that serve as clearing houses for the latest information about the supply and demand for currencies. These markets were created to provide an efficient and effective mechanism to manage currency prices. The individuals and corporations participating in the futures market trade futures contracts to secure a price now for currencies to be delivered later. This transaction, known as hedging with futures, becomes insurance against adverse currency prices.

Other participants are speculative investors who accept the price risk, which is avoided by the hedgers. In contrast to hedgers, the speculators do not plan on handing over or taking delivery of the currencies that they purchase or sell. Rather, they purchase futures contracts with the hope of making a profit. To benefit from a foreign exchange transaction speculators purchase a currency when they anticipate a price increase and sell it when they expect a price decline. In other words, foreign exchange opportunists pre purchases currencies with the anticipation of selling them later at a higher price. Similarly, they pre sell a foreign currency with they plan to purchasing it back at a lower price.

Speculation with futures currency contracts is not appropriate for everyone. A lucky speculator can realize substantial profits very quickly, but he or she can also incur speedily into severe losses. The potential for large profits or losses, in relation to the initial commitment of capital, stems from the fact that trading with futures contracts is a highly levered form of speculation.

To purchase a futures contract, speculators only have to invest a relatively small amount of money, known as *margin*, which provides them with the opportunity to control assets having a much larger value. Therefore, the leverage of futures trading favors a speculator when the price of a currency moves in the direction anticipated by the investor. However, the investment is lost if currency prices do not behave as expected.

HEDGING WITH FUTURES CONTRACTS

To describe how futures contracts are used to hedge, consider the prospect of investing in Mexican Treasury bills, better known as Certificados de Tesoreria or Cetes. Historically, these Mexican financial instruments offer a higher return than comparable U.S. Treasury bill rates. This combination of factors turned Cetes into an attractive, but risky, investment possibility.

The risk associated with holding a peso-denominated security and the fact that there were not appropriate instruments to hedge peso investments deterred many foreign investors from taking advantage of the high return offered by the Mexican government debt instrument. The introduction of futures contracts in pesos, offered by the CME and other exchanges, opened up the door to hedging peso-denominated assets and liabilities. The availability of the new financial tools helped to lower the premium risk associated with investing in pesos and to increase the inflow of foreign direct investment into the Cetes market.

To invest in pesos or in any other currency, the major consideration is the NPV of the venture measured in terms of the currency of the investor.

To estimate the NPV in dollar terms of a Cetes purchase, consider the case of a U.S. investor pondering a MxP$952,381investment on a 91-day Cetes contract with a face value of MxSP$1,000,000. During the planning period, the spot rate is MxP$10/$1, the return on Cetes is 15%, and the U.S. discount rate is 5%. Given this information, the NPV of investing $95,238, to purchase a MxP$1 million is $6,085. This result indicates that the Cetes investment yields a return that is $6,085 higher than a return on a similar investment in the United States.

For more details on the estimates used to arrive to this conclusion, see Table 10.1, and the calculations presented below.

NPV (\$) of a peso investment = − initial investment + dollar present value of peso investment

Estimating the initial dollar investment is easy. It is simply the peso investment multiplied by the spot rate, which equals \$95,238.

Initial dollar investment = peso investment × the spot rate

= MxP\$952,381 × \$1/MxP\$10

= (MxP\$952,381/MxP\$10) × \$1

= 95,238 ×\$1

= \$95,238

This investment let the U.S. investor purchase MxP\$1 million on June 1. If the spot rate happens to be \$0.099/MxP\$1 at the maturity of the Cetes, the investor will get back the equivalent of \$99,000.

Future dollar value of peso investment = face value of the Cetes × spot rate 91 days later

FV(\$) = MxP\$1,000,000 × \$0.099/MxP\$1

= MxP\$1,000,000/ MxP\$1 × \$0.099

= \$99,000

The anticipated profit of the spot transaction is \$3,762.

Profit = future value of spot transaction − initial value of spot transaction

Profit = \$99,000 − \$95,238

= \$3,762

The NPV of the spot transition is \$3,715.

NPV(\$) = \$3,762/(1+5%/4)

= \$3,715.

However, to lock-in this profit, the U.S. investor has to cover for exchange rate risk. If he chooses to hedge with futures he has meet the margin requirement, which is equal to \$3,000 per contract. Since there are two contracts, the value of the margin is \$6,000. The margin gives the investor the right to pre sell on June 1, MxP\$1 million. At this date the futures rate is \$0.1/MxP\$1, therefore, the market value of the two futures contracts is \$100,000.

Dollar value of futures contracts = contract size × number of contracts × futures rate

FV(\$) = MxP\$500,000 × 2 × \$01/MxP\$1

= MxP\$1,000,000/MxP\$1 × \$0.1

= \$100,000

To close the futures position on August 31, the investor needs to purchase pesos buying two futures contracts. If at this time the futures rate is \$0.0976/MxP\$1, the value of the two contracts is \$97,600, which is less than the notional dollar amount received for the sale of pesos on June 1 (\$100,000). Therefore, the futures hedge is providing the investor with a profit equivalent to \$2,400.

Table 10.1
Investing in Cetes, Alternative 1

	Spot transaction	
Date		
01/06	Initial investment	MxP$952,381 × $0.1/MxP$1 = $95,238
31/08	Future value	MxP$1,000,000×$0.099/MxP$1 = $99,000
31/08	Profits	= $99,000 – $95,238 = $3,762
	NPV of spot transaction	$3,762/(1+5%/4) = $3,715
	Futures transaction	
	Pay margin	$3,000 × 2 = $6,000
01/06	Pre sell pesos	1,000,000 × $0.1MxPS$1 = $100,000
31/08	Pre purchase pesos	1,000,000 × $0.0976/MxP$1 = $97,600
	Profits	$100,000 – $97,600 = $2,400
	NPV of futures transaction	– $6,000 + $6,000 + $2,400/(1+5%/4) = $2,370
	Total NPV	= $3,715 + $2,370 = $6,085

Profits from futures transaction = dollar value of peso sale – dollar value of peso purchase
FV($) = $100,000 – $97,600
= $2,400

The NPV of the futures transaction is $2,370.

NPV from futures transaction = profits/(1+5%/4)
= $2,400/1.0125
= $2,370

If the expectations of the U.S. investor regarding spot and futures rates materialize the total NPV of investing in Mexican Cetes is $6,085. See Table 10.1, and Figure 10.1.

To further investigate the NPV of investing in Cetes, the U.S. investor could consider other scenarios, attach a probability to each scenario, and estimate the most likely value of a peso investment. For example, if the pre selling and pre purchasing futures rates are $0.97 and $0.976 respectively, the NPV of investing in Cetes is reduced to $3,123. This decline is explained by the fact that the investor is pre selling dollars cheap and buying them back expensive. Nonetheless, even under this more pessimistic scenario, the NPV of the project is positive. See Table 10.2.

HEDGING WITH OPTIONS CONTRACTS

Currency options enable investors to assess currency variations in the foreign exchange market while protecting themselves against these changes. A currency option contract provides the buyer (or holder) with the right, but no the obligation to exchange a fixed amount of one currency for another at a fixed rate of exchange on the expiry date. The amount, exchange rate, and date to maturity are all pre-determined.

Figure 10.1
Covering Interest Rate Arbitrage with Futures Contracts

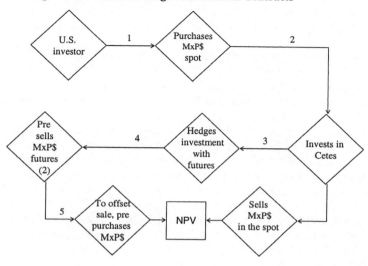

Table 10.2
Investing in Cetes, Alternative 2

	Spot transaction	
Date		
01/06	Initial investment	MxP$952,381 × $0.1/MxP$1 = $95,238
31/08	Future value	MxP$1,000,000×$0.099/MxP$1 = $99,000
31/08	Profits	= $99,000 − $95,238 = $3,762
	NPV of profits	$3,762/(1 + 5%/4) = $3,715
	Futures transaction	
	Pay margin	$3,000 × 2 = $6,000
01/06	Pre sell pesos	1,000,000 × $0.97MxPS$1 = $97,000
31/08	Pre purchase pesos	1,000,000 × $0.0976/MxP$1 = $97,600
	Profits	$97,000 − $97,600 = −$600
	NPV of profits	− $6,000 + $6,000 − $600/(1+5%/4) = −$592
	Total NPV	= $3,715 − $592 = $3,123

There are two types of options contracts: put and call. A *put option contract* confers on the owner a right to sell foreign currency at the *strike price*. The seller (or writer) of a put contract is obligated to buy foreign currency at the request of the owner of a put contract.

A *call option contract* grants the owner a right to purchase foreign currency from the seller of a call contract at the strike price. In this case, the contract seller has to furnish foreign currency if the owner wants to exercise the call contract.

The *exercise* or *strike price* is the price at which the contract buyer has the right to purchase or sell currency. Normally, the strike price is stated in U.S. dollars. Two exceptions to this rule are the Japanese yen, which is quoted in dollars per 100 yen, and French francs, which are stated in French francs per dollar cents.

The expiration dates for options on foreign currencies are March, June, September and December. The last day on which an option can be exercised is the Friday before the third Wednesday of the expiration month.

To purchase on option contract, the buyer of the currency option pays a premium to the seller of the option for the right to exercise the option. The *premium* is the sum of money that the buyer of the option pays to acquire an option contract and is, in effect, the price of the option. It is usually payable on the second business day of the acquisition of the option, and is quoted either as a percentage of any of the two currencies involved in the transaction or in points. A pip or point is the smallest unit by which a currency can change. For example the price of a $/€ option can be quoted as a percentage in dollars (%$), as a percentage in euros (%€), dollar points per euro, or euro points per dollar. For example, if the spot rate is $130/€1 and the option rate is $131.15, the pips or points are 15 ($131.15/€1 − $131/€1). One point is equal to one percent of one dollar cent, or one percent of one percent of a euro.

Options contracts may have market value. In the case of a call contract, the option has market value if the spot price of a currency is above the strike price. The market value is the result of the fact that the holder of a call contract can exercise the contract, purchasing currency at the strike price to sell it later in the spot market at a profit.

For example, if the spot price is at $0.93/€1 and the strike price is $0.9/€1, the holder of a call contract can purchase euros at $0.9 in the options market and sell them in the spot at $0.93. This transaction will provide the owner of the call contract with a gross profit of $0.03 per euro traded.

In contrast to call contracts, a put contract has market value if the spot price is below the strike price. For example a put contract on euros has market value if the spot rate is $0.89/€1 and the strike price is at $0.93/€1. Given this scenario the owner of a put contract can purchase euros in the spot at $0.89/€1 and sell them to the writer of the put contract at $0.93/€1. This transaction will net the contract owner a gross profit of $0.04 per euro traded. In the two previous examples the options are *in- the- money*.

Normally, an option whose exercise price is the same or very nearly the same as the spot price, is said to be *at-the-money*. Call contracts with a spot price below the strike price or put contracts with a spot price (or spot rate) above the strike price are classified as *out-of-the-money*. In these two instances, the contracts are worthless because exercising the contracts would lead to a loss.

To purchase an options contract, investors have to pay a premium. The premium of an option can be viewed as having two components: intrinsic and extrinsic value. *Intrinsic value* is the difference between the strike price and spot rates for the same value date. In general, only options that are in-the-money have intrinsic value.

The *extrinsic value* of an option refers to impact of some external factors that may include time to maturity, interest rate differential between two currencies, the difference between spot and strike rates, and the volatility of a currency's premium. The premium is higher when the time to maturity is long, when the difference between interest rates and spot and strike is high, and when the currency is volatile. The extrinsic value is determined by the expected value of the contract, which is the weighted average of the possible range of values. The premium can be viewed as a lottery outcome. For example, consider the case of a game of chance having four out of one hundred chances to draw a $10,000 prize. The price of purchasing a ticket to participate in this lottery is as follows:

Price = probability of winning × prize
Price = 0.04 × $10,000 = $400

Options are priced in a similar fashion. Throughout the lifetime of an option, there are an infinite number of final outcomes; consequently, there is an infinite number of expected values that can be analyzed to determine the price of the option.

Once the premium is determined, it becomes the only cost of an option transaction because there are no commission charges or fees. Consequently, the maximum loss that can be incurred by the holder of an option contract is the premium paid for the option. In contrast, the sellers, whose only benefit is the premium, may incur in unlimited losses when they sell an option contract.

The Black Scholes Model

Fischer Black and Myron Scholes paved the way for the $84 trillion derivatives market with a complicated book which essentially set out a way to provide a future value for securities, including currencies. The Black Scholes formula is now the accepted standard for pricing options and its influence propelled the authors of this notion to fame and eventually, the Nobel Price for economics to Scholes. The application of the formula also brought infamy to Scholes for his role in the 1988 debacle of the hedge fund Long Term Capital.[1]

The original Black Scholes formula for the price of an European call option has five parameters, four of which are directly observable: S, the price of the asset, E, the exercise price, r the riskless interest rate, and T the time to maturity of the option.[2] The Black Scholes formula is as follows:

(10.1) $$C = N(d_1)S - N(d_2)Ee^{-rt}$$
$$d_1 = \frac{\ln(S/E) + (r + \sigma^2/2)T}{\sigma T^{1/2}}$$

$$d_2 = d_1 - \sigma T^{1/2}$$

where:
C = price of the call
S = price of the asset
E = strike price
r = riskless interest rate (the annualized continuously compounding rate on a safe asset with the same maturity as the option).
T = time to maturity of the option in years
σ = standard deviation of the annualized continuous compounded rate of return on the asset

ln = natural logarithm

e = the base natural log function (approximately 2.7183)

N(d) = probability that a random walk draw from a standard normal distribution
will be less than d

To understand this model, it is convenient to divide it into two parts. The first part $N(d1)S$ provides the expected benefit from acquiring an asset outright.. The second part of the model, $N(d_2)Ee^{-rt}$, provides the present value of paying the strike price on the expiration day (European option). The fair market value of the call option is calculated by taking the difference between these two parts.

In a further development of this model, Merton derived the formula for the value of a put by substituting for C in the put-call parity condition.[3] The resulting formula for the value of the put is:

(10.2) $P = (N(d_1) - 1) S + (1 - N(d_2)) Ee^{-rt}$

This model was generalized by Merton to allow for a constant continuous dividend when the model is applied to estimate stock options.[4]

(10.3) $C = N(d_1) Se^{-dT} - Nd(d_2)Ee^{-rt}$

$d_1 = \dfrac{\ln(S/E) + (r - d + \sigma^2/2)T}{\sigma T^{1/2}}$

$d_2 = d_1 - \sigma T^{1/2}$

In the real world neither the volatility (σ) nor the dividend of the asset (d) are known with certainty. The empirical evidence on studies conducted to investigate the behavior of these variables indicates that both vary stochastically. However, the parameters of this model can be easily calculated using a spreadsheet and information on cumulative standard normal distribution of the asset.[5] A calculator with software developed to estimate call and put premiums for currencies can be found in http://www.kumade.com.

To estimate option prices (premium) for call and put option contracts an investors needs to have information on spot, forward, volatility, time to maturity and delivery of the option contracts, and choose a strike price. See Table 10.3.

With this information at hand it is possible to estimate, with the appropriate software put and call premiums. For example, on April 22, 2002, the Bank of Montreal was quoting the following spot and 30-day forward rates: $1/¥131.89 and $1/¥131.15.[6] This difference implied -74 pips or points. With a volatility of 13 and a strike price of $1/¥135, the price of a 30-day Japanese yen call premium, measured in dollar terms is ¢0.54 per ¥100 (or $0.0054/¥100). A put premium is equal to ¢3.46 per ¥100 ($0.0346//¥100).

In the cases previously discussed, the put premium is higher than the call premium because the buyer of the option contract has chosen a very high strike price, relative to the spot price, to sell Japanese yens to the writer. The higher premium should be viewed as a defensive move on the part of the writer to overcome potential losses associated to the chance of having to purchase Japanese yens at the strike price solicited by the buyer.

The estimation of call and put premiums for the Japanese yen over 30, 90, 180, and 365 days are described in Table 10.4.

Table 10.3
Japanese Investment in the United States

Quotes	Spot	Strike	Premium		
			Call	Put	
Number of shares					1,000
Stock price	$100	$100	$6.74	$4.35	
Stock dividend yield					3%
Stock volatility					0.2
U.S. risk-free interest					5%
Japanese discount rate					2%
Currency rates					
$/¥100	$0.7703	$0.7634	$0.00069	$0.01454	
¥100/$1	1.2982	1.3099			
Yen volatility					10

Hedging a Payable in the Options Market

To explain how to use options contracts to hedge, consider that on March 28, a U.S. importer agrees to purchase a shipment of Swiss cheese for delivery on April 15 at a cost of Swf375,000. The importer has the choice of paying the import bill at any time between March 28 and April 15. Within this period, the Swiss franc can appreciate. If this happens, the U.S. firm will have to pay a larger amount of dollars to settle the Swiss franc account payable. To avoid this inconvenience, the U.S. corporation can hedge the Swiss franc payable with call option contracts.

The value of the account payable stands at Swf375,000, but the size of a Swiss franc options is only of 125,000 units. Therefore, to fully hedge this liability, the U.S. firm has to purchase three options contracts for maturity the third Wednesday of April at the strike price of $0.48/Swf1.

Number of options contracts = Swiss franc liability/options contract size
= Swf375,000/Swf 125,000 = 3

To purchase the call contracts, the U.S. firm has to pay a call premium equivalent to $0.0085/Swf1. Therefore, the total cost of purchasing one Swiss franc is $0.4885.

Cost of one Swiss franc = strike price + call premium
= $0.48/Swf1 + $0.0085/Swf1
= $0.4885/Swf1

Table 10.4
Options Pricing, Japanese Yen

Days	Spot ¥/$1	Forward ¥/$1	Pips	Strike ¥/$1	σ	Call price ¢	¥ pts	Put price ¢	¥ pts
	131.89								
30		131.15	−74	135	13	0.54	71.8	3.46	456
90		128.89	−300	135	13	1.15	152.0	5.02	663
180		128.97	−292	135	13	1.85	244.0	6.38	842
365		124.34	−755	135	13	2.06	27.0	10.10	1337

If the contracts are exercised, the total cost of each call contract is $183,187.

Total cost of the call contract = (strike price + premium) × contract size × number of contracts

= ($0.48 + $0.0085) × 125,000 × 3

= $0.4885 × 125,000 × 3

= $183,187

For more details in this transaction, see Table 10.5.

The acquisition of the three call contracts provides the U.S. firm with a *ceiling cost*. That is, the total cost of the Swiss franc account payable cannot exceed $183,187. However, if the spot price of the Swiss franc is less than $0.48 per Swiss franc, the U.S. importer may end up paying less than $183,187.5 at any time within the life of the contract. This is because if the Swiss franc depreciates, the U.S. firm can buy Swiss francs cheaper in the spot than in the options market.

The hedging example also shows that call contracts should not be exercised if the spot rate is less than the strike price. It also indicates that the premium is irrelevant to the decision on whether to exercise an options contract because the premium is a sunk cost that is incurred, regardless of the actions of the holder.

Hedging an Account Receivable

To provide an illustration of how to hedge a receivable using options contracts, consider the case of a U.S. multinational exporting a tennis shoes cargo to Japan valued at ¥50,000,000. Proceeds from the export are due in 90 days, let us say, May 15. Given the existing economic situation in Japan, the U.S. multinational fears a devaluation of the yen. To avoid an exchange rate loss, the U.S. firm can hedge the yen account using put option contracts.

To fully hedge the Japanese receivable the U.S. firm can purchase four options contracts at the strike price of $0.8/¥100. The price of the option (premium) is $0.0121/¥100. Therefore, if the contracts are exercised, the total revenue is $98,487.5.

Put contract revenue = (strike price - put premium) × contract size × number of contracts

= ($0.8 - $0.0121) × (12,500,000/100) ×4

= $0.7879 ×125,000 × 4

= $98,487.5 × 4

= $393,950

Table 10.5
Total Cost of Hedging the Swiss Franc Account Payable

Number of options contracts:	3
Type of contracts purchased:	call contracts
Strike price per franc:	$0.48/Swf1
Plus call price per franc:	$0.0085/Swf1
Total cost per franc:	$0.48+ $0.0085 = $0.4885
Total cost of payable:	$0.4885 × 125,000 × 3 = $183,187

A summary of the calculations used to arrive at the final cost of the option is detailed in Table 10.6.

Hedging with put options guarantees the holder a floor revenue because the total values of the yen receivable cannot fall below $393,950; however, the proceeds of a put contract can be higher if the spot price of the yen exceeds the strike price of $0.8/¥1.

The previous discussion also indicates that put contracts should not be exercised when the spot rate is higher than the strike price.

Investing with Options

Options contracts allow shareholder to modify their risk exposure on local currency investments, avoid exchange rate risk on foreign ventures, and obtain the highest possible return on local and overseas investment programs, while setting a ceiling to investment losses. Previous sections provided an explanation of how options limit the risk exposure of payables or receivables stated in a terms of a foreign currency. This section goes a step forward, it describes how to use options contracts to modify and diversify risk. To understand how an investor can benefit from options contracts, consider the case of Ms. Satoko, a Japanese investor wanting to purchase 1,000 U.S. stock selling at $100 per share, providing a dividend yield of 3%, and having a volatility of 0.2, at the time the risk-free interest rate in the United States is 5%.

The Japanese investor wants to undertake this venture because she believes that the price of the U.S. shares can increase to $112.5 within the next 90 days, if the U.S. economy meets its anticipated growth rate. However, if this is not the case, the price per share may drop to $89. Most of the financial analysts that Ms. Satoko has consulted believe that there is an 80% probability that the U.S. economy will meet its growth expectations. In spite of these assurances, Ms. Satoko is still concerned about a stock price decline that could be worsened if the yen appreciates against the dollar.

To ease Ms. Satoko's worries, Mr. Tagi, a Japanese financial expert has suggested her to hedge both the strock price and the exchange rate risks with options contracts. He also advised her to invest in the U.S. stock market only if the net present value of the transaction is positive because this will be the only reason to undertake the investment.

On April 25, 2002, Mr. Tagi provided Ms. Satoko with call ($6.74) and put ($4.35) premiums for a strike price of $100 per share. These premiums are quoted on per unit basis. Regarding currency options, Mr. Tagi also provided information on call ($0.00069/¥100) and put ($0.01454/¥100) premiums on the Japanese yen for a strike price of $0.7634/¥100). The size of a Japanese options contract is 12.5 million yens. The spot rate at this date was $0.7703/¥100. See Table 10.3.

To help Ms. Satoko to estimate the NPV of the transaction measured in yens, Mr. Tagi prepared the following notes.

The first action, he explains, should be to determine the value of the initial investment ($-I_0$) in yen terms. This happens to be ¥1,141,529.

Table 10.6
Total Revenue of the Put Option Hedge

Number of options contracts:	4
Type of contracts purchased:	put contracts
Strike price:	$0.8/¥100
Plus call price per franc:	$0.0121/¥100
Total revenue per 100 yens:	$0.8/¥100 − $0.0121/¥100 = $0.7879/¥100
Total cost of payable:	$0.7879 ×12,500,000/100 × 4 = $393,950

Initial investment $(-I_0)$ = [dollar cost of hedging the stock price + dollar cost of covering exchange rate risk] × spot rate

= ($6740 + $2,053) × ¥100/$0.7703

= (8,793/$0.7703) × ¥100

= 11,415 × ¥100

= ¥1,141,529

A subsequent step is to estimate the dollar cost of hedging the stock price, which is equal to $6,740.

Dollar cost of hedging the stock price = number of shares × call premium on the stock price

= 1,000 × 6.74

= $6,740

An additional action is to hedge for exchange rate risk. The cost of this transaction is $2,053.

Dollar cost of hedging exchange rate risk = (number of shares × anticipated price share × strike price) × currency put premium

= 1,000 × $107.8 × ¥100/$0.7634 × $0.01454/¥100

= ($107,800/$0.7634) × ¥100 × $0.01454/¥100

= 141,210 × $0.01454

= $2,053

Given these two hedges, the anticipated price of a share is $107.8.

Anticipated share price = probability of high price × high price + probability of low price × low price

= 0.8 × $112.5 + 0.2 × $89

= $107.8

Given that Ms. Satoko has hedged using options is not possible to determine the exact final outcome of the transaction, because this will depend on the performance of the spot rate. However, the implementation of the two hedges suggests that the worse possible outcome is the loss of the premium on the stock and currency contracts, which is equivalent to ¥1,141,529. This event will occur only if the future spot price of the U.S. shares falls below $100.

In the planning period of the U.S. investment, Ms. Satoko is expecting to purchase shares cheap ($100) and to sell them expensive (at more than $100), most likely at $107.8. She is also anticipating not to exercise the contracts if the stock price is below $100, because, if she does, her losses will increase.

Another possible outcome on this transaction is having Ms. Satoko exercising the options by purchasing stock at $100 and selling it at the anticipated price of $107.8. Under this alternative scenario the NPV of the U.S investment is a loss equivalent to $-¥148,971$ if the U.S. discount rate is 8%.

NPV of U.S. investment = $-$ initial investment $+$ {[number of shares $\times$ (anticipated stock price $-$ strike price of stock)/(1 $+$ U.S. discount rate/4)] $\times$ spot rate }

$= -¥1,141,529 + \{1,000 \times (\$107.8 - \$100)/(1 + 8\%/4))] \times ¥100/\$0.7703]\}$

$= -¥1,141,529 + [\$7,800/(1.02) \times ¥100/\$0.7703]$

$= -¥1,141,529 + [(\$7,647/\$0.7703) \times ¥100]$

$= -¥1,141,529 + (9,927 \times ¥100)$

$= -¥1,141,529 + ¥992,700$

$= -¥148,791$

These losses (¥148,791) however, are not a secure outcome. The NPV of the U.S. investment can be positive, if the spot price of the stock at the time of the expiration of the contract is higher than the anticipated price of $107.8 per share. Another factor that could contribute to raise the NPV of this transaction is the future spot rate of the Japanese yen.

If at the time of the maturity of the currency contracts the spot rate is less than the strike price of $0.7634/¥100, Ms. Satoko could let the option contracts expire and purchase yens cheaper in the spot. In this instance, with the same amount of dollars she could be able to purchase a larger quantity of yens. For further details on the U.S. investment results see Table 10.7.

SUMMARY

This chapter examined the currency futures and options markets, and reviewed some of the institutional characteristics and mechanisms of these markets.

Both the currency futures and options markets can be applied to hedge and speculate. In the first market, the futures contracts have to be settled at their expiration date. By contrast, currency options give the owner of a contract the right to buy (call options) or to sell (put options) the amount of the currency specified in the options contract.

Futures contracts are standardized contracts that trade in organized exchanges such as the CME and other exchanges.

Option contracts are sold on both organized and over the counter markets. There are two types of options, American and European. The American option provides the owner of the contract with the ability to exercise an option contract at will, within the life span of the contract. The European option is more limited in scope and can be exercised only at the date of expiration of the contract.

Unlike forward contracts, the futures contracts are not designed to suit the needs of traders, when referring to contract size and date to maturity. Given these limitations, traders using futures contracts to hedge often have to settle their account payables and receivables in the spot market on dates not matching the maturity of the futures contracts. The spot transactions may lead to a gain or loss that is usually counterbalanced by losses or gains experienced in the futures markets at the closing of a trader's position.

Table 10.7
Summary, Japanese Investment in the United States

Cost of hedging the stock price	$1,000 \times \$6.74 = \$6,740$
Cost of hedging exchange rate risk	$1,000 \times \$107.8)/\$0.7634 \times \$0.01454 = \$2,053$
Anticipated stock price	$0.8 \times \$112.5 + 0.2 \times \$89 = \$107.8$
Total cost of hedging ($)	$\$6,740 + \$2,053 = \$8,793$
Total cost of hedging (¥)	$-\$8,793 \times ¥100/\$0.7703 = -¥1,141,529$
NPV: worse possible scenario	Loss of premiums $= -¥1,141,529$
Anticipated PV	$1,000 \times (\$107.8 - \$100)/1.02) \times ¥100/\$0.7703$ $= ¥992,700$
Anticipated NPV	$-¥1,007,555 + ¥992,700 = -¥148,791$

If traders pre-sell a currency using futures contracts, they can close their position in this market, prior to the expiration of the contracts, by pre purchasing the same amount of currency in the same market. If a multinational corporation wishes to hedge an account payable using options, they can do so by purchasing a call contract. To acquire a call contract, the multinational has to pay a fee, known as call premium. The premium is the price of the option and is paid on per unit basis. A call contract provides the firm with a "cost ceiling." However, if the currency depreciates in the spot market the trader may pay less than expected.

If an exporting firm wants to hedge an account receivable, they can do so by buying a put contract. To acquire this contract the firm has to pay a put premium. A put contract provides the firm with a "revenue floor." However, if the currency appreciates in the spot market more than anticipated, the exporting corporation may end up having revenue higher than expected.

PROBLEMS

1. You purchased a call option contract on Swiss francs. The price of the call is $0.02/Swf1 unit. At the settlement of the option, the spot rate is $0.46/Swf1. Should the call option contract be exercised if the strike price is $0.45/Swf1? The contract size on Swiss francs is 62,500.

2. A trader sells a put option on Canadian dollars. The price of the put is $0.03/C$1, the strike price is $0.75/C$1, and the put contract size is 50,000 units (Canadian dollars). At the exercise of the option, the spot rate is $0.72/C$1. What is the amount of profit or loss from this transaction?

3. A trader purchases a put option contract on British pounds. The put premium is $0.05/£1, the strike price is $1.50/£1, and contract size is 12,500 units (British pounds). At the purchase of the put contract, the spot rate is $1.51/£1. As time passes, the spot rises continually to $1.62/£1 by the settlement date. What is the profit or loss from this transaction?

4. A speculator purchases a call option contract in euros. The price of the call is $0.0082/€1, the strike price is $0.96/€1, and the contract size is 62,500 euros. At the purchase of the call contract the spot rate is $0.98/€1 and rises

continuously to $1.02/€1 by the settlement date. What is the profit or loss from this transaction?

5. A speculator purchases two put option contracts on Canadian dollars for $0.0025/C$1 at the strike price of $0.6823/C$1. At maturity, three months later, the spot rate is $0.6771/C$1. The size of the option contract on Canadian dollars is 50,000 units. What is the profit or loss from this transaction?

6. A speculator purchases two call option contracts on Canadian dollars for $0.013/C$1 at the strike price of $0.6823/C$1. At maturity, three months later, the spot rate is $0.6771/C$1. The size of the option contract on Canadian dollars is 62,500 units. Did the speculator have a dollar profit or loss?

7. A firm sells five put option contracts in euro at a $0.0105/€1 premium. The strike price is $1.15/€1. At maturity, three months later, the spot rate is $1.186/€1. The size of the option contract on pounds is 62,500 units. Did the writer (selling firm) have a dollar profit or loss?

8. A corporation sells 10 call option contracts on British pounds at a $0.017/£1 premium. The strike price is $1.5750/£1. At maturity, three months later when the contract is exercised, the spot rate is $1.5896/£1. The size of the option contract on pounds is 62,500 units. Did the writer of the contracts (selling firm) have a dollar profit or loss?

9. A Japanese speculator sells two put option contracts on Canadian dollars. The put premium is $0.03/C$1. The strike price in the contract is $0.55/C$1. The spot at the time of maturity of the contract is $0.52/C$1. If the speculator sells the Canadian dollars immediately after receiving them, what is the net profit to the Japanese resident of the transaction if the put contract size is 62,500?

10. To promote its British exports, Dai-Kal has created an inventory of finished goods in London. The value of the British inventory on July 1, 2002, is £500,000, and the spot and December futures rates for the same date are $1.64/£1 and $1.60/£1, respectively. The futures contract size in British pounds is £62,500. The company wants to hedge the foreign exchange rate risk on the 1,000 units of finished goods inventory held when 50% of the exchange rate change can be offset by raising the pound sale price. How could Dai-Kal hedge with futures contracts? On December 1, Dai-Kal sells all its British inventories at a price of £500. At that date, the spot and futures rates are the same at $1.50/£1.

    a. What should Dai-Kal do to close its position?

    b. After the futures position is closed, did the company have a capital gain or loss in this futures transaction?

Case A: American Thermoplastics in Japan

The U.S. corporation American Thermoplastics specializes in the manufacturing and distribution of custom-printed binders. The products of this company are widely used in corporate and professional association meetings. One important customer is the Allied Social Sciences Association (ASSA), whose number of associates exceeds 10,000.

Customers, such as ASSA, have permitted American Thermoplastics to reach large economies of scale. This in turn allowed the company to invest heavily in machinery and equipment and to train and hire highly specialized personnel. This combination of elements has let the corporation reach and maintain a high market share in the United States. At this stage, all the marketing efforts of American Thermoplastics are concentrated in maintaining their share of the U.S. market.

Recently, American Thermoplastics received an order from Japan Overseas Development Corporation (JOI), which is a Japanese government institution specialized in providing funding, marketing, and business intelligence services to Japanese corporations. The Japanese request was placed by JOI and accepted by American Thermoplastics on March 17. It consisted of an order for customized binders, broken down into three deliveries of 100,000 units for each delivery date. The first was due on May 16, 2000. The remaining deliveries were due on August 14 and December 4 of the same year. The prices of the customized binders vary. Considering the large size order and the relatively large degree of similarity between the different binders ordered, American Thermoplastics decided to apply the same price to the three orders at $1.56 per binder.

Normally, Thermoplastics requires six working days to deliver an order in the United States. However, considering that the Japanese request has to be reviewed by customs, American Thermoplastics decided that a more realistic delivery period is a 15-day lead time.

Given the limited international exposure of Thermoplastics, the management of the company has requested to be paid at delivery in dollars. This request has posed a problem for JOI. Government institutions in Japan can only price their services in Japan in terms of local currency, the Japanese yen. Therefore, JOI has to quote the price of the binders to Japanese customers in yen before delivery of the binders. These circumstances worry the managers of JOI because it exposes the institution to foreign exchange rate losses due to a possible depreciation of the yen against the U.S. dollar.

The expectation of a foreign exchange loss is a very problematic issue for JOI, since this corporation is government owned as is a not for profit corporation. These institutions in Japan are subject to very strict budgetary rules. As such, funding even a small loss is a major issue for JOI, given that it must engage in complicated and lengthy negotiations with the Japanese Treasury. To hedge the exposure, JOI has decided to purchase futures contracts that commit the institution to pre sell yen.

The futures contracts present several challenges. First, their maturity does not meet JOI's commitment to pay in dollars. For example, the first delivery is on May 6; however, the futures contracts mature the third Wednesday of June.

The remaining orders present the same mismatch problem. A second challenging aspect of these contracts is that the yens have to be pre sold in bulk packages of 12.5 million units. This will force JOI to pre sell more or fewer yen than they would have to otherwise.

Mr. Mitsunobu Koike, JOI's foreign exchange specialist, has tried to soothe the management worries by assuring them that the maturity mismatch also has a positive aspect in that, it may lead to gains. In addition, Mr. Koike has to let JOI know that to participate in the futures market, traders only need to deposit at the exchange a relatively small amount of cash to guarantee the transaction. This deposit is known as margin. It varies from trader to trader, but Mr. Koike has secured a $3,000 margin per contract.

The value of the margin may go up or down during the life of a futures contract, due to the gains or losses experienced by the contract in the market. The exchange does not let the value of the margin fall below 80% of its initial value. Consequently, if a trader experiences losses exceeding 20%, he has to replenish the margin in a period not to exceed 48 hours.

The management of JOI has asked Mr. Koike to provide an estimate of the number of contracts JOI has to purchase and an evaluation of potential gains and losses that JOI could experience if the predictions about upcoming spot and futures rates become a reality.

Mr. Koike has also explained to the Japanese management other peculiarities associated with the futures market. One of them is related to the managerial accounting of the futures transaction. In the specific case of the transaction with American Thermoplastics, the order was placed by JOI on March 17 in dollars. Therefore, the transaction measured in yen has to be recorded in the accounting system of JOI at the spot rate prevailing this date. At the settlement of the first transaction on May 16, the spot rate can be different. A discrepancy between the March and May spot rates generates an accounting foreign exchange rate or loss.

In the case of the futures transaction, there exists the possibility of foreign exchange rate gain or loss. For instance, on March 17, JOI pre sells yen. Once the transaction is settled in the spot market on May 1, JOI will not need to hold futures contracts any longer. Therefore, JOI has to close the futures position. To do so, it has to buy back yens on May 16. At this date, the futures rate may be different from the one existing on March 17 when the yen were pre sold. Just like the spot transaction, the discrepancy between March and May futures quotations may generate foreign exchange gains or losses. The information required by JOI to hedge the transaction using futures contracts is provided in Case A Table 10.1.

CASE PROBLEMS

1. How can JOI hedge the exchange rate risk using futures contracts?

2. Given the expectations about the spot rate in the future, indicate whether hedging is a good idea. To justify your answer, provide a detailed analysis of the potential gains and losses by JOI if it hedges the exposure with futures contracts.

3. Indicate whether JOI should incorporate expected futures losses in the price of the binders to the Japanese customers to cover for potential losses resulting from the hedge with futures. These expectations should be based on the assumption that the forthcoming spot and futures rates meet the exchange rate anticipations listed in the information provided.

4. Estimate the number of futures contracts that JOI needs to hedge the foreign exchange rate exposure. To determine the anticipated gains or losses JOI needs to estimate the gains and losses in the spot and futures markets at the settlement of the contracts, assuming that the anticipated spot and futures rates hold true.

Case A Table 10.1
Japanese Yen (CME), 12.5 million, $ per yen (.00)

	Open	High	Low	Settle	Lifetime High	Lifetime Low
Mar 00	0.7736	0.7768	0.7700	0.7734	0.9375	0.7512
June 00	0.7837	0.7870	0.7810	0.7832	0.9090	0.7637
Sept 00	0.7960	0.7960	0.7930	0.7931	0.8695	0.7735
Mar 01				0.8132	0.8315	0.8260

Expected Rates $/100yen	Spot	Futures Rates
17-Mar	0.7738	
16-May	0.7875	0.786
14-Aug	0.7838	0.79383
04-Dec	0.7939	0.7987

Case B: Digisolve, Risk Management in South Africa

Digisolve is a South African company established in 1993 by local entrepreneurs Ron Watson and Martie Bezuidenhout, with the purpose of supplying computer business solutions at competitive prices to business in South Africa. This was not an easy task, given the challenges posed by the macroeconomic and microeconomic environment of South Africa. These challenges included high trade barriers, extensive capital controls, a limited supply of well-trained technicians, a poor infrastructure, a low level of urbanization, and an expensive and cumbersome telecommunications industry.

In spite of these shortcomings, Digisolve soon achieved financial success. The founders of the company attribute the financial success enjoyed by Digisolve to its 24-hour service and support that the company provides to customers and the high quality of the products supplied. These products include brand names of global leaders such as Microsoft, Compaq, and Novell.

In 1996, Ron and Martie met with executives of South Africa Tourist Internet Solutions (SATIS), which is a local company established to provide the local hospitality industry with networking and system solutions, e-commerce consulting, messaging, and programming to seek an strategic alliance. After a brief evaluation of the strengths and weakness of the two companies, the presidents of both entities agreed to merge. Currently, the merger is operating as a single business unit under two different names. In addition to providing professional services related to computer and telecommunications industries, the merger expanded into the marketing and distribution of software and hardware in South Africa and some of the neighboring countries. This move helped to increase the business activity of the merger, which has experienced brisk growth due to the enormous and untapped economic potential of South Africa.

This country has a territory of 1,219,080 square kilometers (about 470,689 square miles), a population of 42.8 million, and a density of 35.1 persons per square kilometer. It is located on the southern tip of the African continent and is bordered by the Indian and Atlantic Oceans on the southern and western sides. Namibia is to the northwest, Botswana to the north, Zimbabwe to the northeast, and Mozambique to the east.

Pretoria is the capital of South Africa, which recognizes several official languages, including English, Afrikaans, Xhosa, Zulu, Sotho, and Venda.

In 1994, the country was divided into nine regions or provinces. Western Cape, Gauteng, KwaZulu-Natal, Eastern Cape, Northern Province, Northern Cape, Free State, North West Province, and Mpumalanga.

The initial purpose of this territorial breakdown was aimed at separating the different ethnic groups of South Africa. However, as time passed by, this territorial breakdown helped to create within the different regions a variety of living styles, job employment opportunities, and markets. In fact, South Africa is so diverse that has been labeled it the "rainbow nation" because of so many cultures in one country.

One of the living styles in South Africa, open to adventurous and well-fit individuals, is the opportunity of hiking the Garden Route which features some of most spectacular forest and mountainous trails in the world along the country's pristine coastline. Other alternatives are backpacking, cycling, and skiing on sunny alpine resorts.

For daring individuals willing to take chances, South Africa offers scuba diving, snorkeling, white-river rafting through the Cedarburg mountains, bridge bungi jumping, paragliding, and hang gliding over cliffs of more than 112 meters, and diving with white sharks in their natural habitat.

A more relaxed and family-oriented individual can visit the Wild Cheetah and Wildlife Center in the foothills of the Magaliesberg or the world-famous Kruger National Park which has a territory of more than 2 million hectares and was established in 1898 to protect local wildlife.[7] Other alternatives are a tour to the Kapama Private Game Reserve or the Leopard Lodge Game Farm and Function Venue.

For a person with a bent for culture, South Africa provides tours to museums and visits to the clinics of world-known witch doctors, traditional healers, and medicine makers, whose medical advice is often sought by Hollywood movie stars, politicians from all over the world, and the common layman of South Africa.

While Digisolve and SATIS have thrived, the country has not. Six years after the end of apartheid and the transfer of power from the white minority to a freely elected government, democracy remains strong, but the economy is not growing as fast as it was anticipated.

The lackluster pace of economic growth experienced by the country over a decade that has prevented South Africa from reaching higher levels of prosperity has several roots. One of them is the inability of the government to generate a strong level of confidence among foreign investors. Nelson Mandela and current president Thabo Mbeki worked hard to attract foreign direct investment. However, the surge of the AIDS epidemic in South Africa and political violence in neighboring Zimbabwe have greatly undermined these efforts.

These shortcomings have not impeded the expansion of computer and telecommunication industries in the country. To satisfy the brisk local demand for hardware and software, Digisolve negotiated in 1998 the right to market and distribute the company's and Microsoft's products in South Africa. The signing of this agreement committed Digisolve to import from Germany 22.5 million euros in computer-related products each year.

During the first three years of this agreement, the company was able to meet the sales target requested by Compaq. Analysis of the sales structures of Digisolve revealed that 65% of the German imports are sold at home in terms of rand, the local currency of South Africa, at a 30% profit margin net of local taxes. The remaining 35% are re-exported to neighboring African countries at the same profit margin. The bulk of imports from Germany are received at the beginning of each quarter, in batches of equal value. Each quarterly delivery is invoiced in euro and is payable in 90-days.

The re-exporting of German imports to other African countries occurs mostly through the Internet. These exports are delivered at the beginning of each quarter, invoiced in 90-day U.S. dollar accounts payable.

To export to other African countries, Digisolve requested the guarantee of an irrevocable letter of credit. SATIS also extended the use of its professional expertise to other African nations from which it imports services and equipment.

Currently, these imports stand at $3 million per year, distributed evenly each quarter.

While reviewing the situation of the company, Ron and Martie noticed volatility in currency markets, reflected in a depreciation of the rand, and rising oil prices had increased the risk of inflation. Mr. Mboweni was confident that Central Bank policies would help South Africa reach the anticipated inflation target of 3% to 6% at the end of the year 2002.

Just hours before the announcement made by Mr. Mboweni in Pretoria, Interntional Monetary Fund (IMF) official Michael Novak indicated to members of the South African parliament that the rand was undervalued and in the view of the IMF there was no need to raise interest rates to protect the rand.

Novak was emphatic, stating that the decline in the dollar price of the rand was temporary and that a rise in interest rates would only help to undermine the economic recovery of the country.

In spite of the assurance on the part of the central bank and the IMF, Ron and Martie became concerned about the short-term effects of a possible depreciation of the rand. These fears were heightened by a further review of the economic situation of South Africa, revealing that in the year 2000, the dollar price of a rand had fallen 17%. The South African currency was trading in the spot at Rnd7.46/$1.

While the dollar was trading in the spot at $0.8657/€1, the one-year interest rate in South Africa was at 10.1%. Anticipated spot rates were as follows:

December 1, 2001	$0.8398/€1
March 1, 2001	$0.8425/€1
June 1, 2001	$0.8449/€1
September 1, 2001	$0.8473/€1

The futures contract size for the euro and the rand in the Chicago Mercantile Exchange (CME) are 125,000 and 500,000 units, respectively.

After consulting with several organizations specializing in futures, the best Digisolve was been able to accomplish was to have some anticipation of the futures quotations for the first day of December 2000 and March 2001. These quotations stand at $0.8386/€ and $0.8410/€1. This lack of information stems from the great of deal of instability surrounding the European currency.

Regarding the rand, it is anticipated that the futures quotations for this currency in the CME, will be as follows:

December 1, 2000	$0.1311/Rnd1
March 1, 2001	$0.1292/Rnd1
June 1, 2001	$0.1283/Rnd1
September 1, 2001	$0.1268/Rnd1

Companies operating in emerging markets, like South Africa, normally cover exchange rate risk using a spot or money market hedge. In few instances, when forward contracts are available, companies can limit their risk exposure by buying or selling currencies in this market. The information required to hedge an international transaction in South Africa is provided in Case Tables 10.1 and

10.2. Case Table 10.3 provides a long-term perspective regarding the behavior of the South African currency in the foreign exchange market.

CASE PROBLEMS

1. Assess Digisolve's degree of transaction risk in terms of rands and dollars.

2. Propose methods to hedge the exchange rate risk in each case.

3. Investigate which hedging method is best for Digisolve. To respond to this question, you have to consider hedging with money market, forward, and futures contracts.

    Note: To estimate the degree of exposure in rands and dollars, Digisolve has to consider the value of imports from Germany, measured in euros, the rand value of sales in South Africa; and the dollar value of exports and imports from and to South Africa

Case B Table 10.1
Interest Rates, October 2000

Currency	Overnight	Seven-day	30-days	90-days	180-days	365-days
Euro	4.28	4.13	4.38	4.56	4.53	4.66
Pound	5.50	5.75	5.94	6.13	6.25	6.41
Swiss franc	2.75	3.06	3.16	3.38	3.69	3.91
US $	6.66	6.50	6.56	6.75	6.75	7.00
Yen	0.03	0.03	0.06	0.16	0.25	0.34
Singapore $	1.75	2.50	2.75	2.69	2.75	2.94

Case B Table 10.2
Currency Rates, 2000-2001

Euro	$/€	Futures	$/€	$/rand
Spot	0.8657			
90-days forward	0.8603	Dec-00	0.8564	0.1326
180-days forward	0.8635	Mar-01	0.8598	0.1314
365-days forward	0.8691	Jun-01	0.863	0.13
		Sep-01	0.8754	0.1286

NOTES

1. Paterson, Lea, "Thinkers fashion a cutting edge for theory." London, England: *The Times*, Saturday, March 2, 2002, p. 47.
2. Black, F., and Scholes, M. "The Pricing of Options and Other Corporate Liabilities." *Journal of Political Economy*, vol. 81, May-June 1973.
3. Bodie, Z., and Merton, R. Finance. Upper Saddle River, NJ: Prentice Hall, 200, p. 399.
4. Merton, Robert, "Theory of Rational Option Pricing." *Bell Journal of Management Science*, vol. 4, Spring 1973.

5. Kumade Project, "FX Options Pricing, (BSGK European)." http://www.kumade.com/. (Accessed April 19, 2002).

6. Bank of Montreal, Economic Research and Analysis, "Currency Spot and Forward Rates." http://www.bmo.com/economic/regular/fxrates.html. (Accessed April 19, 2002).

7. A hectare is a surface measuring 10,000 square meters or 111,089 square feet.

SUGGESTED ADDITIONAL READINGS

Bernstein, J. *How the Futures Markets Works.* 2nd ed. Englewood Cliffs, NJ: Prentice Hall, 2000. http://www.liffe.com/. (Accessed April 26, 2002).

Eiteman, D., et al. *Multinational Business Finance.* 9th ed. Reading, MA: Addison Wesley Longman, 2001. See Chapter 6.

Hull, J. *Introduction to Futures and Options Markets.* 3rd ed. Englewood Cliffs, NJ: Prentice Hall, 1998, http://www.liffe.com/. (Accessed April 24, 2002).

Hull, J. *Options Futures and Other Derivatives.* 4th ed. Englewood Cliffs, NJ: Prentice Hall, 1999. http://www.liffe.com/. (Accessed April 20, 2002).

Kline, D. *Fundamentals of the Futures Market.* New York, NY: McGraw Hill, 2000. http://www.liffe.com/. (Accessed November 11, 2002).

Lofton, J. *Getting Started with Futures.* 3rd ed. New York, NY: Wiley & Sons, 1997. http://www.liffe.com/. (Accessed April 20, 2002).

Nasdaq. "Understanding Options." http://options.nasdaq.com/asp/option_info.asp. (Accessed April 26, 2002).

11

Managing Economic Risk

In the year 2000, a retailing company based in Phoenix, Arizona, was assessing whether to expand into northern Mexico. The initial version of the expansion project considered opening stores in major urban centers located within 500 miles of the Arizona-Sonora border. To assess a preliminary version of the business plan, the Chief Financial Officer of company had to overcome the roadblock of how to deal with exchange rate exposure in the long run.

The event previously described suggests that multinational corporations considering a global project will expect some type of exchange rate risk. Since the fulfillment of these expectations is not certain, companies are always exposed to an exchange rate risk known as *economic exposure*.

This risk permeates the various activities of a multinational. Therefore, its prevention should concern all key decision makers. They should work together to develop marketing and production initiatives directed to maintain the profitability of a firm and its subsidiaries in the long run.

The aim of this chapter is to provide an explanation of what constitutes economic risk. It will also introduce the finance tools required to manage this risk. To meet the proposed goals, this chapter:

- Describes the different variations of economic exposure.
- Discusses the different strategies available to deal with economic exposure.
- Analyzes the short, medium, and long-term consequences of exchange rate trends on the value of a firm.
- Suggests preventive measures that can help multinationals cope with economic risk.

MANAGING ECONOMIC EXPOSURE

Economic exposure to exchange rate risk refers to the effect of unexpected changes in the exchange rate on the dollar value of cash flows generated by overseas business ventures. Unexpected variations in the exchange rate modify the dollar value of: foreign currency cash flows and equity. In the first case, economic exposure is labeled *operating cash flow exposure*. In the second instance, it is referred to as *equity exposure*.

An example of operating cash flow exposure is provided by the increase in the dollar cash flows reported by the Mexican subsidiaries of GM, Ford, and Chrysler after the unexpected and large peso devaluation in December of 1994. The cash flow gains were traced back to the decline in the dollar value of operating assembly plants in Mexico. They were also related to the increase in the volume of car and truck exports from the subsidiaries of the U.S. automakers to the United States.

Another example of operating cash flow exposure is provided by the effect of the continuous appreciation of the Taiwanese dollar observed in the 1980s and 1990s on operating cost and revenues of manufacturing plants located within Taiwan. Operating costs, while steady in local terms, rose in dollar value. Operating revenues, in turn, fell as a result of the higher prices exhibited by the products of Taiwan in world markets due to the continuous appreciation of the local currency.

An instance of exchange rate equity exposure is illustrated by the experience of the McDonald's in Asia. After the massive devaluation of several of the Asian currencies in 1997, the revenues generated by the U.S. corporation in the Far East, while steady in term of Asian currencies, declined substantially in dollar value, prompting a reassessment of McDonald's stock on Wall Street.

MANAGING OPERATING CASH FLOW EXPOSURE

To provide an explanation of what constitutes operating exposure and how to· measure it, consider the case of a U.S. multinational having a Swiss subsidiary. The European company manufactures and distributes its output in Switzerland. Consequently, it generates cash flows in Swiss francs. The U.S. owners of the Swiss subsidiary prefer dollar cash flows to Swiss francs cash flows. For instance, if the Swiss franc cash flows are Swf2, 000,000 per year and the expected exchange rate is $0.4/Swf1, the anticipated dollar cash flow of the Swiss subsidiary is $800,000. However, if the exchange rate deviates form its forecasted value and happens to be $0.35/Swf1, the dollar value of the Swiss franc cash flows will decline to $700,000.

Anticipated cash flows = Swiss franc cash flow × the anticipated spot rate
= Swf2,000,000 × ($0.4/Swf1)
= Swf2,000,000/Swf1) × $0.4
= 2,000,000 × $0.4
= $800,000

Actual cash flow = Swiss franc cash flow × the actual spot rate
= SwF2,000,000 × ($0.35/Swf1)
= Swf2,000,000/Swf1) × $0.35

= 2,000,000 × $0.35
= $700,000

The exchange rate deviation from its anticipated value could be deemed by the management of the U.S. multinational either as permanent or temporary, and will adjust to the new expectations. If managers consider that the change in the exchange rate is permanent, they will change their expectations about the cash flows. If the variation is regarded to be passing, then dollar cash flow expectations will not change.

MEASURING CASH FLOW EXPOSURE

Operating cash flows consist of revenues minus operating costs. The statement of a cash flow shows all the cash that flows into and out of the firm during a period of time. It differs from the income statement, which shows only revenue and expenses.

The cash flow statement focus on what is happening to the firm's cash flow position over time, because even very profitable firms are exposed to financial distress if they run out of cash. Paying attention to the cash flow statement allows the management of a firm and the investors interested in purchasing stock of a firm, the ability to judge whether a corporation is building up or drawing down its cash. In addition, cash flow analysis will let them understand the reasons behind cash flow outcomes.

To provide an example of operating cash flow, consider the information presented in Table 11.1 for the subsidiary of a U.S. corporation operating in Chile. In this presentation the total cash flow, or change in cash and marketable securities, is the result of three activities: operating the manufacturing facilities, investing in the business, and financing the activities of the corporation

The cash flow from operating activities consists of cash flows generated by the sale of the company's products in Chile, less the cash outflows for expenses such as materials and labor. The net result of is a cash inflow amounting to $26 million. The cash flow from the investing activity is a $90 million cash outlay applied to fund investment in new plant and equipment.

The cash flow from financing activities includes an outflow to pay dividends and an inflow resulting from the acquisition of new debt. The net outcome is an inflow of $84 million generated, mostly, by short-term borrowing.

The net impact of the three activities is a net inflow of $20 million. This is generated when the exchange rate is at $0.001487/ChP$1. At this rate, the total cash flows generated by the subsidiary in Chile is ChP$13,449.9.

However, the focus of operating exposure is not on the total cash flows but rather on operating income, which happens to be $26 million or ChP$17,484.87.

The operating cash flow exposure of a subsidiary is the *percentage response of dollar operating cash flows to a 1% change in the dollar value of a foreign currency.* This relationship is also known as the *exchange rate elasticity of cash flows* (ε), which can be expressed as follows:

(11.1) $\quad \varepsilon = [(CF_1/CF_0) - 1] \times 100/ [(E_1/E_0) - 1] \times 100$

Table 11.1
Cash Flows, Chilean Subsidiary of a U.S. Corporation

Cash Flow from Operating Activities	Dollars	Chilean Pesos
Net income (price times quantity of units sold)	$24	16,139.88
plus depreciation	$30	20,174.85
less increase in accounts payable	$10	6,724.95
less increase in inventories	$30	20,174.85
plus increase in accounts receivable	$12	8,069.94
Total cash flow from operation	**$26**	**17,484.87**
Cash flow from investing activities		
less investment in plant and equipment	**$90**	**60,524.55**
Cash flow from financing activities		
less dividends paid	$10	6,724.95
plus increase in short term debt	$94	63,214.53
Total cash flow from financing activities	**$84**	**56,489.58**
Change in cash and marketable securities	**$20**	**13,449.90**

ε is the elasticity response of dollar cash flows to a 1% change in the exchange rate, CF is the expected dollar value of the cash flows in period t, and E is the expected dollar value of one unit of foreign exchange in period t.

To provide an illustration of how to estimate the exchange rate elasticity of cash flows, assume that the European subsidiary of a U.S. multinational is having a $100 cash flow when the exchange rate is $0.8/€1. An anticipated appreciation of the dollar to $0.76/€1 will lower the expected dollar value of the cash flows to $92.

If the expectations are fulfilled the value of the elasticity is 1.6. This means that an anticipated dollar appreciation of 1% will lower the dollar value of European cash flows by 1.6%.

Exchange rate elasticity of cash flows (ε) = % change in cash flows/% change in the exchange rate

$\varepsilon = \{[(\$92/\$100) - 1] \times 100\} / \{[(0.76/0.8) - 1] \times 100\}$
$= (-8\% / -5\%)$
$= 1.6\%/1\%$
$= 1.6$

Solving Equation 11.1 for the dollar value of the cash flow in period one (CF_1), the following equation is obtained:

(11.2) $CF_1 = [(CF_0) \times \{1 + \varepsilon \times [(E_1/E_0) - 1]\}$

Equation 11.2 implies that the adjusted dollar value of operating cash flow (CF_1) is equal to the original dollar cash flow (CF_0) times one plus the elasticity (ε) times the percentage change (in a decimal format) in the dollar value of one unit of foreign exchange $[(E_1/E_0) - 1]\}$.

To provide an illustration of how to apply Equation 11.2, consider the previous information given on the European subsidiary.

$CF_1 = [\$100 \times \{1 + 1.6 \times [(0.76/0.8) - 1]\}$
$= \$100 \times (1 + 1.6 \times -0.05)$
$= \$100 \times (1 - 0.8)$
$= \$100 \times 0.92$
$= \$92$

This result indicates that the U.S. manager is anticipating a cash flow of \$92 with the dollar appreciating from \$0.8/€1 to \$0.76/€1.

THE EXCHANGE RATE ELASTICITY

From the previous example it is possible to conclude that the numerical value of the elasticity (ε) may be positive or negative, and it may be greater than one, or less than one. If the value of (ε) is positive and greater than one, let us say 1.6, the anticipation of a 1% dollar appreciation will lower the expected dollar value of the foreign subsidiary's cash flows by 1.6%. Similarly, a forecasted depreciation of the U.S. currency by 1% will increase the dollar value of operating cash flows by 1.6%. If the value of the elasticity (ε) is negative, it will lead to opposite results.

FACTORS DETERMINING OPERATING EXPOSURE

The experience with exchange rate changes indicates that operating cash flows are uncertain and that this uncertainty is a function of at least three factors: 1) the capability of a firm to adjust prices when there is a change in the exchange rate, 2) the response of demand to changes in the exchange rate; and 3) the response of demand to shifts in the competitive position of a firm, occurring as a result of an unexpected variation in the dollar value of the home currency.

CONVERSION EXPOSURE

The uncertainty surrounding the dollar equivalent of a given stream of foreign currency cash flows, known as *conversion exposure,* can be exemplified by the case of U.S. multinationals owning subsidiaries in Argentina. Given the monetary turmoil of this country, U.S. companies are not certain about the dollar value of the cash flows that will be generated by their subsidiaries in the South American nation.

Pure conversion exposure is very rare, because it is assumed that the only factor affecting the foreign cash flows is the variation in the exchange rate. This implies that a change in the exchange rate does not affect the price and volume of sales of local firms. But this is not always the case. In fact, local firms usually adjust their local prices in response to changes in the exchange rate, and consumers respond to the variation in local prices by changing their pattern of consumption.

PRICE EXPOSURE

The ability of a firm to adjust prices after an unexpected change in the exchange rate is known as *price exposure*. It is characterized by the difficulties faced by a banana farm in Venezuela to raise the price of the commodity in lieu of a devaluation of the local currency. By contrast, a distributor of luxury cars in the same country will not have problems raising the price of the vehicles after a devaluation of the Bolivar, the currency of Venezuela. To design appropriate pricing policies in this context, a firm has to have information detailing prices, sales, and exchange rate trends to estimate the various elasticities required to judge the effect of a change in the exchange rate on operating income. If the local currency is devaluated and the firm knows that the absolute value of the price elasticity of exports is higher than one, let us say 2, the appropriate pricing policy is to maintain the existing price structure.

Price elasticity of exports = % change in the quantity of exports/% change in the exchange rate

$$= [(Q_{x1}/Q_{x0}) - 1]/[(E_1/E_0) - 1] = 2\%/1\%$$

This approach will lead to higher revenues since the increase in the volume of exports (2%) will more than offset the loss in the dollar value of export revenues prompted by the devaluation of the local currency (1%). Lowering the local price is also a sound policy. This pricing strategy generates even higher revenue than steady pricing. However, the strategy of lowering prices is not always recommended because it invites price retaliation in domestic and foreign markets that could lead to cutthroat competition.

If the absolute value of price elasticity is less than one, it means that the output of the firm is price inelastic. That is, an increase in the local price will not deter consumers from buying the output of a firm. In this case, the best pricing policy given a depreciation of the local currency is to raise prices. The rationale for this suggestion rests on the fact that a price increase will result in a less than proportional decline in volume of sales. Therefore, revenue after the devaluation will remain steady or will increase.

DEMAND EXPOSURE

The response of demand to a change in the exchange rate labeled as *demand exposure* is typified best by the observed increase in the volume of exports of a country when the home currency depreciates. Sales are a function of price and income. Price, in turn, is a function of changes in the exchange rate. For example, devaluations lower the foreign currency price of home output. As a consequence of this change, the volume of sales of local firms in world markets will increase. The degree of sales improvement in foreign markets will depend on the numerical value of the price elasticity of exports.

COMPETITIVE EXPOSURE

The shift in competitive position experienced by local firms when the local currency depreciates is referred to as *competitive exposure*. For example, it has been observed that the foreign demand for the services provided by assembly plants in Central America, increases when local currencies depreciate.

It also refers to the long-term effect of a steady appreciation of the home currency on a firm's revenue and operating income. Normally, steady appreciations of a local currency result in lower revenue and operating income.

To explain this concept, consider the case of AT&T's operations in Singapore in the 1980s. The currency of this country, the Singaporean dollar, appreciated steadily against the U.S. dollar. The appreciation of the local currency contributed to increase the standard of living of Singapore. As a result, local sales of AT&T products in the local market increased in volume. This change brought an increase in revenues and operating income measured both in terms of local currency and U.S. dollars.

The success enjoyed by AT&T in Singapore attracted the attention of its competitors and more companies entered into Singapore. The additional competition brought a lower market share and lower sales volume for each competitor in Singapore. Eventually, increased competition led to price declines, which may further eroded the dollar value of AT&T and other companies operating in Singapore.

THE DETERMINANTS OF OPERATING COST EXPOSURE

Operating expenses normally include expenditures on local and foreign inputs and raw materials. As such, a variation in the exchange rate affects the cost incurred by a firm when it uses inputs or raw materials of external origin.[1]

Unlike domestic input, the price of the foreign raw materials, parts, and labor, used to manufacture locally rises immediately with a depreciation of the local currency. This change increases the cost of operating expenses, which in turn, lowers the local value of operating income. The total effect of depreciation on operating expenses depends, ultimately, on the proportion of local and foreign input content and the flexibility of a firm to adjust the input mix.

Devaluations have also indirect effects on operating expenses. They increase the volume of exports. This in turn makes firms increase inventories and expand the value of accounts receivable in order to meet the excess demand for exports generated by the devaluation. To fund these two items the firm has to incur in additional overhead expenses and working capital expenditures.

CONTROLLING OPERATING EXPOSURE

The effects of a change in the exchange rate on operating income indicates that sustained exchange rate trends can have a meaningful impact on pricing policies, corporate revenues, and operating expenses.

Price changes brought about by exchange rate changes alter the competitive position of a firm at home and abroad. To respond to these changes management has to adjust the production processes or the marketing mix to accommodate the structure of the firm to the new set of relative prices. By carrying on with the necessary marketing and production adjustments, multinationals can either counteract the harmful effect of a variation in the exchange rate or capitalize on the opportunities presented by a change in the value of a currency.

To implement the appropriate production and marketing policies, management has to understand the distinction between nominal and real exchange rates. This is important because this distinction has serious implications on the firm's decision on exchange rate risk. Nominal currency changes that are fully offset by inflation differentials do not constitute a real change in the exchange rate. Therefore, they do not change the relative price mix. In contrast, a real exchange rate entails a material degree of exchange rate risk because it affects the competitive position of local firms and their foreign competitors.

To prepare for anticipated or actual exchange rate changes, a firm can pursue various actions related to marketing, promotion, product selection, and pricing strategies. To implement these strategies, firms have to consider the length of time that real change is expected to persist. For example if a temporary appreciation shortens an exporting firm's market, then the best strategy is to maintain foreign currency prices at existing levels.

To implement the most convenient marketing and production strategies, exporting firms may want to keep in mind several of the following factors:

- The diversity of the firm's markets
- The price elasticity of the company's imports and exports
- The degree of competition at home and abroad
- The cost structure of the company

MANAGING EQUITY EXPOSURE

Equity risk is measured as the percentage response in the dollar value of equity to a 1% change in the dollar value of a foreign currency. This relationship is presented in Equation (11.3).

Exchange rate elasticity of equity $\varepsilon(e)$ = % change in the value of equity/% change in the exchange rate

(11.3) $\varepsilon(e) = \{(\text{equity}_1/\text{equity}_0) - 1] \times 100\}/\{[(E_1/E_0) - 1] \times 100\}$

where $\varepsilon(e)$ is the elasticity response of dollar equity value to a one percentage change in the exchange rate. Equity is the expected dollar value of the stock price of a company in period t. E is the dollar value of one unit of foreign exchange in period t.

Solving Equation (11.3) for the dollar value of equity in period one (equity$_1$), the following equation is obtained:

(11.4) $\text{Equity}_1 = \text{equity}_0 \times \{1 + \varepsilon(e) \times [(E_1/E_0) - 1]\}$

Equation (11.4) expresses the new value of equity that is anticipated given the new exchange rate.

To provide an example of how to apply Equation 11.4, consider the case of a U.S. multinational owning a German subsidiary worth $200 million when the exchange rate is $0.9/€1, and the value of the exchange rate elasticity of equity is 2. If the dollar appreciates permanently to $0.86/€1, the dollar equity value of the German will decline to $182.22 million.

$Equity_1 = equity_0 \times \{1 + \epsilon(e) \times [(E_1/E_0) - 1]\}$
$= \$200 \times \{1 + 2 \times [\$0.86/\$0.9 - 1]\}$
$= \$200 \times [1 + 2 \times (- 0.04444)]$
$= \$200 \times (1 - 0.0888)$
$= \$200 \times (0.91)$
$= \$182$

ECONOMIC EXPOSURE: THE CASE OF MEYER TOOLS INC.

To provide a comprehensive example covering in detail many of the relevant aspects of economic exposure, consider the case of the U.S. company Meyer Tools, which wants to diversify its investment portfolio and is planning to acquire the Spanish firm Herramientas Castellanas.

The current financial situation of the Spanish firm is described in Table 11.2. It presents the balance sheet for years 2000 and 2001, the income statement for year 2001, and the statement of cash flow for 2001. All the initial information is stated in terms of euros.

Herramientas Castellanas manufactures in Spain using 50% of materials and labor from Spain. The other 50% is largely composed of U.S. imports. The tools produced by this company are mostly sold within the European Union (80%) and invoiced in euro. The remaining 20% is exported to the United States and invoiced in dollars. Currently, the spot rate is $0.86/€1, but some believe that the real exchange rate will adjust permanently to $0.91/€1. Herramientas Castellanas estimates that the exchange rate elasticity of exports and imports is 1.8. Given this scenario, Meyer Tools wants to investigate the impact of a dollar depreciation on operating cash flows and the value of the Spanish firm.

Table 11.2
Herramientas Castellanas, Balance Sheet, 2000 and 2001

ASSETS (€ million)	2001	2001	Change
Cash	100	120	20
Accounts receivable	80	90	10
Inventory	120	130	10
Total current assets	*300*	*340*	*40*
Plant & equipment	400	500	100
Accumulated depreciation	100	120	20
Net plant & equipment	*300*	*380*	*80*
Total assets	600	720	120
Other information			
Paid in capital	200	200	0
Retained earnings	100	110	10
Price per share (euro)	200	210.6	10.6
LIABILITIES(€ million)	**2000**	**2001**	**Change**
Accounts payable	60	70	10
Short-term debt	*90*	*190*	*100*
Total current liabilities	*150*	*260*	*110*
Long-term debt	150	150	0
Stockholder's equity	*300*	*310*	*10*
Total liabilities	*600*	*720*	*120*

Table 11.3
Herramientas Castellanas, Cash Flows, 2001

Income Statement (€ million)	
Sales (20% exports + 80% domestic)	200
Less cost of goods sold (domestic)	55
less cost of goods sold (foreign)	55
Gross margin	90
Less general selling and administrative expenses	30
Operating income	*60*
Less interest expense	20
Taxable income	40
Income tax @ .28	10
Net income	*30*
Earnings (euro) per share, one million shares	24
Dividends	20

Cash Flow Statement	
Cash flow from operating activities	
Net income	30
plus depreciation	20
less increase in accounts payable	10
less increase in inventories	10
plus increase in accounts receivable	10
Total cash flow from operation	**40**
Cash flow from investing activities	
less investment in plant and equipment	-100
Cash flow from financing activities	
less dividends paid	20
plus increase in short term debt	100
Total cash flow from financing activities	**80**
Change in cash	**20**

DOLLAR DEPRECIATION AND THE INCOME STATEMENT

The simulation on the possible effect of a dollar depreciation from $0.86/€1 to $0.91/€1 is presented in Tables 11.4 and 11.5. The first one shows the effect of dollar depreciation on the income statement. The second table shows the effect of the dollar depreciation on the cash flow statement.

Line 1 of Table 11.4 shows the sales of the Spanish company in the year 2001 (€200 million). Also presented in column A1 (alternative 1) is the dollar value of sales for the same year at the existing exchange rate of $0.86/€1 ($172 million). The last column A2 (alternative 2) displays the anticipated dollar value of sales at the new exchange rate of $0.91/€1, amounting to $176.4. This information indicates that the dollar value of sales will improve, with the dollar depreciation, from $172 million to $176.4 million.

Sales (A1) = € sales × exchange rate
= €200 × ($0.86/€1)
= (€200/€1) × $0.86
= 200 × $0.86
= $172

Table 11.4
Herramientas Castellanas, Income Statement, 2001

Income Statement ($ million)				
		2001	**A-1**	**A-2**
1	Sales (20% exports + 80% domestic)	€200	$172.0	$176.4
2	Less domestic cost of goods sold	€55	$47.3	$50.1
3	Less foreign cost of goods sold	€55	$47.3	$42.4
4	Gross margin	€90	$77.4	$84.0
5	Less selling & admin expenses	€30	$25.8	$27.30
6	*Operating income*	*€60*	*$51.6*	*$56.7*
7	Less interest expense	€20	$17.2	$18.2
8	Taxable income	€40	$34.4	$38.5
9	Income tax @ 28%	€10	$8.6	$9.1
10	*Net income*	*€30*	*$25.8*	*$29.4*
	Earnings per share (one million shares)	€24	$25.8	$29.4
	Dividends	€20	$17.2	$18.2

Sales (A2) = domestic sales + exports
Domestic sales = (80% × €200) × ($0.91/€1)
= (€160/€1) × $0.91
= 160 × $0.91
= $145.6

$\text{Exports}_1 = \text{exports}_0 \times \{1 - \varepsilon(\text{exports}) \times [(E_1/E_0) - 1]\}$
= (0.2 ×$172) × {1 − 1.8 × [0.91/0.86 − 1]}
= $34.4 × {1 − (1.8 × 0.0581)}
= $34.4 × (1 − 0.1046)
= $34.4 × 0.8954
= $30.8

Therefore,
Sales (A2) = domestic sales + exports
= $145.6 + $30.8
= $176.4

Line 2 of Table 11.4 shows the cost of raw materials and inputs produced in Spain in terms of euros (€55), the dollar cost given the rate of $0.86/€1 ($47.3), and the cost in dollar terms at the anticipated exchange rate of $0.91/€1 ($50.1).

Dollar cost of local inputs (A1) = value (€) × the spot rate
= €55 × $0.86/€1
= €55/€1 × $0.86
= 55 × $0.86
= $47.3

Dollar cost of domestic inputs (A2) = €55 × $0.91/€1
= €55/€1 × $0.91
= 55 × $0.91
= $50.1

Line 3 of Table 11.4 presents the cost of raw materials of external origin in terms of the European currency (€55), the dollar cost at the rate of $0.86/€1 ($47.3) and the dollar cost at the anticipated dollar rate of $0.91/€1 ($42.4).

Dollar cost of foreign inputs (A1) = € value × the spot rate

= (€55) × ($0.86/€1)

= (€55/€1) × $0.86

= 55 × $0.86

= $47.3

Dollar cost of foreign inputs (A2) = cost of imports

Cost of imports$_1$ = imports$_0$ × {1 − ε(imports) × [(E$_1$/E$_0$) − 1]}

= $47.3 ×) {1 − 1.8 × [0.91/0.86 − 1]}

= $47.3 × {1 − (1.8 × 0.0581)

= $47.3 × (1 − 0.1046)

= $47.3 × 0.8954

= $42.4

Line 6 of Table 11.4 describes operating income in terms of the European currency (€60), at the rate of $0.86/€1 ($51.6) and at the anticipated rate of $0.91/€1 ($56.7). The comparison of these results points to an improvement in the financial performance of the Spanish company under the expected exchange rate.

Line 10 of Table 11.4 presents net income in European terms (€30), at the spot rate of $0.86/€1 ($25.8), and at the anticipated rate of $0.91/€1 ($29.4). These results also point to an improvement in the performance of the Spanish company under the anticipated change in the exchange rate.

DOLLAR DEPRECIATION AND CASH FLOWS

Line 11 of Table 11.5 only repeats the information provided in the income statement.

Line 12 of Table 11.5 presents information included in the balance sheet. The addition of lines 11 and 12 provide an estimate the narrowest concept of operating income, often used by multinationals as the *true* cash flow from operation. In terms of European currency, this is equal to €50.

The dollar value of this operating cash flow, estimated at $0.86//€1 is equal to $43. At the anticipated rate of $0.91/€1, the dollar value of the cash flow is equal to $47.6. The comparison of the two results indicates that the company will be better off, if the new exchange rate sets in.

Line 16 of Table 11.5 provides the dollar value of operating cash flows, as the accounting profession evaluates them. The information provided by this approach reinforces the perception that the Spanish company will be better off under the anticipated exchange rate, given that the dollar cash flows raise from $34.4 to $38.5 million.

PRESENT VALUE OF CASH FLOWS

The last step to be taken to judge the impact of the anticipated change in the exchange rate on the value of the Spanish corporation is to investigate the impact of this change on the present value of operating cash flows.

Table 11.5
Herramientas Castellanas, Cash Flow Statement, 2001

Cash Flow Statement			
Cash flow from operating activities	**2001**	**A-1**	**A-2**
11 Net income	€30	$25.8	$29.4
12 plus depreciation	€20	$17.2	$18.2
13 less increase in accounts payable	€10	$8.6	$9.1
14 less increase in inventories	€10	$8.6	$9.1
15 plus increase in accounts receivable	€10	$8.6	$9.1
16 Total cash flow from operation	**€40**	**$34.4**	**$38.5**
17 Cash flow from investing activities			
18 less investment in plant and equipment	-€100	-$86.0	-$91.0
19 Cash flow from financing activities			
20 less dividends paid	€20	$17.2	$18.2
21 plus increase in short term debt	€100	$86.0	$91.0
22 Total cash flow from financing activities	**€80**	**$68.8**	**$72.8**
23 Change in cash Flow	€20	$17.2	$20.3

To complete this step, it is assumed that the change in the exchange rate occurs a year from now, that the change lasts four years, and that the appropriate rate to discount the project is 6% per year The anticipated dollar devaluation will be reflected in an increase in operating cash flows, measured as net income plus depreciation, equivalent to roughly $5 million per year.

This information, presented in Table 11.6, indicates that the present value of the Spanish corporation under the current spot rate of $0.86/€1 is equivalent to $181.13 million. Under a rate of $0.91//€1, the present value of cash flows is anticipated to increase to $198.6 million. Therefore, if Meyer purchases the Spanish company, and if the change in the exchange rate takes place as it is expected, then Meyer will obtain a capital gain of $17.47 million.

Table 11.6
Herramientas Castellanas, Present Value of Cash Flows

Period	Current cash flow ($0.86/€1)	PV of cash flow	Anticipated cash flow ($0.91/€1)	PV of cash flow	Difference
0		$181.13		$198.60	$17.47
1	43	$40.57	43	$43.00	
2	43	$38.27	48	$42.36	
3	43	$36.10	48	$39.97	
4	43	$34.06	48	$37.70	
5	43	$32.13	48	$35.57	

MARKETING MANAGEMENT OF EXCHANGE RATE RISK

Currently, Herramientas Castellanas is well positioned since it is producing within the European Union and is able to compete both in the United States and Europe. However, while the financial analysis points out to the fact that Herramientas Castellanas will be better off under the anticipated exchange rate, the management of the firm needs to be aware of some of challenges that the company will have to meet to preserve the anticipated gains. First, the management of the European company has to remember that from the perspective of foreign companies, especially U.S. multinationals, a strong euro is a golden opportunity to gain market share in Europe at the expense of local rivals. They also have to consider that Japanese companies can also use their dollar cost advantage to carve out market share against European competitors in markets outside Europe and the United States.

PRICING STRATEGIES

The information provided indicates that the products sold and the inputs purchased by the Spanish company are elastic since all the elasticity value is higher than one. Given these facts, the Spanish company will be faced with some tough choices. Does it maintain the same price to preserve the anticipated gain in its profit margin at the risk of losing market share? Or does it lower prices to preserve market share while losing the profit margin edge?

The answers to these difficult questions are not simple, since they are the subject matter of empirical testing and mathematical simulation. In principle, prices should be lowered only if the price change increases the net present value of cash flows. Otherwise, the price change should not be implemented. Similarly, policies geared to maintaining or increasing market share only makes sense when they improve the NPV of cash flows. This is the only way to improve shareholder's wealth. Optimization of cash flows happens when firms follow the standard economic proposition of setting the price that maximizes profits, by equating marginal revenue with marginal cost.

Some managers operating in countries experiencing a strong currency are often tempted to exercise international price discrimination. The managers of Herramientas Castellanas may be tempted to implement this strategy. However, they should consider the danger associated with this strategy. This strategy is illegal and invites retaliation. Therefore, a pricing policy of this nature should be avoided.

PROMOTIONAL STRATEGY

Given that a strong euro will help to attract more competition into Europe, then the management of Meyer should plan the implementation of measures that can help to preempt future competition. An obvious and wise action is to increase the marketing budget in areas designed to promote the company's products in key European countries and in the United States. In addition, they need to hire a pool of specialized sales personnel well trained in international trade.

PRODUCT STRATEGY

Under the competitive strain of a currency appreciation, local companies may also want to upgrade their research budget to identify weak and cost ineffective products and to design cost competitive brands featuring new and more attractive quality features. In the process of eliminating and introducing goods, a company should always keep in mind the useful principle of equating marginal cost with marginal revenue. This will help to keep managers abreast of what products to eliminate and how much to offer of each one.

INPUT MIX

Herramientas Castellanas is currently importing raw materials and parts from the United States. Therefore, a depreciation of the dollar will help the company to remain cost competitive. To reinforce this advantage, the company should consider a critical review of its input mix and consider increasing the proportion of U.S. inputs in the manufacturing process, if this is technically possible. The Spanish company should also consider a more aggressive sourcing policy where entire manufacturing process could be turned to more cost competitive foreign suppliers. In addition, the firm should consider the redesign of their manufacturing processes to introduce innovations that can create more cost competitive entities. Additionally, Meyer Tools should consider training programs designed to increase local labor productivity, given that the international cost of domestic labor will increase with the appreciation of the euro.

SUMMARY

Strong temporary changes in the exchange rate or permanent changes in real exchange rates create a risk known as economic risk. This risk affects all the different aspects of running a multinational corporation. Therefore, managing economic risk should be the responsibility of all important policymakers, especially those involved in global finance and in operation.

Exchange rate risk may take the form of an appreciation or a depreciation of the home currency. An appreciation leads to short-run and medium-term gains in operating cash flows. However, in the long run, it attracts more diversified and cost competitive rivals. To prevent and preempt this competition, local firms have to establish coordinated programs involving the different aspects of management to develop and run an effective foreign currency exposure program.

Within the context of this program, the financial manager should be responsible for providing accurate assessments of the impact of currency risk on the different items of the balance sheet, the income statement, and operating cash flows.

Based on the financial information, the marketing managers should provide effective and well-structured programs aimed at increasing the promotion of crucial products in key local markets. In addition, they should spend time reviewing the product mix in order to eliminate weak and cost ineffective products and to introduce more cost effective products displaying more advanced quality features.

Personnel and operation managers should devise programs directed at enhancing the input mix, improving the productivity of local labor, and improving sourcing in order to change the entire manufacturing processes to more cost effective foreign suppliers.

In the case of currency devaluation, the responsibility of the financial managers remains unchanged. However, marketing managers should focus on designing appropriate export entry strategies and hiring the personnel skilled in the introduction and promotion of products in foreign markets.

PROBLEMS

1. Over the past six months Hair Inc., had sales of 5,000 bottles of shampoo for normal hair per week in Argentina. After the dollar appreciation against the Argentinean peso the local price of shampoo rose from AP\$8 to AP\$10, sales in the shampoo in the South American country declined to 3,000 bottles.

   a.   What is the exchange rate elasticity of demand for Hair Inc. shampoo?

2. Exports of patio and lawn furniture from the United to Europe has been estimated using a sample of 36 observations as follows:

   Demand $= 8.25 + 1.25_t - 2.75D1_t + D2_t + 3.5D3_t + 1.5E_t$
   t = time period (quarter)
   $D_{1t} = 1$ for first quarter of observation
   $\quad$ 0 otherwise
   $D_{2t} = 1$ for second quarter observation
   $\quad$ 0 otherwise
   $D_{3t} = 1$ for second quarter observation
   $\quad$ 0 otherwise
   E = anticipated \$/€1spot rate
   E_1 (first quarter) = \$0.913/€1
   E_2 (second quarter) = \$0.911/€1
   E_3 (third quarter) = \$0.909/€1
   E_4 (fourth quarter) = \$0.901/€1

   a.   Using the previous information forecast exports of patio and lawn furniture for each one of the fourth quarters of the year 2003.

3. German Airlines manufactures small pleasure use aircraft, most of which are for exports to the Unites States. Based on past experience, exports appear to be a function of the price of the airplanes and the exchange rate. Based on the information provided:

a. Estimate the U.S. price elasticity of demand using 2001, 2002, and 2003 data.

b. Forecast exports assuming that the exchange rate will remain constant but the local price of exports measured in euros will increase by $500 from the 2003 level.

Year	Exports	Euro price	Exchange rate
2001	525	€ 7,200	$0.94/€1
2002	450	€ 8,000	$0.91/€1
2003	400	€ 8,000	$0.98/€1

Case: Giant Manufacturing and Economic Risk

Taiwan is an island located between Japan and the Philippines and was established as a nation independent of China in 1949. The economy of this relatively young nation is deeply rooted in market principles. Nonetheless, the government plays a major role in its developing and planning. For very long, political conflicts between China and Taiwan kept both nations isolated from each other. However, after the passing away of the Cold War leaders, the international relationship between the two nations has improved tremendously. So much, that 1977, Taiwan became one of the most important investors in the People's Republic.

The Island has a very limited endowment of natural resources. To prosper and grow, it had to join the rest of the world to access other nations' factors of production. To promote the global integration of Taiwan, the government created one of the most sophisticated communications networks in Asia, and Taiwan, in this activity, is only second to Japan in the region. To pay for the imports of raw materials, the local industry was forced from the beginning to become export oriented. However, subsequent increases in labor cost led to a restructuring of the economy from a labor-intensive to a capital-intensive manufacturing base. This industrial transformation, however, did not change the exporting spirit of the local firms. One of the areas where Taiwan has excelled in exporting is the bicycle industry. At the beginning of the 1980s, some American companies wanted to buy bicycles from Japan, but the Japanese industry was not interested and let go, what would turn out to be an extremely profitable activity. When the market peaked in the mid 1980s more than 60 companies were assembling bicycles for exports. In 1991, the industry reached a milestone when Taiwan became the largest exporter of bicycles, and the value of export exceeded, by the first time in the history of the industry, a \$1 billion benchmark.[2] Most of these exports were manufactured in the Taichung region which is the world leader in the production of bicycles since it accounts for 90% of the national production of bicycles, and 80% of the manufacturing of related parts.

The domestic market for bicycles is very small and amounts to 700,000 units per year. The key markets are located in the United States, the European Union, and Japan, and the two leading manufacturing companies are Giant and Merida.

GIANT MANUFACTURING

It was founded in 1972 in Tachia, 20 kilometers from downtown Taichung, a port city in western Taiwan. This company is both the largest producer and the largest exporter of bicycles in the world. The initial success enjoyed by this company was based on two management attributes: imagination to turn a problem into an advantage, and the ability to differentiate between a fad and an enduring shift in consumer demand. Giant's management was given the opportunity to display both attributes in the 1980s.

Giant's ability to turn a problem into an advantage was first display in 1981 when the workers of Schwinn, at that time the largest manufacturer of bicycles in the United States, went on a strike at the company's main factory in Chicago. Schwinn's management, unwilling to seek a settlement entered into a partnership with Giant, closed the Chicago plant and sent its engineers and equipment to Taiwan. Under this partnership, Schwinn committed to providing technology, engineering expertise, and volume sales. In return, Giant devoted to manufactured and exported the product to the United to be marketed under the Schwinn banner. By 1984, Giant was shipping 700,000 units a year to its partner in the United States. However, in 1985, the business relationship between the Taiwanese and U.S. corporation collapsed when Schwinn decided to terminate his association with Giant. The decision taken by the U.S. corporation left Giant without its most important customer, however, what appeared to major setback was turned by Giant's management into an advantage. Forced to find new markets, the management of the Taiwanese company decided that it was time to introduce the bicycles with a company's brand name in Europe in 1981 and later in 1987 in the United States. To attract distributors Giant offered its customers Schwinn quality bicycles at a 15% discount.

In 2002, the company had more than 4,500 employees, sales equivalent to $425 million sold in shops around the world in 50 countries and in 17 owned-company stores. However, at this time unlike the golden period of the 1980s, Giant and in general the bicycle industry in Taiwan began to feel the pinch of international competition and the impact of the appreciation of the Taiwanese dollar against the U.S. currency. Both effects took their toll on both Taiwan's bicycle industry and Giant's sales. For example, in the year 2000, the exports of Taiwan had declined from 9,484 units in 1996 to only 5,325 units in the year 2000 (See Case Table 11.1). The maturity reached by the bicycle industry worldwide also hurt Giant's competitors. For example, top brands, such as those made by Huffy and bankrupt Derby Cycles were struggling to survive in the year 2001.[3]

INNOVATION AT GIANT

In the opinion of the management of Giant, the development of new products is as important as manufacturing. In the view of the company's management, one of the strengths of Giant is its ability to introduce new product lines within the context of an international approach. About three quarters of the products sold by Giant abroad are the same. But for the remaining Giant allows the regional managers the freedom to specify products that they think can have a local appeal.

To support innovation the firm spends 2% of net profits to support the work of sixty-five designers and development engineers. One of the latest developments of Giant was the introduction of an electric battery-powered bike.

EXCHANGE RATE RISK MANAGEMENT

From its inception, Giant was born as a global company. Therefore, exchange rate exposure has always been a problem. To begin with, most of the sales are to the U.S. market. However, as time has passed, competing in this market has become an increasing problem due to the sustained appreciation of the local currency against the U.S. dollar. Other major headaches are the increasing volatility of the yen, cut throat competition exacerbated by various developments in the world economy, including the United States.

The management of Giant is very convinced that the time has come to re-evaluate the firm's exchange rate risk management by establishing healthy pricing, export, and exchange rate policies that can help Giant stabilize revenues in Taiwanese dollars. To accomplish this goal, Giant has hired the services of a U.S. consulting firm to provide some answers to the company questions. This company has estimated the elasticity of price, exchange rate, and time.

The price elasticity reflects the percentage response of quantity to a one percent change in the domestic price of bicycles and is usually represented as the ratio of percentage change in quantity of exports over the percentage change in price

Price elasticity = [(anticipated quantity of exports/current quantity of exports) − 1]/[(expected price of bicycles/current) − 1]
$= [(Q_a/Q_c) - 1]/[(P_a/P_c) - 1] = -0.034$

The exchange rate elasticity describes the percentage response of quantity of exports to a one percent change in the exchange rate, and is usually represented as the ratio of percentage change in quantity of exports over the percentage change in the exchange rate (Tw$/$1).

Exchange rate elasticity = [(anticipated quantity of exports/current quantity of exports) − 1]/[(expected spot rate/current spot rate) − 1]
$= [(Q_a/Q_c) - 1]/[(E_a/Ec) - 1] = -0.98$

Time elasticity reflects the percentage response of quantity to a one percent change in the efficiency and or quality of the bicycles produced in Taiwan. It is usually represented as the ratio of percentage change in quantity over a period that can be a quarter of a year, six months, or a year.

Exchange rate elasticity = [(anticipated quantity of exports/current quantity of exports) − 1]/(period)
$= [(Q_a/Q_c) - 1]/period = 0.0039$

The consulting company also investigated the relationship between the dollar price of Taiwanese bicycles as a function of the quantity of exports, and the exchange rate. As it should be expected, the consulting firm found a negative relationship between price and quantity, and the exchange rate (Tw$/$1). These results imply that an excess supply of bicycles lowers the dollar price of the item, and that an appreciation of the Taiwanese dollars is increasing the Taiwanese exports of bicycles. The first result is consistent with the expected theoretical relationship between dollar price and quantity of exports. The second elasticity is consistent with economic theory only if Taiwanese dollar appreciations are met by more than proportional increases in the price of bicycles in overseas markets where Giant is exporting its bicycles.

The consulting firm also studied the long term cost structure of the Taiwanese company and found that in the long run the fixed cost is zero. Similarly, it was reported that variable cost of producing a bicycle is $94.35 and that exchange rate and time also play a role in determining the cost of structure of Giant. Time is included to reflect efficiency or the lack of. The cost information is included in Case Table 11.1.

Provided that the consulting company has found the relevant information on price and cost, both Giant and the consulting firm are ready to embark on an analysis to determine how good is the pricing strategy of the firm, and how this strategy has influenced output. To carry on with this analysis, both the consulting firm and Giant are planning apply the conventional approach of equating marginal revenue to marginal cost. The company has advised Giant to apply the following procedure, assuming an exchange rate of Tw\$33.1/\$1 and a time value of one year (t = 1):

Total revenue = price × quantity
Total cost = fixed + variable cost
Profit = total revenue − total cost
Marginal profit (change in profit/change in quantity) = 0

Solving the previous equation by Q will provide the volume of exports that maximize the revenue of the firm. This information can be compared against the current pricing policy to judge the performance of Giant and in general the Taiwanese bicycle industry. Case Table 11.3 presents company's information and a summary of the financial performance of Giant.

CASE PROBLEMS

1. Please help the Taiwanese bicycle industry to find the price and quantity that maximizes export revenues.

2. Given the previous information issue an assessment of the marketing management of exchange rate risk.

3. Considering the findings in question 1, what do you think about the pricing strategy of the Taiwanese bicycle industry and the current volume of exports? Should the bicycle industry change its pricing policies or should it keep the current one?

Case Table 11.1
Taiwan Bicycle Industry, Variables

Price = 225 − 0.0036Q − 3.7XR
Total revenue = 102.5Q − 0.0036Q^2
Total cost = 45.4 Q − 17,023XR + 25,679t
Total cost = -0.05 + 45.4 Q − 563,464 + 25,678.7
Total cost = −537,782 + 45.4 Q
Profit = 537,782 + 57Q − 0.0036Q^2
Marginal profit = 57 − 0.0072Q

Note: Q = quantity of exports in thousand unit, XR = exchange rate, and t is time.
XR = 33.1 and t = 1

Case Table 11.2
Taiwan Bicycle Exports, 1984-2000

Period	Exports (units, thousand)	Exports Change %	Value ($, thousand)	Value Change %	Price ($)	Exchange Rate (Tw$/$1)
1984	6,328		281,596		44.50	39.6
1985	7,442	17.60	300,359	6.66	40.36	39.8
1986	10,239	37.60	418,058	39.19	40.83	39.9
1987	9,685	−5.41	547,009	30.85	56.48	32.0
1988	7,151	−26.20	484,981	−11.34	67.82	28.1
1989	5,200	−27.30	425,256	−12.31	81.78	26.4
1990	8,942	71.90	909,938	114.00	101.80	26.8
1991	9,831	9.90	1,112,762	−87.61	111.47	26.8
1992	8,427	−14.30	972,897	762.80	115.50	25.1
1993	8,621	2.30	1,044,779	7.39	121.20	26.3
1994	8,751	1.51	988,338	−5.40	112.90	26.4
1995	9,064	3.57	1,066,380	7.90	117.70	26.6
1996	9,484	6.92	984,186	−7.71	101.60	26.5
1997	8,826	−6.94	862,355	−12.38	97.70	32.4
1998	8,388	−4.96	896,993	4.02	95.54	32.4
1999	7,782	−7.22	760,274	−15.24	97.69	31.7
2000	5,325	−31.57	558,240	−26.57	104.80	33.1

Source: Japan Bicycle Promotion Institute, December 2001

Case Table 11.3
Giant, Financial Performance

Financial information	2001	1995
Sales ($ million)	425	330.00
Operating expenses	402	312.00
EBIT	23	18.00
Interest	14	9.00
Taxes	1	1.00
Profits	10	8.00
Total assets	358	278.00
Total fixed assets	286	187.00
Fixed assets	110	71.75

Source: www.hoovers.com/co/capsule/9/0,2163,55179,00.html (Accessed May 6, 2002)

NOTES

1. A change in the exchange rate has inflationary consequences, which force an increase in the price of local inputs at a later stage.

2. Taiwan Bicycle Company Profile, "The Past, Present, and Future of Taiwan's Bicycle Industry," http://www.biketaiwan.com/TBC/en_tbc.htm (Accessed May 2, 2002).

3. Hoover's Online, "Giant Manufacturing Co., Ltd," http://www.hoovers.com/co/capsule/9/0,2163,55179,00.html (Accessed May 2, 2002).

SUGGESTED ADDITIONAL READING

Shapiro, A. *Multinational Financial Management*. 6th ed. New York, NY: John Wiley, 1999. See Chapters 10 and 11.

12

Interest and Currency International Swaps

The process of globalization provides enormous international expansion opportunities, and risks, even for companies focusing on the domestic market. In the case of the U.S. fast food industry, which was born with the intent of serving regional markets in the United States, sales and profits abroad are growing faster than at home. To finance the expansion required to serve the world market, while keeping interest rate and exchange rate risks as low as possible, multinationals use swap contracts.

Swap contracts evolved from the parallel loan concept, which was devised by multinational firms to circumvent cross-border capital controls. To understand how a parallel loan agreement worked, consider the case of Nestlé in China. This is a profitable subsidiary of the European firm, which has operated in China for a number of years. However, the repatriation of profits made in China to Switzerland would meet the continuous resistance of the Chinese Central Bank. The attitude of the Chinese monetary authorities became a source of tension between Nestlé and the Chinese government. The latter institution often delayed the remittance of profits without the benefit of an interest payment, for periods lasting a year or longer. The Chinese government's rationale for the delay was grounded in the belief that the exchange control would encourage Nestlé and other multinationals operating in China, to invest these profits locally to further enhance employment opportunities for the Chinese labor force.

In search of ways to avoid the exchange controls imposed by China, Nestlé found that there was no local law preventing multinationals from lending funds raised in China to foreign corporations interested in investing in the Asian country, in return for payments in non-Chinese currency to the parent in

Switzerland. Taking advantage of this loophole, the Swiss Company began engaging in trading Chinese profits to be delivered within China, in exchange for non-Chinese currency payments to Switzerland.

The aim of this chapter is to provide an explanation of what constitutes a swap contract and to provide the tools required to execute them. To meet this goal, this chapter:

- Provides an explanation of what constitutes a swap.
- Discusses the mechanism and structure of interest rate swaps and currency swaps.
- Shows how swaps can be used both to fund the business activities of multinational corporations and to hedge exchange rate risk.

INTEREST RATE SWAPS

An interest rate swap is an arrangement between two parties to trade dollar interest payments for a specific period, by a mutually agreed amount. The principal is a *notional principal* simply used in swap contract as a benchmark used to estimate the interest payments to be swapped. As such, under an interest rate swap, the parties never exchange principal.

The time to expiration of interest rate swaps ranges from less than 1 year to 15 years. In practice, most swaps fall within a 2 to 10-year period. Interest rate swaps can be stipulated as trade coupon payments or basis points. Basis points are estimated as 1% of 1%.

In a *coupon swap*, one party pays fixed interest, which is estimated considering a notional amount, and receives, from the counterpart a floating interest estimated with the same notional principal. In a *basis swap*, each company trades floating coupon payments priced in terms of basis points.

Coupon swaps are negotiated with consideration to different parties having different risk preferences. For example, some investors prefer to fix the return on their investments, while others prefer floating rates. Borrowers also look at risk in a variety of ways. Some are more attracted to fixed interest debt, whereas others prefer floating rate debt. These contrasting views are the heart of an interest swap. Another factor playing a role in interest swaps is the credit rating of the borrowers and their needs for financing. Some borrowers are able to borrow at low fixed rates but prefer to borrow at floating rates. Others have an advantage by borrowing at low interest amounts in terms of floating rates but prefer to borrow at fixed rates.

The discrepancy between credit ratings and scale of preferences is the basis for trading interest rates payments that will benefit the borrowers in two ways. First, it will let them borrow at a lower rate than they would otherwise. Secondly it will let the intermediary engineering a swap to earn a profit. An interest rate swap can be based on the strengths of each borrower. If this is the case, the swap is negotiated considering *absolute advantage*, that is, on the fact that one borrower is better borrowing at a fixed rate while the other is more efficient borrowing at a floating rate.

Interest rate swaps can also be arranged in the case where a borrower is better than his counterpart at borrowing on both fixed and floating rates. In this instance, an interest swap can be worked out considering *comparative advantage*. Swaps based on comparative advantages are usually typified by interest rate swap transactions.

To explain how interest rate swaps based on comparative advantages can be negotiated, consider the case of two corporations wanting to borrow $10 million for two years. Party A can borrow at a 7% floating interest rate and a 5.5% fixed interest rate. Party B, in contrast, can borrow the same principal at a floating rate of 9%, and fixed at 6%. At a first glance, it is clear that Party A can borrow at lower interest rate than Party B. Therefore, Party A has absolute advantages borrowing either at floating or fixed rates. A more careful analysis reveals that Party A has a comparative advantage of 22% borrowing at a floating rate and a comparative advantage of only 8% borrowing at a fixed rate, as shown in Table 12.1.

Given these circumstances, a smart financial intermediary will realize that these conditions are ripe to arrange a swap that can benefit him and the two borrowing entities. To benefit from the situation faced by the two borrowers, the financial intermediary could encourage Party A to trade a stream of payments stated at a 7% floating interest rate in exchange for a payment stream priced at less than 5.5% fixed, for example, 4.75%.

Similarly, the bank, acting as intermediary, should try to convince Party B to trade a stream of interest payments priced at a 6% fixed in exchange for a payment stream priced at less than 9% fixed, for example, at 8.75%.

If the transaction is engineered along the rates previously stipulated, the financial intermediary will gain an interest rate profit of 1.75% in the transaction with Party B while losing 1.25% in the transaction with Party A. All together the transaction will net a 0.5% profit to the financial intermediary:

Net gain to intermediary = (8.75% – 7%) + (4.75% – 6.00%)
= 1.75% – 1.25%
= 0.5%

The swap transaction also will benefit the parties because it will lower their cost of borrowing. For example, Party A will enjoy an interest rate reduction of 0.75%:

Party A, interest reduction = 4.75% – 5.5% = –0.75%.

Similarly, giving the swap arrangement, Party B's interest expense will be reduced by 0.25%:

Party B, interest reduction = 8.75% – 9.0% = –0.25%.

The benefits of the swap to the three parties are described in Figure 12.1.

Table 12.1
Comparative Advantages in Borrowing

Party	Floating interest rate	Fixed interest rate
A	7.0%	5.5%
B	9.0%	6.0%
Interest rate difference	7% – 9% = –2.0%	5.5% – 6.0% = –0.5%
Comparative advantage	– 2%/9% = –22.0%	– 0.5%/6% = –8.0%

Figure 12.1
Interest Rate Swap

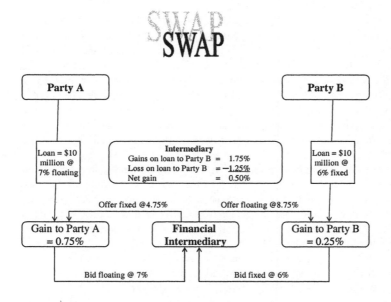

INTERNATIONAL CURRENCY SWAPS

The term *currency swap* describes a transaction between two borrowers that is coordinated by a financial intermediary. Under a swap agreement, one party agrees to make periodic payments in a given currency, for a specific period, in order to meet a liability incurred by the other party in terms of the said currency. In return, the second party agrees to do the same thing on behalf of its counterparty but in a different currency.

A currency swap is possible when the parties involved in the transaction have absolute or comparative advantages in borrowing and when each one of the streams of payments to be swapped has the same present value, regardless of whether the streams are stated on fixed or fluctuating interest rates.

THE CASE OF ABSOLUTE ADVANTAGES IN BORROWING

To explain a currency swap engineered on the basis of absolute advantages in borrowing, consider the case of two multinational corporations, one from the United States and the other from Germany. The U.S. company needs to borrow €1,123,596 for four years. The German firm, in turn, needs to borrow $1,000,000 for the same period. The existing spot rate is $0.89/€1. Giving this spot rate, the two principals are equivalent in terms of either dollars or euros.

Each company is highly respected in its home country and can borrow at premium interest rates locally. However, outside of their local financial markets, their borrowing ability is somewhat limited. Table 12.2 describes the credit ratings of each company on both the United States and Europe.

Table 12.2
Case of Absolute Advantages

	Borrowing Interest Rates	
	Dollar	**Euro**
U.S. company	6.0%	5.0%
German company	7.5%	3.5%
Absolute advantage of German company	$7.5\% - 6.0\% = 1.5\%$	$3.5\% - 5\% = -1.5\%$

The U.S. company has an absolute advantage of 1.5% borrowing dollars as compared with its German counterpart. The European firm, in turn, has an absolute advantage of 1.5% borrowing euros. This means that the U.S. Company is better at borrowing in dollars, and the German company has an advantage at borrowing euros.

The fact that each corporation possesses absolute advantages borrowing at home provides grounds for a swap agreement where the financial intermediary earns an interest rate profit, and each participating firm lowers its cost of borrowing in foreign exchange. The total interest rate gains of this currency swap amount to 3% and can be distributed among the participants in many different ways.[1]

Under a scenario in which the gains of the currency swap are shared evenly, the U.S. and German companies can borrow simultaneously $1,000,000 at 6% and €1,123,596 at 3.5%, as described in Figure 12.2. Next, the two firms can deliver the principal of each loan to the financial intermediary, which will make the $1,000,000 available to the German firm at 6.50% and deliver the €1,123,596 to the U.S. firm at an interest rate of 4%.

Under this agreement, the U.S. firm will be able to borrow euros at 4%. This will represent a 1% savings in the cost of borrowing euros. Similarly, the German firm can borrow dollars at only 6.5%, which is 1% below the cost that this firm can borrow dollars.

The benefit to the intermediary is a 1% per year profit. It receives the dollar principal from the U.S. firm at a bid rate of 6% and transfers it to the German company at an offer rate of 6.5%. This transaction provides a 0.5% per year gain. With respect to the German principal, the intermediary receives euros at bid rate of 3.5% and transfers them to the U.S. firm at an offer rate of 4%. This transfer also yields 0.5% profit to the bank.

Upon swapping principals, each firm has benefited from a 1% reduction in the interest cost of borrowing. However, the two companies are still exposed to exchange rate risk. The U.S. company must make four semiannual coupon payments in euros at the expiration of the swap contract two years later. The German company also has a foreign exchange liability. It has to make four semi-annual dollar coupon payments and pay back the dollar principal two years from now.

Figure 12.2
Absolute Advantage Case

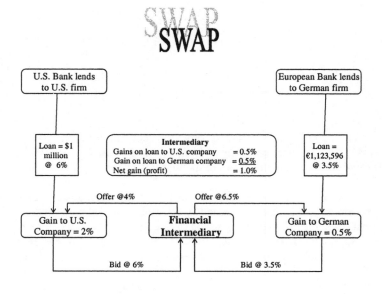

To eliminate the exchange rate risk involved in the transaction, each firm may further agree to swap the stream of payments. To cover the exchange rate risk, the U.S. firm has to commit to make four semi annual dollar coupon payments of $32,500 each plus the repayment of the principal ($1,000,000) at the expiration of the contract, on behalf of the German firm. This stream of payments is shown in line 3 of Table 12.3.

In turn, the German firm must agree to meet four semi annual payments of €22,472 each plus the repayment of the principal at the expiration of the swap contract on behalf of the U.S. firm. The liabilities to the German company are also described in Table 12.3.

If the currency swap agreement goes this far, both firms lower their cost of borrowing foreign currency and eliminate the exchange rate risk associated with external borrowing.

A CASE OF COMPARATIVE ADVANTAGE IN BORROWING

In the previous example, it is easy to justify a swap agreement, since each participant has absolute advantage borrowing locally. However, there are cases where a company can borrow at lower rates than its counterpart in all markets. Would a currency swap still makes sense under this scenario for the company exhibiting absolute advantages in borrowing in all markets?

Table 12.3
Description of the Dollar/Euro Swap Agreement

Line	Item	0	1	2	3	4
1	Exchange rate	$0.89/€1				
2	Principal swapped	$1,000,000				
3	Coupon swapped @ 6.5/%/2		$32,500	$32,500	$32,500	$1,032,500
4	Discount factor @ 6.5%/2	1	0.969	0.938	0.909	0.88
5	PV of coupon payments		$32,500 × 0.969 = $31,477	$32,500 × 0.938 = $30,486	$32,500 × 0.909 = $29,527	$1,032,500 × 0.88 = 908,510
6	Accumulated PV	$1,000,000				
7	Principal swapped	€1,123,596				
8	Coupon swapped @ 4%/2		€22,472	€22,472	€22,472	€1,146,068
9	Discount Factor @ 4%/2	1	0.980	0.961	0.942	0.924
10	PV of coupon payment		€22,472 × 0.98 = €22,031	€22,472 × 0.961 = €21,599	€22,472 × 0.942 = €21,176	€1,146,068 × 0.924 = €1,058,790
11	Accumulated PV	€1,123,596				

To provide an answer to this question consider two companies, one from the United States and the other from Brazil. The U.S. corporation needs to borrow BR$2,500,000 real for four years. The Brazilian firm needs a $1,000,000 loan for the same period. The two companies can borrow at fixed interest rates in dollars and real (BR$) as shown in Table 12.4, when the spot rate is at $0.4/BR$1.

The previous information indicates that the U.S. firm can borrow at lower interest rates in either one of the two currencies. The most relevant aspect of this information is the fact that the difference between the rates offered to the companies is not the same in both markets. For example, in the dollar market, the U.S. company has a 2% competitive edge against the Brazilian company. In terms of Brazilian reals, the advantage of the U.S. company is only 0.5%. This difference in the interest rates means that the U.S. corporation has absolute advantages borrowing in both markets but a comparative advantage of 25% borrowing dollars.

Comparative advantage = dollar difference / Brazilian firm's cost of borrowing dollars:

$= -2\%/8\%$

$= (-0.02/0.08) \times 100$

$= -0.25 \times 100$

$= -25\%$

This situation provides financial intermediaries with an opportunity to organize a swap that can benefit them and the companies entering into the swap agreement. To obtain this benefit, the companies have to borrow along their comparative advantages.

Table 12.4
Comparative Advantages in Borrowing

	Borrowing Interest Rates	
	Dollar	**Brazilian real**
US company	6.0%	10.5%
Brazilian company	8.0%	11.0%
Interest rate differential	6% − 8% = −2.0%	10.5% − 11% = −0.5%
U. S. firm's comparative advantages	−2%/8% = −25.0%	− 0.5%/11% = −4.5%

The U.S. company can borrow in dollars at 2.0% less than the Brazilian company, but the Brazilian company can only borrow Brazilian reals at 0.5% higher than the U.S. entity. Therefore, the net benefit of this transaction in only 1.5%.

Swap's total interest rate benefit = U.S. company's interest cost advantage − Brazilian company's interest cost disadvantage
= 2% − 0.05%
= 1.5%

A swap agreement can be negotiated on the base of an equal distribution of the benefits, that is a gain of 0.5% for the U.S. and Brazilian companies, and 0.5% for a financial intermediary arranging the swap. If this is the case, the U.S. company could borrow $1,000,000 at 6%, and the Brazilian company BR$2,500,000 at 11%. If the loans are executed, the companies have to turn the principals to the financial intermediary to let him or her to transfer the dollar principal to the Brazilian firm at 7.5% and the Brazilian reals to the U.S. firm at 10%. This transfer nets the intermediary a profit of 5%, and helps the Brazilian company to save 0.5% interest on the dollar loan. In a similar fashion, the U.S. firm saves 0.5% on the real loan.

Figure 12.3 describes the nature of the transaction and the benefits that each party receives from this transaction.

Up to this point, the U.S. and Brazilian companies have realized interest savings of 0.5% each, but they are still exposed to exchange rate risk. The U.S. firm has the commitment of making four annual real coupon payments to the financial intermediary. The Brazilian corporation has to make four yearly dollar coupon payments.

To eliminate exchange rate risk, the U.S. firm may further agree to take over the dollar coupon payments and the repayment of the dollar principal at the maturity of the dollar loan on behalf of the Brazilian corporation. By the same token, the Brazilian company has to agree to take over the real loan on behalf of the U.S. firm. If the two firms agree to swap the two streams of payments, they are voiding exchange rate risk.

The swapping of principal and interest payments is shown in Table 12.5. This table lists the spot rate at the time the transaction is taking place ($0.4/BR$1). The principals swapped—the U.S. firms turns to the intermediary $1,000,000, the Brazilian company delivers BR$2.5 million. The U.S. company agrees to make four coupon payments of $75,000 each plus the payment of the principal at the end of Year 4. Therefore, in Year 4 the U.S. company is paying $1,075,000.

Figure 12.3
Comparative Advantages Case

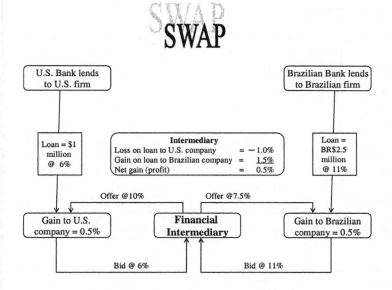

The Brazilian company in turn, agrees to make four coupon payments of BR$250,000 each plus the repayment of the principal and the coupon payment at the end of Year 4. That is, in Year 4, the Brazilian company is making payment totaling BR$2,750,000.

The present value of the U.S. liabilities is $1,000,000. Similarly, the present value of the Brazilian commitments is BR$2,500,000, which multiplied by the spot rate is equivalent to $1,000,000. The details of the swap transaction and the commitment of each company to the swap are described in detail in Table 12.5.

Valuation of Currency Swaps

To determine the value of a currency swap in the absence of default risk the financial intermediary has to dissect the swap transaction. In the previous swap contract, the U.S. corporation has agreed to make dollar coupon payments at 7.5% to the financial intermediary, in exchange for receiving 10% coupon payments in Brazilian reals.

This transaction entails the financial intermediary to receive a dollar coupon payment from the U.S. corporation, which constitutes an asset for the financial intermediary. The market value of this asset is the present value of the dollar payment stream. The acquisition of these assets creates a liability in Brazilian real.

Table 12.5
Description of the Dollar/Real Swap Agreement
(in thousands, except the spot rate quotation)

Spot rate = $0.4/BR$1

ITEM	0	1	2	3	4
Principal	$1,000				
Coupon @ 7.5%		$75.00	$75.00	$75.00	$1,075.00
Discount factor @ 7.5%	1	0.93	0.87	0.80	0.75
PV		$75 × 0.93 = $69.76	$75 × 0.87 = $64.90	$75 × 0.80 = $60.73	$1,075 × 0.75 = $804.96
Total PV	$1,000				
Principal	BR$2,500				
Coupon @ 10%		BR$250.00	BR$250.00	BR$250.00	BR$2,750.00
Discount factor @ 10%	1	0.91	0.83	0.75	0.68
PV		BR$250 × 0.91 = BR$227.27	BR$250 × 0.83 = BR$206.61	BR$250 × 0.65 = BR$187.82	BR$250 × 0.68 = BR$1,878.28
Total PV	BR$2,500				

The market value of this liability is the present value of the real payment stream. Consequently, the value of the swap transaction is equal to the present value of the dollar asset less the dollar value of the real liability, measured in dollars.

(12.1)   NPV ($) = PV ($) – PV (BR$) × E

where NPV($) is the dollar net present value of swap, PV($) is the present value of dollar receipts, PV(BR$) is the present value of liabilities in terms of Brazilian real, and E is the spot rate prevailing at the time when the swap is negotiated expressed in terms of the number of dollars per one Brazilian real. ($/BR$), or more generally speaking, in terms of the number of dollars per unit of foreign exchange.

To provide an example of how to assess the market value of a swap from the perspective of a financial intermediary, consider the case of a U.S. firm that has agreed to a currency swap. The contract commits the U.S. firm to a $1 million principal at the maturity of the swap contract, and to make five semi annual dollar coupon payments at 2.5% to the financial intermediary when the semi annual dollar market interest rate is 2.0%. The contract also stipulates a 125 million Japanese yen principal payment at the maturity of the swap to a Japanese corporation, plus five semi annual yen coupon payments at 1% when the semi annual yen interest rate is 0.75%. At the time of the swap transaction, the spot rate is $0.8/¥100.

The present value or market value of this swap transaction is $11,344.

Swap value = NPV($) = Present value of dollar receipts (dollar bond, B$) – dollar present value of yen payments (yen bond, B¥)

NPV($) = PV(B$) – PV (B¥) × the spot rate

= [PV(B$ – (PV (B¥) × E]

= $1,024 – ¥126,528 × ($0.8/¥100)

= [$1,024 – (¥126,528/¥100) × $0.8]

= $1,024 – (1,265.28 × $0.8)

= $1,101 – $1,012

= $11.344

Further details on the present value of the swap are provided in Table 12.6.

KEY CONSIDERATIONS IN SWAP CONTRACTS

An international currency swap is a contract related to the exchange of cash flows stated in different currencies that can take many different values. These different values may depend on how the participating entities agree to distribute the benefits, and the level of the exchange rate. As such, there is no limit to the variety of swaps that can be negotiated, given two principals and their interest rates. The variables determining the value of an international cash flow are the principal in each currency, the cost of borrowing and lending in each currency, the spot rate, and the expiration period of the swap contract.

The most widely used swap is a *fixed-for-fixed currency swap*. This is known as the basic "plain vanilla swap." Under a plain vanilla currency swap, the cash flows of the swap are based upon the future cash flows of two fixed-coupon bonds in two different currencies. This case is used extensively to explain the currency swap concept in this chapter.

Another popular swap is the *fixed-for-floating currency swap*. Under this agreement, one of the payment streams is stated on a fixed coupon rate in one currency, and the other payment stream is based on a floating rate note on the second currency. This currency swap is also referred to as a cross-currency swap.

Another well-liked swap is the *off-market swap*. In this case, the parties agree to exchange cash flows having different present values, given a certain spot rate. Obviously, the party receiving the cash flow with lower present value is compensated with a balancing payment from the party receiving the higher present value cash flow. This balancing payment can take place at the mutual agreement of the two partners or at any time within the life span of the swap contract.

ESSENTIAL INGREDIENTS IN A SWAP NEGOTIATION

A swap contract is normally a long-term commitment for all the parties involved. Therefore, to engage in a successful and risk-free swap, the engaging parties have to investigate the credit risk of their counter party and the reputation of the financial intermediary. The focus should be more on the financial intermediary, since this entity acts as the party guaranteeing the swap.

Table 12.6
Dollar Present Value of a 3-Year Dollar/Yen Swap
(Semiannual, and in thousands, except the spot rate quotation)

Spot rate = $0.8/¥100
Principal = $1,000
Principal = ¥125,000

Period	0	1	2	3	4	5
Coupon receipts @						
5%/2 = 2.5%		$25.00	$25.00	$25.00	$25.00	$1025.00
Discount rate @ 4%/2						
= 2%		0.98	0.96	0.94	0.92	0.91
PV		$24.51	$24.03	$23.56	$23.10	$928.37
Total PV	$1,024					
Coupon payments @						
2%/2 = 1%		¥1,250	¥1,250	¥1,250	¥1,250	¥126,250
Discount rate @ 1.5%/2		0.99	0.99	0.98	0.97	0.96
= 0.75%						
Present value		¥1,241	¥1,231	¥1,222	¥1,213	¥121,620
Total PV	¥126,528.00					
Total NPV	$1,012.00					
Value of the swap	$11.34					

SUMMARY

Multinational corporations can use creative financing to achieve various goals. These include reducing their cost of borrowing and reducing exchange rate risk. This chapter focused on two of these techniques: interest rate swaps and international currency swaps.

In an interest rate swap, there is no exchange of a principal either initially or at the expiration of the contracts. These contracts only involve the exchange of two interest-payment streams calculated on the base of a notional amount. Interest rate swap contracts can take the form of an exchange of a fixed interest rate coupon for a floating interest rate coupon. It can also take the form of the exchange of a stream of payments based on a floating rate in exchange for another stream also estimated on the base of a floating rate, where each payment stream is priced in terms of basis points. A basis point is 1% of 1%.

Currency swaps refer to transactions where each party exchange principal and the interest payment associated to that principal over the stated life of a swap contract. This transfer of principal and coupon payments stated in two different currencies helps multinationals to lower their cost of borrowing and to hedge the currency risk.

Currency swaps can take many forms. The most popular swap contract is known as plain vanilla, where the parties trade fixed interest rate coupon payments stated in dollar terms for fixed coupon payment stated in non dollar currencies.

PROBLEMS

1. A Japanese company wishes to borrow dollars. In contrast, a U.S. multinational wishes to borrow yens. The amounts required by the two companies, in existing spot rates, are the same in either of the two currencies. These two companies have been quoted the interest rates describe in the table below. These interest rates are net of taxes.

Company	Yen Rate	Dollar Rate
U.S.	5.0%	9.0%
Japanese	6.5%	10.0%

Design a swap that will net the financial intermediary 20 basis points profits per year. The swap should be engineered in such a way that it will be equally attractive to the two companies. Finally, ensure that all the exchange rate risk is transferred away from the companies to the bank.

2. German company wishes to borrow dollars. A U.S. company wants to borrow euros. They have been quoted the following yearly rates for semi-annual coupon payments.

Company	Euro Rate	Dollar
German	4.0%	7.0%
U.S.	3.5%	5.5%

Design a swap that will distribute the benefits evenly.

3. Suppose that the dollar interest rate is 5.5% per year, while the euro rate is 4% per year. The existing spot rate is $0.9/€1. Under the terms of a swap agreement, the financial intermediary pays 3% per year in euros and receives 6.5% in dollars. The notional principals are $10 million and the equivalent in euros. There are four semi annual payments. What is the value of the swap to the financial institution?

4. A bank has entered into a four-year currency swap with a U.S. company. Under the term of the swap, the bank receives interest at 3% per year in Swiss francs and pays interest at 6% per year in dollars. Interest payments are semi annual. The principals traded are $7 million and Swf10 million. If the U.S. company defaults at the end of Year 3 when the exchange rate is $0.4/Swf1 and the interest rates are 3% and 5% in Swiss francs and dollars, respectively, what is the value of the swap after the default of the U.S. company?

Case: Sumitomo Bank, Swapping in Asia

THE BANK

Sumitomo Bank Capital Markets Inc. (SBCM) is a subsidiary of the Sumitomo Bank, a Japanese financial intermediary. SBCM was approved as a dealer in the U.S. swaps market in 1989. It was the first subsidiary of a Japanese commercial bank to start trading interest rate swaps. Beginning with a staff of 5 in New York, SBCM now has 170 employees in offices located in New York, London, and Hong Kong.

THE PRODUCTS

Over the years, SBCM has become a major player in the market for interest and currency swaps. On a stand-alone basis, SBCM had by the end of 2000, $615 million in equity capital and a Standard and Poor debt rating of BBB2. In derivative product markets, Sumitomo was given AAA rating. An issue with this rating is considered to be a top-quality financial instrument. This rating indicates good asset protection and the least risk of payment impairment within the universe of derivative products.

SWAP CONTRACTS

An interest rate swap is a contractual agreement to exchange a set of cash flows, typically fixed for floating, over a period of time. The size of the swap, or principal, is a notional amount. This concept is used to estimate the value of each cash flow. The term to expiration of swap contracts is determined by customers needs. However, contract ending ranges from 6 months to 30 years. A cross-currency swap, or simply a currency swap, is a contractual agreement to trade cash flows denominated in one currency for a set of payments stated in terms of another currency for a pre agreed time period.

A major difference between a cross-currency swap and an interest rate swap is that the former includes the initial or final exchange of principals stated in terms of different currencies, as well as two sets of interest payments stated in two currencies.

Swap contracts may not be fulfilled. Therefore, they usually specify penalties for a party unable to meet its contractual commitment and compensation for those parties hurt by the failure.

As a counter party for derivative product transactions, SBCM offers capital strength and credit quality since the Sumitomo Bank is one of the largest and best capitalized banks in the world.

Another important aspect of the services provided by SBCM is the ability of the bank to provide customers with information on a large number of currencies, a 24-hour quote service, and global coverage. These attentions to clients are possible due to the fact that SBCM operates in Asia, Europe, and North America.

The business philosophy of SBCM is to work together with clients to provide them with advice on interest rates and currency management issues. The bank also helps them to design solutions to mach each customer's needs on a wide variety of financial products under different circumstances.

THE CURRENCY SWAP AGREEMENT

Hyundai opened up a subsidiary in Thailand in 1996. This business unit required dollar funding to meet long-term (8-year) liabilities in this currency.

In an attempt to acquire appropriate funding for the Thai subsidiary, Hyundai was offered dollar loans ranging from 6.5% to 8%. As such, the best Hyundai could do on its own was to borrow in terms of the U.S. currency at 6.5%. By comparison, in the Asian capital markets, the South Korean chaebol could borrow baht at 8.5%.

At the same time, Chrysler was on the verge of acquiring a subsidiary in Thailand. To fund this acquisition and start expenses, the U.S. corporation needed baht, long term. In an initial testing of Asian financial markets, Chrysler discovered that it could borrow baht at 8%, which was an excellent rate in comparison to what other companies from Asia or the United States could get. In dollar terms, it could do better since it was able to obtain 10-year interest rates at 4.5%.

Knowing that both Chrysler and Hyundai were searching for funding in currencies different from their home currency, bank executives Mr. Kawamoto and Mr. Yates decided to contact both companies to offer them SBCM services. Using sound and compelling financial reasons, the two executives convinced both, Chrysler and Hyundai, to enter into a currency swap agreement. To convince Chrysler to join, SBCM argued that the best Chrysler could do was to borrow baht at 8%. Given the conditions existing in the financial markets, it was an excellent interest rate. But, with the help of SBCM it could be better. In meetings with Hyundai executives, the two SBMC bankers used the same line of reasoning.

THE TERMS OF THE SWAP CONTRACT

After several successful meetings, the three parties entered into a swap contract on January 1, 1996, which committed the U.S. company and the Thai subsidiary of Hyundai to trade $10 million and 250.5425 million bahts, respectively. These values amounted to the same principal measured in terms of either one of the two currencies. In addition, each party agreed to meet quarterly coupon payments.

Sumitomo, acting as a financial intermediary, agreed to receive from the Thai subsidiary of Hyundai quarterly baht coupon payments costing the bank 8.5% (bid rate). Chrysler, in turn, agreed to borrow from Sumitomo baht quarterly coupon payments at a 7.5% annual rate. On the other end of the contract, Sumitomo agreed to receive from Chrysler quarterly dollar coupon payments at 4.5% (annual basis) to be transferred to Hyundai at 6% (yearly).

FINANCIAL EVENTS IN ASIA

The swap agreement worked well. However, the financial consequences of the Asian crisis hurt both South Korea and Hyundai. Hyundai's domestic sales collapsed and forced a capital utilization of only 40%. The lack of demand and the buildup of inventories led the South Korean Company to lay off workers both in South Korea and Thailand. More importantly, Hyundai was forced to declare a moratorium on interest payments. The corporate creditors, unhappy with the policies of Hyundai, enforced a drastic management shake-up that transferred the leadership of the company from the founding family to a more professional management team appointed by the creditors. The new management group moved swiftly to eliminate 11 of the 25 subsidiaries held by the South Korean chaebol, and spun off 42 of the 104 business divisions of the conglomerate.

The new Hyundai management team also focused on improving the financial efficiency of the corporation. They considered that it was in the best interest of the company to cut short the swap agreement since they believed that interest rates in the euro market and Thailand would move in a direction that will be beneficial to Hyundai. For instance, in the euro market, they expected a decline in dollar rates. In Asia, they anticipated an increase in baht interest rates.

Sumitomo, with the approval of Chrysler, agreed in November 2000 to cancel the swap contract by the end of this year, provided that both the bank and Chrysler would be compensated for any losses associated to this change in the contract.

MARKET CONDITIONS, FIRST QUARTER 2001

Mr. Yates anticipated by January 2001 a spot rate of bht38.545/$1. Regarding interest rates, Mr. Yates believed that at the beginning of the first quarter of 2001, the dollar and baht rates will be 6.6% and 11%, respectively.

If these conditions prevailed, Mr. Kawamoto and Mr. Yates would be interested in finding out the value of the compensation to both Sumitomo and Chrysler that would help SBMC to begin a negotiation with Hyundai to settle the swap contract.

CASE PROBLEMS

1. Estimate the benefits of the swap for Sumitomo, Chrysler, and Hyundai.

2. Help Mr. Kawamoto and Mr. Yates to estimate the cost associated to the cancellation of the swap contract for both Chrysler and Sumitomo.

3. Is in the advantage of Hyundai to cancel the swap agreement? To estimate the losses to Chrysler, you have to consider the increase in the baht interest rate from the one provided by Sumitomo (7.5%) to the new market rate (11%).

NOTE

1. The total interest rate gains to be distributed among the three parties is the sum of the advantage that the U.S. firm has over the German company borrowing dollars (1.5%) plus the advantage that the German company has over the U.S. firm borrowing euros (1.5%).

SUGGESTED ADDITIONAL READINGS

Chicago Board of Trade. "Swap Reference Guide." http://www.cbot.com/cbot/www/cont_modular/1,2291,14+483+10,00.html. (Accessed October 2, 2001).

Finance.Wat.ch. "Currency Swap." http://finance.wat.ch/TermFinance/en/en000583.htm. (Accessed October 14, 2001).

Finance Wat.ch. "Interest Rate Swap." http://finance.wat.ch/TermFinance/en/en000583.htm. (Accessed October 14 2001).

Finance Watch.com. "Plain Vanilla Swap." http://finance.wat.ch/TermFinance/en/en000583.htm. (Accessed October 14 2001).

Green Interest Rate Swap Management. "What is an Interest Rate Swap?" http://home.earthlink.net/~green/ (Accessed October 16, 2001).

Investopedia.com. "Interest Rate Swaps, What Does It Mean." http://www.investopedia.com/terms/i/interestrateswap.asp (Accessed October 14, 2001).

Shapiro, A. *Multinational Financial Management*. 6th ed. New York, NY: John Wiley, 1999. See Chapter 16.

13

Valuing a Foreign Business

Expanding opportunities in world markets are providing incentives for large increases in cross-border capital expenditures. Similar to local expenditure projects, international investment ventures need to be assessed to determine their contribution to the value of firms implementing them. To evaluate transnational investment, the financial manager is required to understand the factors shaping the cross-cultural appreciation of the firm's products in foreign markets, the tax complexities involved in overseas investments, and the degree of the firm's exposure to country and exchange rate risks.

The purpose of this chapter is to provide the student of global finance with the analytical tools required to incorporate country and exchange rate risk exposure in the evaluation of international investment projects. To illustrate the application of the tools that will be introduced, this chapter will use examples associated with U.S. corporate investments overseas. Toward this end, this chapter:

- Provides the analytical tools required to evaluate new capital expenditures in the global market
- Examines the different foreign currency and dollar cash flows
- Discusses foreign tax regulations and expropriations
- Analyzes the impact of exchange rate changes on capital budgeting
- Introduces technical procedures allowing the investing firm to rank foreign investment projects

FRAMEWORK TO EVALUATE CAPITAL EXPENDITURES

To evaluate capital expenditures, one can resort to applying various financial tools such as NPV, internal rate of return, or the discounted benefit cost ratio. However, the conventional view in managerial finance is to apply NPV tools to analyze capital budgeting due to the theoretical advantages offered by this approach. This chapter relies heavily on NPV tools to analyze global projects and to examine the different aspects of capital budgeting techniques.

Net Present Value

NPV is defined as the present value of future cash flows discounted at the project's cost of capital less the cash outlay required to meet the initial capital expenditure. The first step in the application of this method is to discount both outflows and inflows. The second step is to take away the capital expenditure outflow from cash inflows. In more specific terms, NPV can be expressed as follows:

(13.1)   NPV = – initial investment + future stream of cash flows

$$= -I_0 + \Sigma CF_i / (1 + k)^t$$

where I_0 is initial investment, CF is cash flow in each period, $1/(1+ k)^t$ is the discount factor, and k is the discount rate. Under the NPV rule, projects are deemed acceptable if the NPV of the project is zero or positive.

To estimate the NPV of a foreign project, it is necessary to have information on sales revenues, operating expenses, depreciation, interest expenses, taxes, the term of the project, and the discount rate.

Sales Revenues

To estimate the revenues related to a foreign project, the firm has to forecast prices, volume of sales, and inflation trends in the host country over a five to seven-year period. Other factors affecting revenues are price control mechanisms, import duties, export subsidies, availability of foreign substitutes for firm's products, cross-cultural differences regarding taste, and income policies of the host country.

Pricing Policies

There are many techniques to estimate prices to market products overseas. If the market is very competitive, the prices are set by supply and demand, and the firm acts simply as price taker. This is often the case for exports and imports of agricultural and industrial commodities. Another widely used method is to set domestic prices equal to marginal revenue. This technique sets the price of exports equal to the domestic price multiplied by the exchange rate. Firms enjoying some degree of market power set the price of exports at average cost plus transportation cost plus a markup. As a general rule, the higher the market power, the higher the markup.

Figure 13.1
Pricing Strategy in Foreign Markets

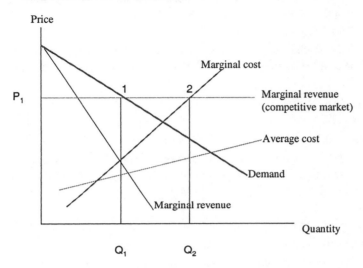

Pricing policies are also related to strategic considerations. Some firms set export prices to maintain a steady profit margin. Other companies prefer to set prices to maintain market share. More recently, many companies in the digital economy have challenged the price notion and are giving away their digital products and services, such as Internet access. The free product policy is implemented with the hope of substituting sales income with marketing revenues.

To provide an example of the aspects related to pricing products in a foreign market, consider the case of a U.S. company planning to establish a new business in Russia. One of the options open to the company is to establish a partnership with a regional government, which will guarantee the company a certain monopoly in a Russian state relatively isolated from the rest of the country. Another possible alternative is to enter in larger and more competitive regions in conjunction with subsidiaries of many other multinational corporations. The second option, most likely, will lead the company to operate in a very atomistic and competitive market.

For the sake of simplicity assume that the company has made some evaluation of the two alternatives and has concluded that the demand and price (inverse demand) functions are as follows:

(13.1) $Q = 100 - 1.25\,P$

(13.2) $P = 80 - 0.8Q$

where Q is the quantity demanded, and P is the anticipated price measured in Russian rubles.

Given the previous equations the company estimates that total revenue (TR) is simply price times quantity, that is,

$TR = P \times Q$
$= (80 - 0.8Q) \times Q$

(13.3) $TR = 80Q - 0.8Q^2$

Similarly, marginal revenue (MR) is simply the change in total revenue attributed to the change in one additional unit sold, that is,

(13.4) $MR = 80 - 1.6Q$

A company's study of the potential costs involved in the Russian operation, suggests that total cost (TC), marginal costs (MC), and profits (π) are as follows:

(13.5) $TC = 75 + 0.15Q^2$

(13.6) $MC = 0.3Q$

            $\pi = TR - TC$

(13.7) $\pi = 80Q - 0.95Q^2 - 75$

If the firm is able to negotiate the joint venture partnership with the Russian government, to optimize profits the company sets marginal cost equal to marginal revenue, as it is shown in point 1 of Figure 13.1.

$0.3Q = 80 - 1.6Q$

Solving by Q, it is found that expected sales are 42.1 million units:

$Q = 80/1.9 = 42.1$ million unit sales per year

Given this output, Russian consumers are willing to pay Rbl$46.3 per unit.

$P = 80 - 0.8 \times 42.1 = $ Rbl$46.3 per unit

Applying the price and quantity information to Equation 13.3, through Equation 13.7 yield the following results on total revenue, marginal revenue, total cost, marginal cost, and profits:

$TR = 80 \times 42.1 - 0.8 \times 42.1^2 = $ Rbl$1,949 million
$MR = 80 - 1.6 \times 42.1 = $ Rbl$12.6 per unit
$TC = 75 + 0.15 \times 42.1^2 = $ Rbl$341 million
$MC = 0.3 \times 42.1 = $ Rbl$12.6 per unit
$\pi = 80 \times 42.1 - 0.95 \times 42.1 - 75$
$\pi = $ Rbl$1,608 million

However, if the company's executives fail to negotiate a partnership with the Russian regional government, the company believes that profit maximization will occur at point 2 of Figure 13.1. Under the scenario of an atomistic and very competitive market structure, to maximize profits the company has to equate marginal cost to price, that is,

$MC = P$
$0.3Q = 80 - 0.8Q$

Under this scenario the potential demand is reduced to 72.7 million of units per year.

$Q = 80/1.1 = 72.7$ millions units per year.

Applying the previous information to Equation 13.2, the company finds that under a competitive market structure the price will decline to Rbl$21.8:

$P = 80 - 0.8 \times 72.7 = $ Rbl$21.8

Table 13.1
Summary of Pricing Strategies in Foreign Markets

	Monopoly	Atomistic
Price	46.30	21.80
Output	42.10	72.70
Total revenue	1,949.00	1,588.00
Total cost	341.00	868.00
Profits	1,608.00	720.00
Marginal cost	12.60	21.80
Marginal revenue	12.60	–36.30
Price elasticity[1]	–1.37	–0.38

Applying the previous quantity and price information to Equations 13.3 through 13.7, the following is obtained:

$TR = 80 \times 72.7 - 0.8 \times 72.7^2 = Rbl\$1,588$ million
$MR = 80 - 1.6 \times 72.7 = Rbl\$36.3$ per unit
$TC = 75 + 0.15 \times 72.7^2 = Rbl\$868$ million
$MC = 0.3 \times 72.7 = Rbl\$21.8$ per unit
$Profit = 80 \times 72.7 - 0.95 \times 72.7^2 - 75$
$Profit = Rbl\$720$ million

The pricing information under the two alternatives evaluated is summarized in Table 13.1

Sales Policies

The volume of foreign sales depends of several factors, such as the relationship between plant capacity, utilization, domestic sales, and competition. If plant capacity is almost exhausted and local competition is very intense, then the firm will likely focus on the domestic market and will export only at the margin. However, if plant capacity is almost exhausted and competition is intense abroad and at home, then the firm has to choose between allocating output to domestic sales or exports, with the certainty that it will lose sales in the market it chooses to minimize. Possible ways to avoid this fate is by increasing the number of shifts, by eliminating products, or by investing in new plant and equipment at home or abroad. In the case of plant expansion, multinationals have to take into consideration the size of markets abroad, the degree of market protection existing in foreign venues, and the cost of transportation. If the foreign markets are small, and tariffs and the cost of transportation are low, then the best expansion alternative is to invest at home and export from home to the foreign market. However, if the foreign markets are large, and the cost of transportation and tariffs are high, then the best option is to invest in foreign plant expansion. Intermediate alternatives to remedy a supply shortage are leasing existing excess plant capacity in domestic or foreign markets or obtain local or overseas sourcing. Any of these options is viable, as long as they return a positive NPV.

Cerveceria Modelo provides an example of excellent management of exporting and global capital budgeting. This successful Mexican brewery producing Corona and Negra Modelo beers is often faced with a shortage of capacity, intense competition at home and abroad, and a very large export market. In every instance that output shortage has become a critical factor in supplying Modelo's fast growing domestic and export markets, the company has always responded with the strategy of investing in plant expansion at home. Some of the reasons shaping this strategy are marketing related. Others are related to global finance. Investing at home is cheaper than investing in the United States, which is the main export market. Operating brewing plants in Mexico is less expensive than operating them in the United States or in other markets where the company has a strong presence. The cost of transportation to the United States is very low, since many of the brewing plants owned by Modelo in Mexico are close to the border with the United States, and the tariffs on Mexican beer exports to this country are low.

Operating Expenses

Operating expenses comprise mainly of manufacturing and administrative expenses. Manufacturing or direct expenses are expenditures in raw materials, parts, and labor incurred by the firm to manufacture the company's output. Administrative expense is the cost related to running a company. Managing these expenses is an important component of the global strategy of a multinational corporation, and a major factor shaping the ultimate value of operating cash flows.

To illustrate the importance of this item, consider the case of Sun Apparel, a U.S. company specializing in the manufacturing of garments under the Polo Brand. This company has headquarters in New York where its output is very labor intensive. To remain competitive, Sun decided to transfer a large portion of its manufacturing facilities to Torreon, Mexico. In this way, the cost of raw materials is the same, but labor expenses are considerably less, with the same or higher quality production. Furthermore, the lead time required to reach critical West Coast markets is less from Torreon than from any manufacturing location in the East Coast.

Depreciation

Depreciation refers to the wear and tear on the capital equipment resulting from the manufacturing of the company's output. It is a non-cash expense that can be estimated using either a straight-line or an accelerated-depreciation method. Under the straight-line method, annual depreciation equals a constant proportion of the initial investment less salvage value.

Accelerated depreciation can be estimated using the rules set by different countries to allow firms an accelerated cost recovery system. In the United States, there are at least six depreciation schedules. These schedules are a very important item to consider in the evaluation of the NPV or the cash flows of a subsidiary because *they reduce taxable income through the annual tax shield equivalent to the value of the depreciation multiplied by the tax rate.*

Interest Expenses

Interest expense refers to the procedure used by the firm to finance capital expenditures and working capital. To fund these expenses, the firm may resort to issuing short-term or long-term debt. Otherwise, it may consider equity funding.

If long-term debt is the preferred funding alternative, the firm has a choice between bonds with fixed coupon rates or convertible bonds to be exchanged into equity at some point in the future. If the firm desires to use equity to finance its capital expenditures, it may choose between issuing preferred and common stock. Preferred stock imposes on the firm the obligation to meet a pre-agreed fixed coupon payment at the end of each fiscal year. In contrast, common stock liberates the firm from this responsibility; since common stockholders are entitled only to a claim on the net income left after the company has met its preferred stock liability.

Taxes

Understanding the implications of the host and home county fiscal laws regarding foreign direct investment is paramount in determining the NPV of cash flows. Carrying out this task is not easy because international projects are subject to numerous taxing jurisdictions, multiple tax regimes, and complex credit provisions.

For example, to export from Arizona to other NAFTA (North American Free Trade Agreement) countries, the exporter has to pay 7.5% local sales taxes if the export product is acquired from a local firm. Also, depending on the nature of the product, it may have to incur a tariff ranging from 0% to 10%. Once the product clears customs, it could be subject to a value-added tax imposed by the importing country. This tax can be as high as 15%. Once exports are sold for final consumption, the customer in the foreign market still has to pay another 5% local sales tax. By the same token, export products can enjoy the benefits of tax subsidies, granted by local, state, and federal levels of government.

Some countries in the Middle East, for example Saudi Arabia, have a clear hierarchy of privileges directed to enhance the competitive position of local companies and joint ventures with high local participation against multinational corporations. For example, only firms with at least 25% Saudi ownership are eligible for tax-holidays and interest-free loans from government credit institutions such as the Saudi Industrial Development Fund. Similarly, only foreign-owned corporations and the foreign-owned portion of joint ventures are subject to the corporate income tax, which can be as high as 45% of net profits.[2]

ESTIMATION OF FOREIGN CURRENCY CASH FLOWS

In this chapter, foreign operating cash flow will be estimated using the *free cash flow* technique. Under this approach, net income is recalculated, by ignoring the interest expense. That is, net income is estimated, as if the company was debt free, even if the company is having some outstanding debt. In a later stage, depreciation is added back to debt-free income, to arrive at the final value of a free cash flow, as shown in the example that follows.

Free Cash Flow Approach	
Revenue	140
Less operating expenses	100
Less depreciation	10
Operating Income (EBIT)	30
Less interest expense	0
Earnings before taxes (EBT)	30
Less taxes @ 50%	15
Net income	15
Plus depreciation	10
Foreign currency cash flow	25

Once foreign currency cash flows are estimated, the next step is to discount the foreign currency cash flows using the WACC. In a subsequent step, foreign currency cash flows are totaled to arrive at a NPV in terms of foreign exchange. In a final step, the foreign currency NPV is converted into dollar terms by multiplying it by an existing spot rate.

To illustrate this technique, consider a two-year project in Brazil costing $65 million, which is expected to provide 100 million Brazilian real each year. If the Brazilian discount rate is 10% and the spot rate is $0.4/BR$1, then the dollar NPV of the project is $4.42 million.

NPV of Brazilian project = – dollar initial investment + PV (BR$) cash flows) × spot rate
$$= -\$65 + [BR\$100/(1 + 10\%)^1 + BR\$100/(1 + 10\%)^2] \times \$0.4/BR\$1$$
$$= -\$65 + (BR\$100/1.1 + BR\$100/1.21) \times \$0.4/BR\$1$$
$$= -\$65 + (BR\$90.9 + BR\$82.64) \times \$0.4/BR\$1$$
$$= -\$65 + (BR\$173.55/BR\$1) \times \$0.4$$
$$= -\$65 + 173.55 \times \$0.4$$
$$= -\$65 + \$69.42$$
$$= \$4.42$$

An alternative procedure to estimate the NPV of a foreign project is by converting the free cash flows from foreign currency into dollars, discounting the dollar cash flows by the WACC in dollars, and computing the NPV of dollar cash flows and inflows.

To provide an example of how to apply this alternative, consider the previous information on the Brazilian project. Except, in this instance the WACC in dollars is 5% and the rates of inflation in Brazil is 10% and 4% in the United States. The rates of inflation are necessary to forecast the exchange rate using purchasing power parity (PPP). Given this scenario, the NPV of the project is $3.44.

Step 1: Exchange Rate Forecasting

Exchange rate (year 1) = spot rate × (1+inflation in Brazil/1 + inflation in the U.S.)
$$= (BR\$1/\$0.4) \times (1 + 10\%)/(1 + 4\%)$$
$$= BR\$2.5/\$1 \times (1.1/1.04)$$
$$= BR\$2.5/\$1 \times 1.058$$
$$= BR\$2.644/\$1$$

Exchange rate (year 2) = spot rate × (1+inflation in Brazil/1 + inflation in the United States)^2
= (BR\$1/\$0.4) × (1 + 10%)^2/(1+ 4%)^2
= BR\$2.5/\$1 × (1.1/1.04)^2
= BR\$2.5/\$1 × 1.119
= BR\$2.796/\$1

Step 2: NPV ($) Estimation

NPV of Brazilian project = – dollar initial investment + [(Brazilian real cash flow (1) × anticipated spot rate in year 1)/(1 + dollar discount factor)^1 + (Brazilian real cash flow (2) × anticipated spot rate in year 2/(1 + dollar discount rate)^2]
= – \$65 + [(BR\$100) × \$1/BR\$2.644)/(1 + 5%)^1] + [(BR\$100 × \$1/BR\$2.796)/(1 + 5%)^2]
= – \$65 + [(BR\$100/BR\$2.644) × \$1/(1 + 5%)^1] + [(BR\$100/BR\$2.796) × \$1/(1 + 5%)^2]
= – \$65 + [(37.818) × \$1/(1 + 5%)^1] + [(35.755) × \$1/(1 + 5%)^2]
= – \$65 + [(\$37.818)/(1 + 5%)^1] + [(\$35.755)/(1 + 5%)^2]
= – \$65 + [(\$37.818)/(1.05)^1] + [(\$35.755)/(1.05)^2
= – \$65 + (\$36.017 + \$32.43)
= – \$65 + \$68.44
= \$3.44

The choice of technique to estimate the NPV depends on where the project is financed. If it is financed in the host country, the procedure described in step 1 should be used. When financed in the home country, then the technique discussed in step 2 is more appropriate.

THE CAPITAL ASSET PRICING MODEL

To estimate the rate of return that compensates an investor for the risk implicit in a specific business activity, it is customary to use the *Capital Asset Pricing Model*.

(13.2) $k = k_f + \beta(k_m - k_f)$

Under the basic tenets of this model in a competitive market, the return associated with an investment in a specific business activity depends on:

- The numerical value of the risk-free rate (k_f)

- The beta index (β), which is a measure of the degree of risk associated with a business activity relative to the market.

- The risk premium (k_m) measured by the difference between the risk free rate and the market return.

The higher the value of beta, the higher the business risk, consequently, a business activity showing a higher beta has to offer a higher return to compensate the investor for the added risk. The beta of a well-diversified portfolio is known as the market beta and is equal to one. This means that the risk associated with a well-diversified portfolio is equal to the market risk.

FINANCING AND RISK

If a new project is fully funded with equity, the appropriate return on equity is measured as follows:

(13.3) $k_s = k_f + \beta_s(k_m - k_f)$

In Equation 13.3, k_s is the expected rate of return on the firm's equity. However, if the capital expenditure is fully financed by issuing debt, then the return on the firm's debt is measured by the following expression:

(13.4) $k_d = k_f + \beta_d(k_m - k_f)$

In Equation 13.4, k_w is the expected return on the firm's debt. In fact, the cost of the debt is calculated by using the cost of debt adjusted for taxes – $k_d \times$ (1 – tax rate).

Another funding alternative to finance a capital expenditure is by using a mixture of debt and equity. To measure the rate of return on projects financed both by debt and equity, it is customary to apply the WACC. The numerical value of this index depends on the proportion of debt (D) and equity (S) to the market value of the firm (V). That is,

(13.5)   WACC = $k_w = (D/V)k_d (1-tx) + (S/V) k_s$

In Equation 13.5 k_w is the weighted average return on a capital expenditure financed by a mixture of debt (*D*) and equity (*S*). *D/V* is the ratio of debt to the total value of the firm, k_d is the cost of debt, *tx* is the corporate tax rate, *S/V* is the ratio of equity to the total market value of the firm, and k_s is the cost of equity.

APPLYING THE CAPITAL ASSET PRICING MODEL

To apply the concepts previously discussed, consider the case of the Spanish company, Ordenadores Alfa. This company is a subsidiary of a U.S. company, Sedona Computers, which is considering a plant expansion program in Spain. To fund this project, it is considering a mix of debt and equity. A review of historical information indicates that equity beta (β_s) is 1.5. Other data suggests that the Spanish risk-fee interest rate (k_f) is 2.5%, and the expected market return on the Spanish portfolio (k_m) is 8%.

Given this information, the cost of equity for Ordenadores Alfa's new project in Spain is 10.8%.

Cost of equity (k_s) = Spanish risk-free interest rate (k_f) + Ordenadores Alfa cost of equity (β_s) × (market return in Spain (k_m) – risk free asset (k_f)

= $k_f + \beta_e \times (k_m - k_f)$

= 2.5% + 1.5 × (8% – 2.5%)

$$= 2.5\% + 1.5 \times (5.5\%)$$
$$= 2.5\% + 8.3\%$$
$$= 10.8\%$$

If the cost of debt (k_d) for Odenadores Alfa is known to be 6%, then the debt beta (β_d) for this company is equal to 0.64.

Debt beta (β_d) = cost of debt (β_d) – return on the risk free asset (k_f) / (the market return (k_m) – return on the risk-free assets (k_f)

$$= (k_d - k_f) / (k_m - k_f)$$
$$= (6\% - 2.5\%) / (8\% - 2.5\%)$$
$$= 3.5\%/5.5\%$$
$$= 0.64$$

If the ratio of debt to the value Ordenadores Alfa (D/V) is 0.5 and the Spanish tax rate is 28%, then the WACC of Ordenadores Alfa is 7.56%.

WACC (k_w) = ratio of debt to firm value (D/V) × the cost of debt (k_d) × (1 – tax rate in Spain) + the ratio of equity to firm's value (S/V) × the cost of equity (k_s)

$$k_w = (D/V) \times k_d \times (1 - tx) + (S/V) \times k_s$$
$$= (0.5) \times 6\% \times (1 - 28\%) + (0.5) \times 10.8\%$$
$$= 3\% \times (78\%) + 5.4\%$$
$$= 2.16\% + 5.4\%$$
$$= 7.56\%$$

Exchange Rate Forecast

A widely used approach to forecast long-term future exchange rates is the purchasing power parity approach (PPP) presented in Equation 13.6. Under this version of PPP, the expected future spot rate (E_t) is a function of the current equilibrium spot rate (E_0) and the ratio of the expected price indexes of both the country hosting the subsidiary, Spain, and the United States.

The future spot rate (E_t) = current spot rate (E_0) × (1 + inflation rate in Europe (i_e)/ 1 + inflation rate in the United States (i_{us})

$$(13.6) \quad E_t = E_0 \times [(1 + i_e)/(1 + i_{us})]$$

To apply this concept, consider the case of Ordenadores Alfa again. The euro is currently trading at $1.01/€1 and the inflation in both Europe and the United States is expected to be 4% and 2%, respectively.

The future spot rate (E_t) = current spot (E_0) rate × (1 + inflation rate in the United States (i_{us})/ 1 + inflation rate in Europe (i_e)

$$E_t = E_0 \times [(1 + i_{us})t/(1 + i_e)^t]$$

Given this information, a four-year forecast of the $/€ in the spot market is given in the last column of Table 13.2.

Table 13.2
PPP Exchange Rate Forecast

Period	(€/$1)	(1+ i_{us})	(1 + i_s)	Exchange Rate Forecast	PPP (€/$1) Forecast
0	$1.01/€1				
1		1.02	1.04	$1.01 \times (1.02)^1/(1.04)^1$	$0.99/€1
2		1.02	1.04	$1.01 \times (1.02)^2/(1.04)^2$	$0.95/€1
3		1.02	1.04	$1.01 \times (1.02)^3/(1.04)^3$	$0.92/€1
4		1.02	1.04	$1.01 \times (1.02)^4/(1.04)^4$	$0.88/€1

Statistical Estimation and Forecast of Exchange Rates

Econometrics is a collection of statistical techniques available to for testing theories by empirically measuring relationships among economic variables. The estimation of an exchange rate using econometric techniques involves the following:

- Identification of the variables.

- Collection of the data.

- Specification of the model.

- Estimation of the parameters of the model.

- Development of forecast.

In this case, the variable that we want to estimate and forecast is the €/$ spot rate. There are several sources to collect data on this variable, for instance the Federal Reserve Bank of St. Louis has historical database called FRED that includes the euro and a selected number of other currencies.[3]

To specify the model the reader can resort to any one of the models specified in Chapter 5. For instance, a popular choice is a modified version of the interest parity condition where the change in the exchange rate is a function of the interest difference between Europe and the United States

$\Delta Et = r_{usa} - r_€$

To estimate the parameters of the model, it is possible to apply the simple linear regression model where the form of the relationship between the two variables is linear.

$Yt = a + bX_t + u_t$

Where Y_t is the anticipated change in the exchange rate, X_t is the interest differential between dollar and euro interest rates, a is the intercept, an u_t is the error term.[4]

Estimating the Cash Flows for Ordenadores Alfa

The Spanish management of Ordenadores Alfa has invested a considerable amount of time researching the computer Spanish market, and they are proposing a new prototype of computer, named SP2001. The details of the project are presented in Table 13.3, which shows estimated annual sales revenue, operating expense, and profits associated with project SP2001. It also shows the estimated capital outlays.

The estimates are assuming that sales will be 10,000 units per year at a price of €1,000 per computer. To implement this project, a new manufacturing facility will be leased for €1.2 million per year, and production equipment will have to be purchased at a cost of €5.8 million. The equipment will be depreciated over a four-year period using the straight-line method. In addition, it is estimated that the company will need €220,000 for working capital. This addition increases the total capital outlay to €6.02 million.

To estimate cash flows, it is necessary to determine the time horizon of the project and the specific process to be used to estimate them. With respect to the aspect related to the life of the project, the natural planning horizon to use in this analysis is the four-year life of the equipment, because at the end of this period, Ordenadores Alfa will have to make a decision about whether to renew the investment.

Table 13.3
Financial Information, Ordenadores Alfa

	Euros
Sales	
10,000 units at a price of €1,000	10,000,000
Fixed cost	
Lease payments	1,200,000
Property taxes	20,000
Administration	600,000
Advertising	500,000
Depreciation	1,450,000
Other	200,000
Total fixed cost per year	**3,970,000**
Variable cost	
Direct labor	200
Materials	100
Selling expenses	120
Other	125
Variable cost per unit	545
Total variable cost for 10,000 units	5,450,000
Total annual operating costs	9,420,000
Annual operating profits	580,000
Corporate income tax @ 28	162,400
Net income or after tax operating profit	**417,600**
Forecasting of initial capital outlay	
Purchase of equipment	5,800,000
Working capital	220,000
Total capital outlay	6,020,000

Table 13.4
Cash Flows, Ordenadores Alfa

Revenue	€10,000,000
Less cash expenses	€7,970,000
Less depreciation	€1,450,000
Operating income	€580,000
Less taxes	€162,400
Net income	€417,600
Plus depreciation	€1,450,000
Cash flow	€1,867,600

The cash flows amount to €1,867,600 each. They are estimated using the free cash flow approach as described below and presented in Table 13.4:

Cash flow = revenues − cash expenses − depreciation − taxes + non-cash expenses (depreciation).

Estimating the NPV of the Spanish Project

To estimate the NPV of the project, it is necessary to complement the cash flow information with discount and exchange rate information. A previous section provides a computation of the WACC for Ordenadores Alfa at 7.56%, which can be used as the discount rate. Also, there are estimates for the exchange rate expressed over a four-year period that will be used to estimate the dollar NPV of the Spanish project.

Finally, it is necessary to have the residual value for the equipment at the end of the four-year period. The natural assumption to make is that the equipment will have no residual value at the end. But working capital will be worth €220,000. The introduction of these assumptions does not mean that the project will be liquidated at the end. It only implies that if the project were going to be liquidated, the company could get back the full €220,000 initially invested in working capital. The project information is summarized in Table 13.5.

- The initial capital expenditure stands at €6.02 million.

- Cash flow per year is estimated at €1,867,600 at the end of years one through four.

- The rate of discount is the WACC estimated at 7.56%.

- There is an additional €220,000 cash inflow at the end of year four.

EVALUATION OF TRANSNATIONAL INVESTMENT PROJECTS

To apply the entire salient points covered in this note, consider the hypothetical case of the U.S. multinational corporation Virtual Office, Inc. This company is planning to establish a $10 million subsidiary in Malaysia to manufacture, distribute, and service all the company's products in this country. The policy of the company is to accept projects showing positive NPVs.

Table 13.5
NPV, Ordenadores Alfa

	0	1	2	3	4
1 CF (€)	−6,020,000	1,867,600	1,867,600	1,867,600	1,867,600
2					220,000
3 DF formula	$1/(1+7.56\%)^0$	$1/(1+7.56\%)^1$	$1/(1+7.56\%)^2$	$1/(1+7.56\%)^3$	$1/(1+7.56\%)^4$
4 DF	1.000	0.930	0.864	0.804	0.747
5 PV of CF (€)	−6,020,000	1,736,333	1,614,292	1,500,829	1,559,710
6 Forecast ($/€1)	$1.01/€1	$0.99/€1	$0.95/€1	$0.92/€1	$0.88/€1
7 PV of CF ($)	−$6,080,200	$1,718,970	$1,533,577	$1,380,763	$1,372,545
8 NPV ($)	−$74,345				

Line 1   Presents the initial investment and the euro cash flow for each year.
Line 3   Shows the discount factor formula used to estimate discount factor values in line 4.
Line 5   Shows the present value of each cash flow shown in line 1.
        PV = cash flow in period t × [1/(1 + discount rate)^t]
Line 6   Describes the PPP exchange rate forecast S($/€1)
Line 7   Presents the dollar value of the cash flows:
        PV ($) = PV (€) × ($/€1)
Line 8   Shows the NPV of the project estimated at −$74,345

To fund the $10 million capital expenditure, there are two proposals. The first one is based on a 100% equity contribution from Virtual Office. The U.S. dollar cost of equity is 8%. The second proposal considers a partnership with a Malaysian firm. In this instance, the partner makes a 40% equity contribution in Malaysian dollars. The cost of equity in Malaysia is estimated at 18%. The remaining 60% can be financed with a debt issue in Malaysian dollars. The cost of borrowing in Malaysia is 14%. The staff of Virtual Office has prepared the cash flows and exchange rate forecast over a five-year period, shown in Table 13.6.

Table 13.6
Cash Flows and Exchange Rate Forecast
(in thousands)

	2000	2001	2002	2003	2004	2005
Investment ($)	−$10,000.00					
CF (M$)		6,240.00	7,090.00	8,650.00	10,520.0	13,080.00
Exchange Rate (M$/$1)		2.90	2.95	3.02	3.00	3.02	3.05
CF ($)			$2,115.00	$2,347.00	$2,883.00	$3,483.00	$4,288.00

NPV of Option 1

To compute the NPV of this option, which is based on 100% dollar equity financing and a U.S. dollar cost of equity of 8%, it is necessary to estimate:

- The dollar value of the cash flows.
- The discount factor.
- The PV of cash flows.
- The NPV of cash flows.

Under the assumptions specified in Option 1, the NPV is equal to $1,739,343. This is detailed in Table 13.7.

NPV of Option 2

Under Option 2 the funding is s combination of 60% debt and 40% equity originating in Malaysia. Therefore, to compute the NPV of this choice, it is necessary to perform the following calculations:

- Estimate the weighted average cost of capital.
- Apply the WACC concept to estimate the Malaysian discount rate.
- Estimate the PV of Malaysian dollars cash flows.
- Use the spot rate to find the present value of case flows in dollars.
- Estimate the NPV of dollar cash flows.

The WACC of the project measured in terms of Malaysian dollars is 12.2%.

$$k_w = (D/V) \times k_d \times (1 - tx) + (S/V) \times k_s$$
$$= 0.6 \times 14\% \times (1 - 0.4) + 0.4 \times 18\%$$
$$= .8.4\% \times 0.6 + 7.2\%$$
$$= 5\% + 7.2\%$$
$$= 12.2\%$$

This rate is used to discount the Malaysian cash flows in Table 13.8. The NPV under this alternative yields a NPV of $797,117.

Table 13.7
NPV, Malaysian Project Under Option 1
(in thousands)

	2000	2001	2002	2003	2004	2005
Investment ($)	−$10,000.00					
CF($)	−$10,000.00	$2,115.00	$2,347.00	$2,883.00	$3,483.00	$4,288.00
DF@ 8%	1.00	0.92	0.85	0.79	0.73	0.68
PV($)	−$10,000.00	$1,958.56	$2,012.75	$2,288.88	$2,560.43	$2,918.69
NPV	$1,739.34					

Table 13.8
NPV, Malaysian Project Under Option 2
(Thousands)

	2000	2001	2002	2003	2004	2005
Investment ($)	−$10,000.00					
CF (M$)		6,240.00	7,090.00	8,650.00	10,520.00	13,080.00
DF @ 12.2%	1.00	0.89	0.79	0.70	0.63	0.56
PV of CF(M$)		5,561,497	5,631,972	6,124,033	6,638,108	7,356,029
PV of CF (M$)	$31,311,640					
Exchange rate	(M$ 2.9/$1)					
NPV ($)	$797,117					

Comparative Analysis

The result obtained for the two financing alternatives studied indicates that under either option, the Malaysian project yields a positive NPV measured in dollar terms, after being adjusted for business and exchange rate risks. Therefore, this project should be accepted because it helps increase the wealth of Virtual Office, Inc.

The NPV calculations conducted under the various assumptions imposed on the project also indicate that Virtual Office will obtain the highest net percent value on this project if it finances the project with equity, since this option yields a higher NPV. However, if the company wants to minimize risk, it should choose the second option, which offers a natural hedge against exchange rate risk because the company is borrowing in local currency to fund the project.

ALTERNATIVE VALUATION METHODS

Mr. Said has just finished his new home. To build it, he used land inherited from his father. To finance the project, he used personal savings, a grant from a company he is working for, and a bank loan. When he was proudly looking a the recently finished new house, and ready to get in, a couple approached him and asked him if he wanted to sell the house,. The strangers offered on the spot half million dollars. Mr. Said, a bit surprised, did not know how to react to the sudden offer. To his amazement, the couple kept on increasing the offer price up to the million dollar mark. After gaining some composure, Mr. Said told the potential buyers to call him later to let him think about the offer. After a while, Mr. Said realized that he did not know the market price of his new home. Consulting with a real state expert he was advised to find the price of a similar home. He found, that a comparable house, in a close neighborhood, having a close resemblance to his, was selling for $950,000. Therefore, Mr. Said concluded that the price presented by the potential buyer was close to market price. He came to this conclusion using what is known as *valuation by comparables*.

An alternative way to decide on the price of the home was to determine the rental value of the new home, and use the present value of the rental value to find out the market value of the house. For example, if Mr. Said's rate of return on the money invested in the house is 8%, and the house market rent is $90,000 a year for twenty-five years, the market value of the house is approximately $960,729. This method of estimating the value of the home is known as the *discount free cash flow model or DFCF valuation method*, thoroughly applied in the previous sections of this technical note.

Different valuation models lead to different results, but the difference between the various procedures should not be very large. However, if different methods produce very dissimilar results, let us say over 20%, it simply means that the assumptions and the information used to valuate the asset should be carefully reviewed.

From the previous discussion it is obvious that the potential buyer of Mr. Said home was offering a fair price, because it was proposing a market price similar to the NPV of rental value and to the value of a comparable home.

The comparables and the DFCF valuation methods are the most commonly applied methods to estimate the value of an asset. However, there are other less popular approaches such as the *liquidation value* and the *replacement value* of a company's asset.

The *liquidation value* is the amount of money that a firm will receive if it splits the company and sells the different components separately. The liquidation value is the *minimum* price a firm expects to receive for its assets. *The replacement value* of an asset is the costs incurred by a company to replace an asset today for another asset of similar quality. In sharp contrast to the liquidation value, the replacement value reflects the *maximum* worth of the asset.

Incorporating Growth

According to the DFCF model, the value of an asset is determined by the capacity of the asset to generate future cash flows. When a buyer purchases a foreign subsidiary or a company overseas, he is buying the entire stream of cash flows that either the subsidiary or he new company area expected to generate in the future.

To estimate the value of either one of these entities, consider a subsidiary in Japan expected to generate ¥100 million per year at perpetuity when the spot rate is ¥297/$1, and the acquiring company's discount rate is 8%. What is the market value of this subsidiary in terms of U.S. dollars? The answer is $420,875. This number was estimated applying a DFCF perpetuity model where the cash flows are expected to remain fixed at perpetuity; that is:

DFCF perpetuity = [Expected annual cash flow/ required rate of return] × spot rate

=(¥100 million/0.8) × $1/¥297

=(¥125 million/¥297) × $1

=$420,875

However, if the cash flows are anticipated to increase 3% per year, the DFCF perpetuity model has to be modified to incorporate growth. In this case, the value of the firm is $437,273.

DFCF perpetuity = [Expected annual cash flow/ required rate of return – growth rate of CF] × spot rate

=(¥100 million/0.8 −0.03) × $1/¥297
=(¥129.8 million/¥297) × $1
=$ 437,273

SUMMARY

This chapter presented extensive and detailed explanations of how to estimate the NPV of projects with cash flows stated in terms of foreign currencies.

To provide the reader with all the unusual tools required to judge how much a foreign project is worth in dollar terms, this chapter reviewed present value techniques and discusses the strategic implications of pricing, output, and international corporate trade policies for purposes of capital budgeting. This chapter also provided various examples describing in a step-by-step fashion how to calculate international discount rates and cash flows under various scenarios, how to forecast exchange rates, and how to compute the NPV of an international project. The chapter closed with a discussion of alternative ways to incorporate the exchange rate into the assessment of foreign investment projects.

PROBLEMS

1. A South Korean manufacturing company currently imports 200,000 units that are used as electrical parts in cars assembled in Korea. The Indian producer buys the parts from a U.S. supplier at a price of W2,000 each. The Indian plant manager believes that it is cheaper to manufacture these parts in South Korea since direct production costs Won1,500 per unit. The equipment required manufacturing the parts in South Korea costs W1.5 million. This investment could be written off for South Korean tax purposes using a three-year depreciation schedule that permits 33.3%, 44.45%, 14.81%, and 7.41%.

   The South Korean plant manager supporting this proposal believes that the local operation will require working capital equivalent to W30 million. However, he argues that this sum could be ignored since it is recovered at the end of the fourth year. The tax rate in South Korea is 35% and the cost of capital is 8%.

   Should this project be accepted?

2. Solo, a U.S. Multinational Corporation engaged in the production and distribution of plastic products, is planning to invest MxP 5,000,000 in a new plant in Mexico.

   Mexican rate of inflation is currently at 8%. It is expected to decline to 6%, 5%, and 5% in three years. The spot rate is $0.111/MxP1. The U.S. rate of inflation is 3%, and is expected to remain at this level for the foreseeable future.

   During the first year of operation, Solo expects to sell 124,000 cases of the plastic products in Mexico. Thereafter, the volume of sales is forecasted to grow at 4% per year. The current price is MxP$35. The pricing policy of Solo is to adjust the price of its products by local inflation.

Labor, material, and parts are estimated at 30% of sales, and administrative expenses at 6% of sales. Depreciation of plant and equipment is based on straight-line depreciation over three years.

Corporate income taxes paid in Mexico are at 30%. The tax credit granted in the U.S. on the taxes paid in Mexico fully offset corporate income taxes in the U.S. That is, the repatriation of Mexican profits is exempt from U.S. corporate taxes. The cost of equity in both Mexico and the U.S. is 12% and 6%, respectively. The company would like to finance the project with 40% equity and 60% debt.

Should Solo invest in Mexico?

3.   Thornton, Inc., a Houston-based manufacturer of disc drive controls, is trying to decide whether to switch to offshore production in Taiwan. Projected yearly net income from the Taiwanese plant is Tai$18 million. Thereafter, revenues are expected to grow 8%. The rate on Taiwanese treasury bills is 4%. The Taiwanese market return is 9%. The Taiwanese beta for the industry is 1.8. The spot rate is Tai$129/$1.

What is the market value of the Taiwanese subsidiary measured in terms of U.S. dollars?

NOTES

1. Price elasticity is equal to the derivative of Q with respect to P multiplied by the ratio of price to quantity = $dQ/dP \times P/Q$.

2. Arab World Online. "Saudi Arabian Investment Climate Statement," www.awo.net/business/invest/sau1.asp. (Accessed June 9, 2002).

3. For further details on this source of data, see Federal Reserve Bank of St. Louis, "FRED an Economics Time Series Database," http://www.stls.frb.org/fred/. (Accessed June 9, 2002).

4. For further details on how to use a linear regression model to estimate and forecast exchange rates, see Neter, J., Kutner, M., Nachtsheim, C., and Wasserman, W. *Applied Linear Regression Models*, 3rd ed. Chicago, IL: Irwin, 1996, Chapter 3.

SUGGESTED ADDITIONAL READING

Shapiro, A. *Multinational Financial Management*. 6th ed. New York, NY: John Wiley, 1999. See Chapters 10 and 11.

14

Value Creation in the Digital Economy

The ability of a foreign subsidiary to create value for its parent company is essentially determined by a combination of internal and external factors. The most important external factors are the size and growth of GDP, and the level and degree of volatility of the exchange rate. The internal ability of a firm to create value is determined, at a large extent, by the profitability of the firm measured as the after tax return on invested capital (ROIC), the cost of capital measured by WACC, and firm's ability to grow. [1]

To provide some understanding of how variations in the level of national income and the exchange rate interact with each other, and how this interaction affects a firm's value creation consider the following examples. Between 1988 and 1993, Mexico achieved remarkable economic progress. All the macroeconomic indicators, with the exception of the balance of payments, showed considerable improvement. Inflation was reduced from 160% in 1987 to 8% 1993. Gross domestic product (GDP) grew at 3% and foreign private capital inflows increased, as did the country's foreign exchange reserves. During this period, a complete structural change and stabilization program took place. As a partial result of all this progress, Mexico was able to join the North American Free Trade Agreement (NAFTA). Nevertheless, in 1994, several adverse economic and political developments brought, at an incredible speed, a crisis that precipitated the devaluation of the peso that led to a massive destruction of firm's value added across industries. By the end of the year 2002, the effects of this crisis were still rattling the country.

Another striking example of how changes in the exchange affect value creation, consider the case of Thailand. In a very short period of time that spanned 25 years, Thailand was transformed from an agricultural based economy into a fast growing industrial country with high-technology products, such as computer accessories and automotive parts. This change promoted a GDP growth that averaged 8.5% between 1990 and 1995. However, as a result of mounting balance of payments problems, in 1997, there was a massive outflow of foreign exchange, which depleted the central bank foreign exchange reserves. The inability of the monetary authorities to stop the outflow of capitals forced them to abandon the existing exchange rate system where the local currency was pegged to the U.S. dollar in exchange for a free-floating regime. All these changes in the modus operandi of the Thai economy tossed the various industries of this country into turmoil, from which they are still trying to recover.

For a very long period of time that spanned decades, the Brazilian firms were saddled with a hyper inflationary environment that hindered their ability to create and accumulate value. Unexpectedly, Brazil witnessed a sudden and drastic decrease in inflation following the presidential elections of October of 1994. The new political party headed by President Fernando Henriquez Cardoso introduced the Real Plan that created a new currency, the real, at rate of $1/BR$1 that was let to float freely. The foreign exchange rate program was complemented with a policy of trade and capital flow liberalization, which allowed Brazilian firms to become fully integrated to the world economy. The plan worked very well. Inflation was reduced to rates of 5%. However, the accumulation of balance of payments problems forced a major devaluation of the real in January of 1999 that changed the parity to $1/BR$2.5. This variation in the dollar price of the Brazilian currency led to a crisis that cause a major disarray both in Brazil and in Mercosur, the South American free trade block.[2]

The analysis conducted by many researchers on the crises experienced by Mexico, Thailand, Brazil and other countries suggests that there is a close relationship among balance of payments results, exchange rate trends, and output. In turn, these factors contribute to variation in firm's value creation. This relationship is deemed as country risk. This refers to the well known fact that firms take crucial business decisions based on expectations regarding the level and direction of output, interest rate differentials between the dollar and other major currencies, and the level and direction of the exchange rates.

This chapter provides a structured and relatively simple economic model to assist global finance executives to understand the relationship between output, the exchange rate, and country and regional risk management. It also explains how monetary and fiscal policies affect real income, the balance of payments, and the exchange rate and how these variables affect value creation. Toward that purpose, this chapter:

- Describes the relationship between national income and international trade.

- Elucidates how output and the exchange rate interact to determine each other.

- Explains the meaning of partial and general equilibrium and their implications for country and regional risk.

- List the drivers of a firm's value creation, and how these drivers are affected by the various aspects of country risk; namely, output, balance of payments, and the exchange rate.

NATIONAL INCOME AND FOREIGN TRADE

The gross national product (GNP) of a nation is equivalent to the market value of all *final* goods and services produced by a nation over a period of time, which is usually a year. The *potential* size of gross national product depends on the endowment of national resources and productivity. The *level of expenditures determines the actual size of GNP*. When potential and actual GNP are expected to be equal, the national economy is anticipated to operate at full employment equilibrium. GNP is estimated by aggregating the expenditures on final goods and services of individuals and families, businesses, governments, and foreigners over the accounting period. Open economy expenditures are usually expressed as:

Open economy expenditures or aggregate expenditures = consumption (C) + investment (I) + government expenditures (G) + [exports (X) – imports (M)]

$GNP = C + I + G + (X - M)$.

The millions of individuals sharing GNP in a country disburse part of their earnings to pay taxes (T_x)., to meet consumption expenditures, and whatever is left, is saved (S). Therefore, the uses of GNP could be described as follows:

$GNP = T_x + C + S$

To pay taxes, households use their share of national income. Whatever is left is known as disposable income which is allocated to satisfy the consumption the consumption of he families. The remaining disposable income is saved. Consequently, in this setting, consumption is viewed as depending on disposable income (Yd):

Y_d= real income (Y) – taxes (T_x).

$Y_d = Y - T_x$

The Current Account

As it was explained in Chapter 7, the current account balance is the sum of the trade, service, income, and transfer balances. All these items are largely determined by the exchange rate and disposable income. If the local currency appreciates or if it is above its market value, it limits the ability of the local firms to compete in foreign markets and to export, which eventually is reflected as deterioration in the current account. A similar outcome will ensue with output growth. This happens because a higher level of real income encourages households and firms to demand a larger quantity of foreign goods, which leads to an increase in imports.

In contrast, if the local currency depreciates, the current account improves. If output declines, the current account tends to get better.

Table 14.1
Thailand, Current Account, 1993-1988
($ billion)

Balance	1993	1994	1995	1996	1997	1998
Trade	−4.3	−3.7	−8.0	−9.5	1.6	16.2
Service	−1.4	−3.8	−4.0	−2.6	−1.6	1.1
Income	−1.4	−1.7	−2.1	−3.4	−3.5	−3.5
Transfer	0.7	1.1	0.5	0.8	0.5	0.4
Current account	−6.4	−8.1	−13.6	−14.7	−3.0	14.2

Variations in the current account and the exchange rate are at the heart of country risk and value creation. For example, in the case of Thailand, a deterioration of the current account was prompted by a gradual overvaluation of the bath against the dollar (Table 14.1). This caused concerns about the level of country risk that eventually, led to a large destruction of firms' values.

The relationship between the current account and the real exchange rate is very complex. A change in the exchange rate affects the flow of goods and services in two ways. The first and more obvious is the value effect. The second is the volume effect.

Value and Volume Effects

After a depreciation, local consumers and firms have to provide more domestic goods to buy the same amount of foreign goods. In contrast, foreigners have to give a lesser amount of their goods to purchase the same amount of imports. This change in the trading relationship between residents and foreigners is known as the *value effect*.

Domestic consumers and local firms usually respond to an increase in the price of imports by purchasing fewer units of the more expensive foreign goods, while foreigners generally increase their demand for domestic goods. This market response is known as the *volume effect*.

The overall result of the value and the volume effect on imports, exports, and consequently the current account, is uncertain. It is very difficult to ascertain in advance whether a depreciation of the local currency will improve or worsen the current account. Ultimately, the response of the current account to depreciation will depend on the relative strength of these two effects.

However, when a currency depreciates, the usual expectation is to have the volume effect outweighing the value effect so that depreciation is anticipated to improve the current account.

Other factors affecting the current account are domestic and foreign disposable income. A rise in local disposable income causes domestic consumers to increase their spending on all goods, including imports. Therefore, an increase in disposable income, assuming foreign income fixed, is expected to worsen the current account. Table 14.2 summarizes how changes in the exchange rate and disposable income affect the current account.

Table 14.2
Exchange Rate, Income, and the Current Account

Current Account

	Variation	Effect on the Balance	
Exchange Rate	Appreciation	Deficit	
	Depreciation		Surplus
Disposable income	Increase		Deficit
	Decrease	Surplus	

THE REAL EXCHANGE RATE AND AGGREGATE DEMAND

A depreciation of the real exchange rate lowers the price of domestic output relative to foreign output and shifts domestic and foreign spending from foreign to domestic goods and services. This shift in spending prompted by depreciation of the real exchange rate lowers the level of sales, profits, and value creation of local firms, while an appreciation has opposite effects. For example, in Table 14.3, the depreciation of the Thai currency in 1997 leads to a large surplus in trade balance in the periods following the devaluation. This trend implied larger volume of sales in the local market, higher corporate profits, and very possible, more value creation.

An increase in real income, assuming taxes are fixed, persuades domestic consumers and local firms to increase their demand for all goods and services. The increase in consumption raises aggregate demand, while the demand for imports lowers it, given that imports are a leakage. Since the effect on consumption is far greater than the effect on imports, an increase in real income should raise aggregate demand, while a decline in income should have opposite results. Aggregate demand is simply the accumulation of firms' sales in a local economy. Normally, the level and variation of the exchange rate and fiscal and monetary policies of a country, as well as political disturbances determine aggregate demand.

Table 14.3
Thailand, Trade, Output, and the Exchange Rate

	1993	1994	1995	996	1997	1998
Trade balance	−4.30	−3.70	−8.00	−9.50	1.60	16.20
Exchange rate Bht/$1	25.54	25.09	25.19	25.61	47.25	38.69
Real GDP ($ billion)	2,481	2,695	2,933	3,095	3,081	2,825

OUTPUT AND THE EXCHANGE RATE

Understanding the short run relationship between the exchange rate and output or real income is critical to comprehending how an open economy operates. It is also significant to understanding and evaluating country risk, and consequently, the impact of external factors on value creation. To build this knowledge, the determination of output is analyzed assuming only changes in the exchange rate. The rest of the variables at this stage are assumed fixed.

Exchange rate depreciation lowers the price of domestic output in foreign markets. This value effect shifts domestic and foreign demands from foreign to domestic output. The fall in the relative price of domestic output, in terms of foreign goods helps local firms to export more than they import. Consequently, depreciation shifts the demand for domestic goods and services upwards. This simply means that the demand for domestic goods and services is higher at each level of output. Firms, in turn, respond to the excess demand for domestic output by expanding output. This expansion of output leads in the aggregate to higher sales, higher profits, and higher value creation.

In general, when the real exchange rate is not in equilibrium with the level of output, the anticipated adjustment on both income and exchange rate introduces an element of country risk that may be of substantial consequences for the country, the firms, and the households. In the case of Thailand, the exchange rate adjustment and the consequent change in the level of output led to an 8.3% decline in output, an increase in the rate of unemployment from 1.9% to 4.2%, decline in local sales, deterioration of firms' profitability, and in many cases to bankruptcy.

The Exchange Rate and the Money Market

There are various definitions of money market. For example, it can be described as the notional location where economic agents buy and sell short term debt instruments. However, in this chapter money market is defined as the notional location where consumers and firms demand local currency and the central bank or the Federal Reserve supplies it. Equilibrium in the money market leads to equilibrium in the foreign exchange market when the prevailing local interest rate is equal to the foreign interest of the largest trading partners of a country. For example, in the case of Japan and the United States, the exchange rate is anticipated to be in equilibrium ($/¥100) when the expected interest rate in the United States is equal to the interest rate of Japan. Interest parity equilibrium between two currencies, for example the dollar and the Japanese yen, can be expressed as follows:

$$R_\$ - R_¥ = [E_{\$/¥} - E_{\$/¥}]/e_{\$/¥}$$
$$\text{if } [E_{\$/¥} - E_{\$/¥}]/E_{\$/¥} = 0$$

then,

$$R_\$ = R_¥$$

$R_\$$ is the anticipated interest rate on one-year dollar deposits; $R_¥$ is the anticipated interest rate on one-year yen deposits; $E_{\$/¥}$ is the parity expected to prevail a year later; and E$/¥ is the predicted price of a yen in terms of dollars.

The Demand for Dollars and the U.S. Money Market

The demand for dollars declines in the international money market when the dollar interest rate falls because a fall in the domestic interest rate makes local assets such as a dollar interest-bearing bank account less attractive to hold. In contrast, a rise in the dollar interest rate increases the demand for dollars in the international financial market.

An increase in output in the United States increases the volume of monetary transactions that are required to meet a higher level of output. These additional transactions compel U.S. residents and multinational corporations to increase their demand for dollars. A fall in output diminishes the need to hold real money. If output is predicted to fall, corporations and individual plan a lesser amount of transactions. As such, they demand less of the local currency for purposes of meeting the transactions required to generate a lower level of output.

With these analytical it is possible to explore the dynamics of short-term equilibrium in the money market. A shift in the demand from money demand probably due to an anticipated increase in output raises the domestic interest rate. The increase in the U.S. interest rate improves the attractiveness of U.S. assets in comparison to foreign assets. For example, a higher rate of return on dollar deposits persuades holders of foreign currency deposits to sell them in order to shift the investment funds to the more profitable U.S. money market. This causes an excess demand for dollars. To induce dollar holders to trade the local currency, the holders of foreign currency deposits offer U. S. residents more foreign currency per dollar. The increase in the foreign-currency prices of a dollar causes a dollar appreciation. The appreciation of the dollar, however, is constrained to be just enough so that the increase in the rate at which it is expected to depreciate in the future offsets the increased interest rate of dollar deposits.

Equilibrium in the Foreign Exchange Market

At this juncture there are two separate functions showing the relationship between output and the exchange rate. One of them is derived from the relationship between the exchange rate and export and imports of goods. The second function is the result of foreign demand for local currency ensuing from variations in the level of the local interest rate relative to a foreign interest rate.

The first relationship describes the perception held by firms producing goods about the relationship between output and the exchange rate. The second depicts the insight of finance companies and banks about the same relationship. A short run equilibrium for the economy as a whole has to lie on both schedules concurrently. This is determined by the intersection of the perception of business producing goods and services and the firms engaged in financial transactions as it is depicted in Figure 14.1. The intersection of these two functions is the only point meeting the general equilibrium criterion, since it is the only point commonly shared by both schedules. At this intersection, the levels of output and the exchange rate consistent with a short-term equilibrium for the economy as a whole are described by Y^* and E^* respectively.

Figure 14.1
Equilibrium, Real Income and the Exchange Rate

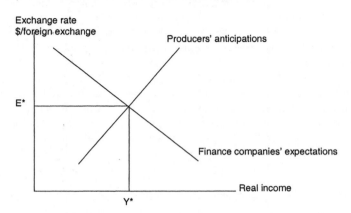

COUNTRY RISK, WARNINGS, AND PREVENTIVE MEASURES

Global firms can succeed only if the world economy offers, in each country, economic and social development. But such an ideal situation requires economic stability that happens only through good *public management*. A country is well managed when there is fiscal responsibility, transparency in the application of public fund, honesty in the disbursement of public money, a healthy private sector, and a good dose of democracy.

Discovering and proposing ways that can assist countries to reach this combination of factors is an extremely difficult task, for two main reasons. First, there are structural differences between countries. As such, it is almost an impossible task to provide a single economic recipe that can help them all. Second, managing a country is a fairly dynamic process that keeps on changing the parameters that are required to arrive to a successful economic development program. What was valid yesterday may not be necessary relevant today. Consider, for example, the public management paradigms in Argentina and Brazil when inflation was rampant. Or consider the case of past Mexico's government policies under the umbrella of a monolithic political party with the approach followed by the first non-PRI administration to public management.

Given the difficulty of applying single-minded economic rules to the complexities faced by the different countries in the world economy, it appears reasonable to meet this challenge with a basic simple approach that can be complemented, for each country with research and common sense, to arrive to suitable economic development programs.

This simple and effective program of economic development should start with the generation of a set of early warning signs that can help policy makers and managers to take the measures that can ensure the prevention of a crisis, rather than its correction once it happens.

Inflationary Signals

A country suffers from inflation when the economy experiences high and sustained increase in the different indices measuring local price levels, such as the consumer price index. In the 1980s, countries experiencing rates of inflation of 10% were considered to be mild-inflationary countries. In the 21st century this rate is too high. Under the standards of the new century, acceptable inflationary standards range from 3 to 5%. Countries exceeding this range of inflation standard will face disruptive changes in the exchange rate or drastic adjustments in public and private expenditures, as well as higher than normal interest and unemployment rates, and very possibly, a high degree of political instability.

Economic Development and GDP

Regarding economic development, GDP is an important variable helping to define this concept and the path to achieve it. For example, the gross domestic product of Russia measured in dollar terms is estimated at $200 billion. This value is a respectable figure suggesting the Russia has a sizable economy. This absolute measure of GDP is important to compare country size, but not sufficient to describe the path toward economic development. This variable alone does not provide enough information to judge the development of a country. To issue a judgment of whether a country is developing, or emerging, it is important to know the rate of growth of the country's GDP. For instance, China has been growing at rates close to 10% per year, but Russia has not. If these trends continue is conceivable to expect China to develop faster than Russia. The Chinese path of growth is unusual. More conventional rates of growth range from 3 to 5% per year, measured in real terms. That is, a 3% to 5% rate of GDP growth above the local rate of inflation. A real rate of GDP growth is obtained by taking inflation away from nominal GDP growth.

Real GDP growth = nominal GDP growth – inflation

A healthy and desirable GDP growth is normally spurred by a prudent relationship between taxes and government expenditures, private savings and investment, and current account surpluses or deficits to GDP.

Government Finances and Economic Development

Many of the crises faced by the emerging markets have been partially attributed to excessive government budget deficits. Therefore, it is strongly recommended that countries stay away from incurring in large government deficits. This is measured as the difference between government revenues and government expenditures.

Government surplus or deficit = taxes – government expenditures

In practice, there are two measures used to determine the size of a government's budget deficit. One of them is the nominal balance, which is equal to total government revenues less total government expenditures. The other is the primary measure, which is somewhat incomplete, given that it ignores the interest expenses of the government. A sound government budget deficit based on the nominal measure should not exceed 3% of the GDP. To have a healthy primary measure, the International Monetary Fund has suggested a 3% government budget surplus. When countries do not meet these standards, they run the risk of losing the confidence of the international financial markets on their ability to meet domestic and foreign currency debt, which may lead to a crisis and consequently losses in local value creation.

Balance of Payments

The analysis of the balance of payments helps to form an opinion about the degree and nature of the country risk faced by a nation. For example, if there is a current account deficit, this may be due to imports of goods exceeding exports, to income payments exceeding revenues, or a combination of both. The analysis of the balance of payments also reveals the degree of imbalance between the current account and the capital account. There is much consensus now that the deficit in the current account should not exceed 3% of the GDP. A current account deficit of this size is considered to be manageable.

A related aspect is foreign exchange reserves that increase with a basic balance surplus and decline with a deficit. The level of foreign exchange reserves held by the central bank of a country has been considered, traditionally, an important variable providing a valid indication of country risk. A nation is considered risky if the level of foreign exchange reserves is low. Foreign exchange reserves are often created to build a mechanism to defend pegged or dirty floating mechanisms. At the end of the last century, countries like Mexico, Chile, and Israel used the exchange rate as an anchor to control local inflation. Later the exchange rate was let to vary within a band. To defend this band, central banks often resort to the use of foreign exchange reserves. In case of an excessive appreciation of local currency, central banks use home currency to purchase reserves. This action creates an excess supply of home currency and a shortage of foreign exchange. By contrast, in the case of an excessive depreciation of the home currency, countries use foreign exchange to purchase home currency. This activity creates an excess supply of foreign exchange and a shortage of home currency.

Generally speaking, the depletion of foreign exchange reserves provides important information about the degree of country risk. Unfortunately, foreign exchange reserves information is not always available. An additional problem is reliability. The information on foreign exchange reserves some times has been manipulated to distract speculation. The Oil Crisis of 1980 that gravely affected the economy of Mexico led to a great deal of speculation against the Mexican peso. To divert it, the Federal Reserves under the chairmanship of Paul Volcker used to lend money to the Mexican central bank temporarily at the end of each month, so that the country could show on its monthly report, issued at the beginning of each month a healthy level of reserves. Once the report was published, the Fed would pull the reserves back to the United States. This measure, while helpful, was misleading. At the end, it only helped to postpone, and perhaps, deepen the crisis that ensued at the end of the administration of President Jose Lopez Portillo. Another aspect playing a critical role in country risk is politics. As a matter of fact, country risk analysis was started by political scientist tying to help business to understand the causes and consequences of the oil crises of the 1970s and 1980s.

The most recent case relating country risk to politics was Indonesia. The long dominance of the Indonesian economy by President Suharto and a handful of political allies was a source of political instability, which finally broke down into the social unrest that still rips the country, its firms, and its citizens apart.

THE DRIVERS OF VALUE CREATION

At this point, it is convenient to recapitulate on the key aspects dealt with in this and previous chapters to conclude this book. One of these significant concepts is after tax return on invested capital (ROIC) from Chapter 1, which is equal to the ratio of after tax EBIT to invested capital:

(14.1) $\text{ROIC} = \{[\text{EBIT} \times (1 - \text{tax rate})]/\text{Invested capital}\} \times E_0$

In Equation 14.1 EBIT are earnings before interest and taxes and invested capital are equal to the sum of cash, working capital, and net fixed assets.

Another key driver is the WACC, which was thoroughly explained in Chapter 13. Linking ROIC and WACC to a firm's growth provides a useful measure of market value added (MVA) previously discussed in Chapters 1 and 13:

(14.2) $\text{MVA} = \{[(\text{ROIC} - \text{WACC}) \times \text{Invested capital}]/(\text{WACC} - \text{Firm's growth rate})) \times \text{Spot rate}$

$= \{[(\text{ROIC} - k_w) \times \text{Invested capital}]/(k_w - g)\} \times E_0$

where g is the firm's growth rate and E_0 is the spot rate. Notice, that for this relationship to hold, WACC has to be greater than g. Otherwise, the relationship breaks down, and the formula is meaningless.

Equation 14.1 can be used to reach several important conclusions regarding the drivers behind value creation. First, for a firm to create value ROIC has to exceed WACC. Otherwise, the firm is destroying value. The difference between ROIC and WACC is known as *spread return*:

(14.3)   Spread return $= (\text{ROIC} - \text{WACC}) \times E_0$

The Importance of the Spread Return Concept

Equation 14.3 suggests that managers should direct their efforts to insure that their firms are maximizing the return spread. This also means that maximizing ROIC alone does not guarantee value creation. This will happen, only if ROIC is greater than WACC. It is important also to point out that managers should not focus on current or historical return spreads, but rather, on anticipated return spreads and on insuring that these expectations are met.

Another important implication of Equation 14.3 is the recognition that sales growth does not necessarily leads to value creation. It is well known that some fast growing firms destroy value. Therefore, what matters from a global finance perspective is a positive relationship between ROIC and WACC. If this relationship is negative for a fast growing firm, it simply means that growth is contributing to speed up value destruction.

To emphasize this important conclusion, consider the information provided in Table 14.4. It shows two firms. One has a high ROIC and is growing very fast at 12%, whereas the second one has smaller ROIC and growing only at 4%. Yet, the slow-growing firm is creating more value ($600 million) for its parent company than the company having a higher ROIC and a high rate of growth:

MVA for firm B = $\{[(\text{ROIC} - k_w) \times \text{Invested capital}]/(k_w - g)\} \times E_0$

= $[(7\% - 5\%) \times 300]/(5\% - 4\%)$

= $(2\% \times 300)/1\%$

= $(0.02 \times 300)/0.01$

= $(1.2/0.1) \times 300$

= $2 \times 300 = 600$ millions

For further details on these calculations, see Table 14.4.

Other key drivers of value creation can be identified by digging deeper into the ROIC concept and finding out what are his basic components by modifying Equation 14.1 as follows:

ROIC = (EBIT/Sales) × (Sales/Invested capital) × (1 – tax rate)

ROIC = Operating profit margin × Capital turnover × (1 – tax rate)

The split up of ROIC shows that a firm can improve value creation by increasing the profit margin and the capital turnover, and points out to the importance of taxes in the process of value creation.

The various drivers, previously explained, and their contributing to value creation are described in Figure 14.2, which also provides an integrated view of what are the variables under control of a financial manager and what are the variables determined by the economic environment, for example, income growth and exchange rate volatility. Figure 14.2 also provides an eagle's view of how to manage a foreign business for purposes of creating value for the parent company.

Managing for Value Creation

To provide an illustration of how to manage the subsidiary of a multinational for value creation, consider the case of the financial manager of a U.S. multinational analyzing the business plan presented by a new management team, which is expected to take over the Mexican subsidiary of a U.S. multinational on December 31, 2002. The new managers are proposing to increase sales from MxP$1.95 billion to MxP$2.24 billion, and profits from the current level of MxP151.67 million to MxP$176.57 million, as it is shown in Table 14.5

Between 2001 and 2002 the Mexican peso appreciated against the U.S. dollar. This trend is expected to continue into the year 2003. Currently (2002), the spot rate is MxP$9.76 and is expected to change to MxP$9.16/$1 by December 31 of 2003. If this is the case, profits measured in dollars will grow from the current level of $15.54 million to $19.28 million in 2003. See Table 14.5.

Table 14.4
Spread Return and Market Value Added

Firm	ROIC	WACC	Spread	Tax rate	Invested capital	Growth rate	MVA
A	0.08	0.07	0.01	0.3	300	0.12	−60.00
B	0.07	0.05	0.02	0.3	300	0.04	600.00

Figure 14.2
Value Creation, Key Financial Drivers

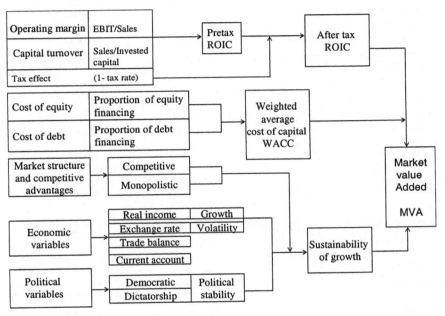

In principle, the business plan proposed by the new management team appears to be improving the performance of the Mexican subsidiary based on the conventional approach of emphasizing sales and profits. However, is the new business program better than the one in place from the perspective of value creation?

The information provided by the new management, rearranged in Table 14.6, reveals a growth in sales from 13% to 15%, and in profits from 12% to 16% from the year 2002 to 2003. Both items exceed the company and industry performances in the year 2002. This enhancement is due to a reduction in the rate of growth of operating expenses from 13% in 2002 to 11% in 2003. However, a closer look at other aspects of the financial statements reveal that the anticipated improvement will be achieved only if the company doubles the rate of growth in capital invested (growth in assets) from 9% in the current year to 18% in the year 2003. The increase in assets is, at a large extent, due to growth in working capital from 15% to 28%, and in the liquidity position of the company from 15% to 20%. If the program is carried on, increasing short-term debt from 20% to 67%, and long-term debt from 11% to 31% will finance it.

Table 14.5
Financial Information, Mexican Subsidiary
(millions)

Invested capital	2001		2002		2003	
Cash	80.00		80.00		70.00	
Working capital	340.00		390.00		500.00	
Net fixed assets	380.00		400.00		460.00	
Total		800.00		870.00		1030.00
Capital Employed						
Short-term debt	50.00		60.00		100.00	
Long-term financing	350.00		390.00		510.00	
Owner's equity	400.00		420.00		420.00	
Total assets		800.00		870.00		1,030.00
Sales		1,720.00		1,950.00		2,240.00
Less operating expenses	1475.00		1672.24		1850.00	
Less depreciation	20.00		25.08		27.75	
EBIT		225.00		252.68		362.25
Less interest expenses	32.00		36.00		110.00	
EBT		193.00		216.68		252.25
Less taxes at 30%	57.90		65.00		75.67	
Net profit (MxP$)		135.10		151.67		176.57
Exchange rate MxP$/$1)		10.12		9.76		9.16
Net profit ($)		13.35		15.54		19.28

The increase in the debt items raises WACC from 9% to 16%. The increase in WACC, in turn, leads to a decline in the growth of the spread from 11% in 2002 to 9% in 2003, in spite of the substantial increase in ROIC from 20% to 25%.

Overall, the plan presented by the new management team shows a higher value creation than the process currently in place. However, the improvement in the growth rate of the spread from 14% to 15% is largely due to the anticipation of 6% appreciation of the Mexican peso against the dollar, which improves the financial performance of the subsidiary when this is measured in dollars. The foreign exchange rate aspect of value creation should not be ignored and should be considered when analyzing the performance of a foreign business. But, it should not be use to rate the business performance of the new management team. Rather, the exchange rate trends should be assessed by the financial management of the parent company as a window of opportunity to be provided by the economic environment of the country.

To estimate growth, for example in sales, the following expression was used:

Growth in sales = {[(sales in period t)/(sales in period t–1)] – 1} × 100
= [(s_t/s_{t-1}) – 1] × 100
= [(1,950/1,720) – 1] × 100
=(1.13 – 1) × 100
= 0.13 × 100
= 13%

In general, the growth formula is as follows:

Growth = [(variable in period 1/valariable in period t–1) – 1] × 100
All the growth estimates are presented in Table 14.6.

Table 14.6
Value Creation, Mexican Subsidiary

Percentage Change from Previous Year	2002	2001
Growth in sales	13%	15%
Growth in net profits	12%	16%
Growth in operating expenses	13%	11%
Growth in assets	9%	18%
Growth in working capital (WCR)	15%	28%
Liquidity position = Short-term borrowing/WCR	15%	20%
Operating profitability (ROIC) = EBIT × (1 – tax rate)/Invested capital =	20%	25%
Variation in the exchange rate	–4%	–6%
Estimation of WACC, and Spread		
Proportion of debt	52%	59%
Proportion of equity	48%	41%
Cost of debt	8%	18%
Cost of equity	11%	12%
After tax cost of debt	6%	13%
WACC	9%	16%
Spread	11%	9%
Spread plus exchange rate gain	14%	15%

SUMMARY

This chapter introduced the concept of country and regional risk, and provided numerical examples of how to use the financial statements of a company to identify and estimate the drivers that are key to the process of value creation in the context of country risk.

Country and regional risk analysis are a very important component of global finance. These two risks are related to economic and political variables. Among the first type of variables playing a role, this chapter lists inflation, GDP, government budget, net private savings, current account, and foreign exchange reserves. These variables and political stability provide the ground to sustain industry and firms' growth.

To provide examples of how to manage a foreign subsidiary for value creation, this chapter provided the financial information of the foreign subsidiary of a U.S. multinational, and used this information to estimate all the key aspects of value creation. The theoretical framework to carry on with these estimates was provided ROIC, WACC, and market value added.

Case: Dell Computers in Europe

The computer industry encompasses electronic computers, storage devices, computer terminals, and computer peripheral equipment. Electronic computers include digital computers of all sizes, as well as computer kits assembled by the purchaser. Computer storage devices are such equipment as magnetic and optical disk drives and tape storage units. Computer peripherals are printers, plotters, graphics displays, and other input/output equipment.[3]

Pricing Strategies in the Computer Industry

Normally, the computer industry is driven by corporate investment expenditures, consumer spending on technology, and real GDP. The personal computer industry is related to consumer spending and as such is highly sensitive to price trends. In the recent past, the growth of the industry was hampered by the monopoly exercised in the microprocessor industry by Intel. However, as Intel introduced new microprocessors to the market, it helped to lower, aggressively, the price of older microprocessors. In the first stages of this trend, the decline in the price of microprocessors did not hurt Intel's profitability very much because the consumers were eager to spend on new path breaking technologies. But as the consumers realized that the old processor were almost as good working with internet applications and new software, the consumers became more reluctant to update their computer equipment. This unwillingness of the consumers to adopt new and more expensive technology reduced the demand for new microprocessors and helped to reduce the price of computers featuring new chips.

Another factor helping to reduce the price of computers and expand the market for lower price PC equipment was standardization in system components disk drives. Without standardization, prices would be too high for the average consumer. As a result of standardization, Microsoft Windows is placed on 83% of all computer systems and Intel microprocessors are found in 85% of all PC's.

Risk in the Computer Industry

The computer industry is a risky business because it is continuously besieged by price wars, short product life cycles, abrupt changes in growth and demand, and the high degree of operating leverage required to compete in the industry. All these factors can and have influence drastically and within very short periods, the profitability and liquidity of the firms operating in this industry.

In spite of these challenges, until very recently, the outlook of the industry was bright due to the growth of the internet worldwide, and the large untapped U.S. and world markets. However, overcapacity, and the decline of economic activity beginning in the year 2000, slowed down the growth of the industry in the United States from 23% in 1999 to 6% in the fourth quarter of the year 2001. The industry experienced a similar trend in Europe where growth decline from 6% in 1999 to -6% in the last quarter of 2001. One bright spot in this picture was the spectacular growth of the Asia/Pacific Rim region where sales growth rose 43% in the year 2001.

The previously discussed sales trends have hurt the major competitors in this industry. For example, Apple Computer reported a net loss of almost $200 million in the fourth quarter of 2000.[4] During the same period, Gateway laid off workers and closed several company-owned stores to cut costs. In March 2001, Micron Electronics announced plans to exit the PC manufacturing business in response to the poor economic performance of the company in this business segment.[5]

Consolidation in the Computer Industry

The short-term prospects of the computer industry has given way to attempts at consolidation on the part of some of the major competitors to root out competition and to seek larger economies of scale or economics of scope from joint non-PC product lines. The trend toward consolidation is not a new phenomenon in the industry, because this business activity is already highly concentrated. In the year 2000, five computer manufacturers accounted for almost 57% of the units shipped.[6] The major players are Compaq (16.1% market share), Dell (14.8%), Gateway (9.3%), Hewlett Packard (8.6%), and IBM (8.0%). The demand for PCs is equally concentrated. In the year 2000, the United States accounted for 40% of the total world market, followed by the European Union (30%), and Japan (10%). DataQuest, a consulting company from California, reported in 1997 that sales of PCs will reach 82 million units, and anticipated sales equivalent to 107 million units at the end of the year 2000, with a market value of $160 billion. [7]

The main factor contributing to the fast pace during this period was the introduction of excellent quality computers priced at less than $1,000. This price and quality enabled many households to acquire a high performance computer at a price that was not imposing a heavy burden on household budgets. Another demand booster was the fact that below $1,000 range price permitted many college students the purchase of computer equipment appropriate to their college tasks and needs. The decline in prices also shifted the laptop market from computer designed to business executive needs to laptops intended for students and academicians.

Dell and the Direct Sales Model

Initially, the distribution of PCs was conducted via retailing sales by local and regional vendors. However, Dell computers pioneered a direct sales model approach where the consumer could order via the Internet a customized computer to be quickly assembled in a centralized location, and delivered within a very short span at a site designed by the customer.

This business model allowed Dell to price its customized computers below retailing price channels. Mail order distribution also contributed significantly to reduce company costs because under this model of retailing Dell did not have to hold large inventories, as its competitors used to do. This approach also helped

Dell to eliminate the price guarantees and incentives that other manufacturers used to pay to distributors.

In view of the success experienced by Dell, other manufacturing companies began to implement the direct sales model by enhancing their physical distribution system and by allowing their distributors to assemble some products before shipment to the customer. This upgrade in the distribution strategy of the companies operating in the computer industry is allowing a continuous flow of manufacturing over the production cycle, a substantial reduction in inventory costs, and a more effective ay to challenge Dell's preeminence in the PC market.

The copycat strategy has helped Dell's competitors to catch up, so much, that Dell's supremacy appears to be in jeopardy. For example, various financial analysts that had purchased Dell's stock and had recommended it to their customers in the recent past, have changed their minds:

"After owning Dell stock for many years, I sold the last of in January because I am not sure how much free cash Dell is really generating for shareholders. Those last two words are critical, because even with the slowdown in PC sales, Dell is generating robust free cash flows. But a great deal of it appears to be going to management and employees in the form of stock options, rather than to share holders."[8]

Dell's revenues are heavily concentrated in the desktop market. In 1999, this segment represented 54% of the company's revenue. For February and November of 2001, it represented 52% and 57% of total sales.

Dell is usually a very rich cash company. Therefore, it is very unusual for this corporation to incur in short-term debt. However, it has acquired long-term debt to take advantage of low costs of borrowing afforded to Dell by its credit ratings. For example, in February of 2001, the company had a total long-term debt of $509 million that increased to 590 by November of the same year. The company does not disclose its cost of debt, but it is estimated that the European subsidiary borrows at a cost of 3.5%, mostly in euro. The company's cost of equity varies across subsidiaries, and it is estimated at 5.4% for Dell's European branch. The sales of Dell's European subsidiary represented 26%, 22%, and 20% of the company's global revenues for January of 1999, 2000, and 2001 respectively, and income taxes are approximately 28% of sales revenues.

CASE PROBLEMS

1. Using the financial information provided in Case Table 14.1 calculate the growth in sales, profits, operating expenses, assets, working capital, liquidity position, operating profitability, the proportion of debt to equity, cost of debt, cost of equity, after tax cost of debt, WACC, spread, and spread plus the percentage change in the exchange rate.

2. Using the information afforded by your response to question 1, find out whether the European subsidiary of Dell is creating value for its stockholders. To facility and guide your estimates use the grid provided below.

	1999–2000	2000–2001
Growth in sales		
Growth in net profits		
Growth in operating expenses		
Growth in assets		
Growth in working capital		
Liquidity position		
Operating profitability (ROIC)		
Variation in the exchange rate		
Debt plus equity		
Proportion of debt		
Proportion of equity		
Cost of debt		
Cost of equity		
After tax cost of debt		
WACC		
Spread		
Spread and % FOREX gain or loss		

3. Using Case Table 14.1, provide a one-year forecast the financial statements
    for the European subsidiary considering a rate of $0.87/€1.

Case Table 14.1
Dell, European Subsidiary, Financial Statements 1999 - 2001

	02/02/01	02/02/00	02/02/99
Total current assets	€2,063	€1,724	€1,348
Property, plant and equipment, net	€217	€172	€121
Working capital	641	559	490
Total assets	€2,921	€2,575	€1,596
Total current liabilities	€1,422	€1,166	€858
Long-term debt	€111	€114	€119
Stockholders' equity	€1,222	€1,192	€539
Total liabilities and stockholders' equity	€2,921	€2,575	€1,596
Exchange rate ($/€1)	$0.92	$0.98	$1.12
Net revenue	€6,932	€5,672	€4,235
Gross margin	€1,401	€1,171	€953
Income before extraordinary loss	€502	418	339
Operating Income	602	€552	€475
Net Income	€502	€418	€339
Europe, proportion of Dell's sales	20%	22%	26%

Source: United States Securities and Exchange Commission, Form 10-Q, II Computers
Corporation, November 2, 2002.

Notes

  1. For further details on the drivers of value creation, see Hawanini, G., and Viallet,
C., *Finance for Executives* 2nd ed. Cincinnati, OH: South-Western, 2002, p. 495.

2. For more details on the crisis that affected Mexico, Asia, and other emerging markets, see Rolf Mario Treuhrz, *The Crisis Manual for Emerging Countries.* Palo Alto, CA: Fabrizio Publications, 2000.

3 Activemedia Corporation, "Industry Environment." http://www.activemedia-guide.com/computer_industry.htm. (Accessed May 3, 2002).

4. Apple Computers, *Annual Report,* 2001. http://204.29.171.80/framer/navigation. asp?charset=utf-8&cc=US&frameid=1565&lc=ens&providerid=113&realname=Apple +computers&uid=3636963&url=http%3A%2F%2Fwww.apple.com%2F. (Accessed May 3, 2002).

5. Micron Electronics *Annual Report,* 2001. http://204.29.171.80/framer/ navigation.asp?charset=utf-8&cc=US&frameid=1565&lc=ens&providerid=113& realname=Micron+Electronics&uid=1721214&url=http%3A%2F%2Fwww.micronpc. com%2F. (Accessed May 3, 2002).

6. According to DataQuest, the increase in the industry concentration increased 40% in a two-year period, from 1998 to 2000. http://www3.gartner.com. (Accessed May 3, 2002).

7. Activemedia Corporation, "Industry Environment." http://www.activemedia-guide.com/computer_industry.htm. (Accessed May 3, 2002).

8. Whitney T., "The High Cost of Dell's Stock Option Program," TheStreet.com. (Accessed May 23, 2002).

SUGGESTED ADDITIONAL READINGS

Caves, R., Frankel, J., Jones, R. *World Trade and Payments.* 9th ed. Boston, MA: Addison Wesley,2002. See Chapter 24.

Duke Education. "Country Risk Analysis." http://www.duke.edu/~charvey/ Country_risk/couindex.htm. (Accessed May 23, 2002).

Krugman, P., and Obstfeld, M. *International Economics, Theory and Policy.* 5th ed. Cincinnati, OH: Addison Wesley, 2000. See Chapter 22.

The PRS Group. "Country Reports." http://www.prsgroup.com/. (Accessed May 23, 2002).

Shapiro, A. *Multinational Financial Management.* 6th ed. New York, NY: John Wiley, 1999. See Chapter 22.

Index

About the Author

FRANCISCO CARRADA-BRAVO is Professor of World Business at Thunderbird, the American Graduate School of International Managment, in Glendale, Arizona. He has taught at Brandeis University, Harvard Business School, and the University of California at Berkeley, and he is the author of several books on global finance.